Letterl

Teacher's Guide

by Gudrun Freese

Consultant
and
originator of Letterland
Lyn Wendon

Published by Letterland International Ltd,
Barton, Cambridge CB3 7AY, UK

Tel: +44 (0)870 766 2629

Fax: +44 (0)1223 264126

www.letterland.com

© Letterland International Ltd 2005

First published 2003

Product Code: TG
ISBN-10: 1-86209-259-1
ISBN-13: 978-1-86209-259-4

British Library Cataloguing in Publication Data

A catalogue record for this book is available from the British Library.

Written by Gudrun Freese

Edited by Sara Wiegand

Educational Consultant: Lyn Wendon, originator of Letterland

Illustrated by Kerry Ingham, Kathy Baxendale and Geri Livingston

Photographs by Steve Lumb

Design by Ken Vail Graphic Design, Cambridge

Cover design by Susi Martin Taylor

Printed in Hong Kong by Printing Express Ltd.

Acknowledgements
The author and publishers would like to thank the following for their help
with the photographs: The staff and children at St. Joseph's RC Primary
School, Norwood and Bishop's Hull Primary School, Taunton; Catriona
Hyland, Gus Hyland, Juliet Maxted and Alexander Maxted.

What is Letterland?

Explain Letterland to your children along the following lines...

When most people look inside a book, all they see are plain, black letters. That's because they haven't been to Letterland and they don't know that every letter is really one of our Letterland friends.

Letterland is the secret place where all the letters live together. The friendly letter people and animals who live there are called the 'Letterlanders'.

Every Letterlander has a special sound, and they love it when we make their sound *just right*. Did you know that they have made up a special trick just to help you learn all their letter sounds? They also have all sorts of other tricks to help everyone learn to read and write.

Would you like to go to Letterland and meet some of the Letterlanders?

To make the imaginative journey to Letterland, you could sing the Letterland Song together, or jump into a giant book, pretend to fly, or simply close your eyes and open them again in Letterland, ready to meet a new Letterlander.

Contents

Foreword

I am delighted to welcome this latest edition that shows how the Letterland system can deliver the aims of the **National Literacy Strategy (NLS)** and its **Progression in Phonics (PiPs)** framework.

Children love to pretend. Any adult who is willing to join them in their make-believe fun becomes special to them. Letterland is a make-believe place, first revealed in the illustrations of the *Letterland ABC Book*. Letterland's pictogram characters are also letter-characters in our real world, so powerful analogies can be drawn between real life and letter shapes, letter sounds and letter functions in words. It then becomes possible to teach the rules of written English using a fable-like instruction language that children want to hear. Letterland targets visual, audial and kinesthetic learners with equal strength.

To really make your Letterland teaching flow, use your story-telling voice and treat it like a shared journey in this new land. You will find the children taking ownership of the alphabet because you capture their imaginations. You are also using well-established learning principles and memory strategies to help you to create a tight link between the abstract letter shapes, their sounds, and their varying functions within words.

It is my sincere desire that using Letterland will provide you with a powerful tool that will not only help you and your children to succeed but also help to impart a life-long love of reading.

Lyn Wendon, Originator of Letterland

Introduction

Letterland's teaching methodology has been the same since its inception over 25 years ago: namely that learning to read and spell is a process that works best when all aspects of a child's intelligence are involved.

Letterland teaching addresses each of these key areas through which we all learn:

- Verbal / linguistic
- Visual / spatial
- Musical / rhythmical
- Logical / analytical
- Bodily / kinaesthetic
- Interpersonal / intrapersonal

Letterland teaching achieves this involvement by presenting children with an engaging parallel realm, which is teeming with analogies drawn from real life. The pictogram characters (the Letterlanders) bring vitality and colour to the plain black letters. An imaginative story logic transforms all the relevant phonic facts and rules into memorable similes, metaphors and fables.

As their teacher, you activate every learning channel by linking letters and their sounds to all the things children already know or are drawn to naturally: intriguing illustrations, story-telling, music and song, rhythm and rhyme, art and craft, movement, play-acting and social interactions.

This latest edition presents all 44 sounds and their major recurring spelling patterns in one book, and is designed to deliver the aims of the National Literacy Strategy's (NLS) Progression in Phonics (PiPs).

Special **new** features include:

- Phonemic Awareness Fast Track covering **a–z** in 2–3 weeks, uniting children of all abilities, including ESL children
- A flexible curriculum containing five, interwoven strands:
  - ✓ Word building
  - ✓ Sight words
  - ✓ Shared reading
  - ✓ Reading by analogy
  - ✓ Assessment
- Engaging child and teacher strategies
- Copymasters (assessment activities, reading and spelling lists, and more…)
- Cross-referencing to PiPs
- Downloadable support materials from www.letterland.com

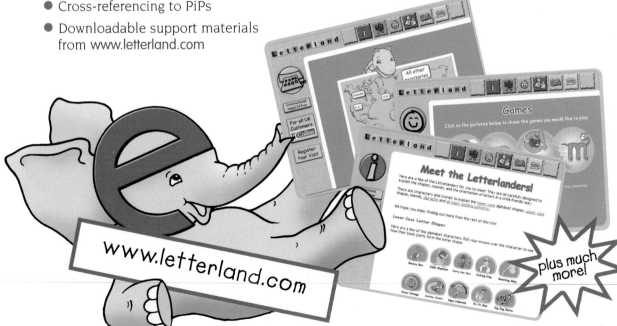

www.letterland.com

plus much more!

Lesson Plan structure

Sections	Assessment outcomes
a–z Phonemic Awareness Fast Track ● An effective way to meet or review **a–z** Letterlanders and learn their letter sounds. ● Extension ideas and assessment outcomes for older or more advanced children ● 10–15 lessons	● Say 26 **a–z** Letterland character names ● Say **a–z** letter sounds in response to plain letters ● Sort words according to initial sound ● Sequence three spoken letter sounds **Extension:** ● Write initial letter in response to a picture ● Read Letterland character names ● Write letter in response to letter sound ● Match **Aa–Zz** upper case and lower case letters ● Read a selection of NLS high-frequency words
Section 1: a–z Word Building ● Focus on each **a–z** letter in more detail ● Build words from the seventh lesson ● Introduce **long vowels**, **ss**, **ff**, **ll**, **ck**, **ng**, **sh**, **ch** and **th** ● Includes a systematic sight words strand ● 40 lessons	● Say **a–z** letter sounds in response to plain letters ● Write letter in response to sound (**a–z**; **ch**, **sh**, **th**) ● Match upper case and lower case letters (**Aa–Zz**) ● Blend CVC/CCVC/CVCC words ● Segment CVC/CCVC/CVCC words ● Read NLS high-frequency words (List 1a)
Section 2: Onsets and Rimes ● Activity ideas for reading and spelling by analogy ● Includes both regular CVC words and sight words ● 10–15 lessons	● Hear onsets and rimes in CVC words ● Blend and segment CVC words in rhyming sets ● Blend rhyming words on the *Letterland Vocabulary Cards* (e.g. b**all**, c**all**, f**all**, h**all**, t**all**, etc.) ● Blend words that rhyme with Letterland character names (e.g. M**ike**: b**ike**, h**ike**, l**ike**, etc.)
Section 3: Beginnings, Middles and Endings ● Activity ideas for focusing on beginning, middle and final sounds in CVC and CVCC words ● Includes CCVCC words with **sh**, **ch** and **th** ● 11 lessons	● Identify and write letter sounds in initial position ● Identify and write letter sounds in final position ● Identify and write letter sounds in medial position ● Blend and segment CVC words and words with **sh**, **ch**, **th**, **ff**, **ll**, **ss**, **ck** and **ng**

Section 4: Consonant Blends
● Activity ideas for teaching consonant blends.
● **bl cl fl gl pl sl**
  br cr dr fr gr pr tr
  sc sk sp st sm sn sw
  scr spl spr squ str shr thr
● 6 lessons
	● Blend CCVC/CVCC words
	● Segment CCVC/CVCC words
	● Read a selection of high-frequency words

Section 5: Digraphs and Trigraphs
● Interactive stories and activities for teaching vowel digraphs and advanced spelling patterns
 	
● **a–e / ai / ay** **o–e / oa / ow** **ow / ou** (cow, ouch) **oo / u** (foot, pull)
  e–e / ee / ea **u–e / oo / ew / ue** **oi / oy** **aw / au**
  i–e / ie / y / igh **ar / or / oor / our** **er / ur / ir** **air / ear**
● 16 lessons
	● Blend and segment words with vowel digraphs and other spelling patterns
	● Read and spell a selection of NLS high-frequency words (List 1b)

Timing and flexibility

The Lesson Plans

Because of Letterland's child-friendly approach, some of you may find that within the first year of teaching Letterland, even your younger children are ready to hear some of the phonic fables from Section 5 of this *Teacher's Guide*. You should feel free to share these digraph and trigraph stories. For example, a child who regularly confuses **was** and **saw** will be helped by the **aw** story on page 137.

There may not be time to cover all of the activities outlined in each Lesson Plan. Simply choose those that focus on the skills and knowledge your children need to develop.

This Guide is yours to use flexibly to meet your particular children's needs.

The Phonemic Awareness Fast Track

It is common for children to learn to recite or sing the traditional 'aee, bee, cee' *letter names* all in one go. Yet in many schools the teaching of *letter sounds* can be drawn out over the better part of the first school year.

The Letterland Phonemic Awareness Fast Track (pages 17–26) introduces a new option: to make an early acquaintance with all the **a–z** sounds and shapes within two to three weeks.

You can use the Fast Track with young children as a quick run through the alphabet before using the in-depth **a–z** lessons in Section 1. Add extension activities to the Fast Track for older or more advanced children, and use them as a quick review of **a–z** letter sounds before launching into word families, consonant blends or digraphs in Sections 2–5.

Letterland strategies

Child strategies

(Pages 143–153) There are eight main strategies or TRICKS for children to use to help them become better readers and writers. Encourage the children to use these strategies during independent reading and writing, or for peer coaching.

Teacher strategies

(Pages 154–161) There are ten main Letterland strategies for teachers.

A quick read through both sets of strategies will give you a good overview of Letterland's methodology. You will be referred to specific strategies in the Lesson Plans.

Assessment strand

There are a few core recommended assessment outcomes at the beginning of each section in this *Teacher's Guide*. Photocopiable assessment materials and *Pupil Record Sheets* will help you measure and record these outcomes.

Phonemic Awareness Fast Track

Activity ideas for assessing the Fast Track outcomes as well as photocopiable *Pupil Record Sheets* are on pages 23–26. Photocopiable *Fast Track Activity Sheets* are in the Appendices section.

Sections 1–5

If you choose not to begin your teaching with the Fast Track, you can still cover some of the Fast Track assessment outcomes for **a–z** during Section 1, using the Fast Track assessment materials.

Most of the remaining assessment outcomes for Sections 1–5 relate to the photocopiable *Reading and Spelling Lists* (including decodable words as well as NLS high-frequency words) at the back of this book. You can download *Pupil Record Sheets* for recording children's reading and spelling vocabulary from www. letterland.com.

Appendices

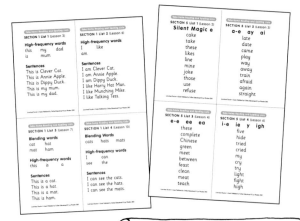

Activity Bank

(Pages 162–170) There are over 20 interactive games and activity ideas for reinforcing letter sounds and shapes, for practising word-building and for language development. Use these activities for reinforcement, revision and for informal, continuous assessment.

Reading and Spelling Lists

(Pages 171–184) With each new phoneme or spelling pattern that they learn, children are able to sound out more words. The *Reading and Spelling Lists* at the back of this *Teacher's Guide* follow the systematic introduction of vocabulary in the Lesson Plans. Section 1 lists also contain a high-frequency words strand. Also included are an *Alliterative Words Grid* and separate NLS high-frequency word flashcards/lists.

Annie's Alphabet Song

Annie Apple, she says 'a...'
She says 'a...'
She says 'a...'
Annie Apple, she says 'a...'
She belongs to Mr A.

Song lyrics

- **(Pages 188–192)** *Letterland Alphabet* and *Handwriting Songs* lyrics.
- *Blends and Digraphs Songs* are in the booklet that accompanies the cassette or CD.
- All of these lyrics make useful shared reading texts.

Why Letterland?

Alphabet sounds made easy

At the heart of Letterland teaching are Lyn Wendon's carefully developed and information-rich **a–z** pictogram characters.

A pictogram is a visual image that is designed to carry information. Letterland pictograms carry information about each letter's shape and sound. By just starting to say each character's name, children discover the sounds that letters make in words. In effect they 'see' the letter sound. **A**nnie **A**pple, **ă** …

Letterland pictograms work in accordance with recognised principles of memory which engage all learning styles. The result is accelerated letter recognition and quick progress in phonics.

Recall routes for digraphs and spelling patterns

Letterland uses interactive storytelling to explain new sounds and spelling patterns. These stories build on what children already know about single letter sounds. For example, why don't Sammy Snake and the Hat Man make their usual sounds in words like **sh**e and **sh**oe? Children know the Hat Man **h**ates noise. (It gives him a **h**orrible **h**eadache.) So when Sammy starts hissing beside him, he hushes Sammy up: **sh!**

There are stories like this one to explain all the phonemes and advanced spelling patterns featured in PiPs. Each one provides a ready recall route to the relevant sound.

For stories and pictograms to explain any spelling patterns that are not included in this book, look at the Letterland Advanced range. www.letterland.com.

Learning with all the senses

One of Letterland's strengths is its multisensory approach to letter/sound recognition. Children can become the letters and role-play the way they behave in words. They can sing about each pictogram's sound and shape as well as draw, write, listen and look. Children talk about the characters and bring them into craft activities. The Letterlanders become friends, motivating children to find out more about them.

More about pictograms

Linking sounds to letter shapes

There are no obvious reasons for a particular sound to be represented by a particular letter or group of letters. Each Letterlander becomes the reason for a letter's shape and sound. Look at **B**ouncy **B**en, the **b**rown **b**unny with a **b**ig **b**lue letter. His head and ears make sense of the otherwise abstract **b** shape. Children easily remember that this character is called Bouncy Ben. Now they already have all the information they need to link letter sound and letter shape within one audio-visual image. The character name acts as a cue for the letter sound: just start to say Bouncy Ben's name, 'b...'. That is the sound his letter makes in words.

Reading Direction

Letterland pictogram characters like to look or move in the Reading Direction (to the right)*. The Reading Direction is an orientation cue built into each Letterland pictogram. For example, it makes sense to write the downstroke for Bouncy Ben's ears first, then add the circle for his face, so he can face the Reading Direction as he bounces along.

Simple built-in picture cues and logic like this have helped children to avoid the common problem of reversing similarly shaped letters, such as **b** and **d**, **p** and **q**, and to orientate all the other letters correctly.

* Except for Golden Girl, Quarrelsome Queen and Zig Zag Zebra. And there are good reasons for these exceptions!

Child-friendly metalanguage

Letterland pictograms make it possible to talk about phonic concepts without jargon, *using language children already have* to talk about letters, sounds and concepts (metalanguage). In this book, suggestions for what teachers say to their students appear as **bold blue text**.

● Child-friendly language about shapes

Lower case letters: Pictogram designs turn letter shapes into body parts, making your instruction language fun and easy for children to understand.

The Hat Man's Handwriting Verse
Hurry from the Hat Man's head
down to his heel on the ground.
Go up and bend his knee over
so he'll hop while he makes his sound.

Capital letters: There is always a story to link lower case letter shapes to upper case letter shapes:

When the Hat Man has a chance to start a name, he is so **happy** that he does a **handstand**. He still whispers his usual sound, 'hhh…' and he even keeps his hat on!

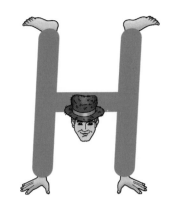

- Child-friendly language about sounds

Pictogram characters have personalities and names, so you can talk about them like friends, and sing about the sounds they make in words. For example:

Annie Apple's Alphabet Song

Annie Apple, she says 'ă…'
She says 'ă…', she says 'ă…'.
Annie Apple, she says 'ă…'
She belongs to Mr A.

- Child-friendly instruction language

Because each pictogram is a personality, you can correct children gently by asking, How does Clever Cat like us to make her letter? And which way does she like to look? And motivate them with, Clever Cat loves it when we make her sound like this, 'c…', 'c…', 'c…'.

Picture-coding

Picture-coding is the process of adding Letterland pictogram details to a plain letter shape. By doing this, children become the animators of lifeless letters. The drawing process is fun. As the children bring the letter shapes to life, they make the letter shapes their own. Picture-coding also greatly increases attention to the shape, sound and orientation of each letter.

You can also use picture-coding on the board, on worksheets or cards to draw attention to target sounds within words.

Letterland materials

Essential
- *Letterland Teacher's Guide*
- *Letterland Picture Code Cards*
- *Letterland ABC Book*
- *Letterland Alphabet Songs Cassette* or *CD*
- *Letterland Vocabulary Cards*
- *My Letterland Reading Booklet* – free download available on our website!
- *Letterland Classroom Wall Frieze*

Highly recommended
- *Letterland Handwriting Songs Cassette* or *CD*
- *Letterland Blends and Digraphs Songs Cassette* or *CD*
- *Word Bank Copymasters*
- *Blends and Digraphs Copymasters*
- *Letterland Early Readers*

For a complete range of *Copymasters*, *Workbooks*, *Readers*, full colour *Big Picture Code Cards*, videos, games and more, please visit www.letterland.com.

Picture Code Cards

- Double-sided cards featuring all the phonemes and spelling patterns in the *Teacher's Guide*.
- Useful example words on the plain letter side, as well as a brief version of the Letterland digraph story, where applicable.
- Use for introducing the characters, role-play, phonemic awareness, language development activities, word building, finger tracing and more.
- Available in straight or pre-cursive letter shapes

Letterland ABC

- Letterland's best-selling classic, updated with new artwork.
- Use for presenting each **a–z** character (see Section 1).
- Use for 'Phonemic awareness and language development' (see Section 1).
- Use the 26 scenes to bring the world of Letterland to life.

Vocabulary Cards

- 78 cards featuring words/pictures for each **a–z** letter sound.
- Picture-coded words on the backs of the cards develop phonemic awareness of initial sounds. Also available on a photocopiable grid (see page 171, *Alliterative Words Grid*).
- Over 250 rhyming words help develop the strategy of reading by analogy. NLS high-frequency words are featured in the lower right corner. All of these rhyming words are also featured on the six photocopiable *Rhyming Words Lists* included in the pack.

Wall Frieze

- Perfect for a permanent display of alphabetical order.
- Useful for finger tracing (keep at comfortable height!)
- Useful for linking upper and lower case letter shapes.
- Available in both straight and pre-cursive fonts.

Wordbank Copymasters

- Covers all digraphs and trigraphs in Section 5.
- Summarises each story (recall route) for each new sound.
- Space for adding new words that children find in their reading books.
- Provides examples of picture-coding.

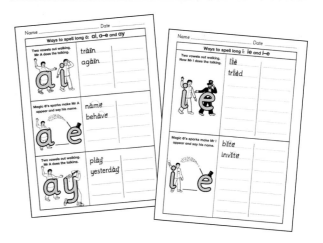

Alphabet Songs

- The *Alphabet Songs* are available on both cassette and CD.
- Invaluable for getting correct **a–z** sounds into children's heads.
- Parents appreciate this fun and effective pronunciation model.
- Use the memorable lyrics as shared reading texts. These lyrics are on pages 190–192 of this book.

> Teachers who use the *Alphabet Songs* report that they make a significant contribution to children's ability to learn and remember letter sounds.

Blends and Digraphs Songs

- Available on both cassette and CD.
- Songs featuring most of the remaining phonemes and spelling patterns (after **a–z**) contained in this *Teacher's Guide*.
- Include consonant blends and digraphs and vowel digraphs.
- Use the lyrics (provided in the accompanying booklet) as a fun and effective resource for shared reading activities.

Handwriting Songs

- Available on both cassette and CD.
- Provide a memorable way of learning how to form all 26 **a–z** letter shapes, by associating them with the body parts of the Letterlanders.
- Songs use language and concepts that the children already have, promoting learning by association. Lyrics for these songs are on pages 188–189 of this book.

Blends and Digraphs Copymasters

- A good resource for teaching and revising blends and digraphs covered in this *Teacher's Guide*.
- Reinforces / consolidates lessons after **a-z**.
- Covers all spelling patterns in Sections 3, 4 and 5 of this *Teacher's Guide*.

Early Readers

- Ideal for guided reading.
- Controlled vocabulary readers for consolidating phonic skills.
- Readers to support most phonemes and spelling patterns in the *Teacher's Guide*.
- Teaching suggestions in each book.
- Gradual inclusion of essential high-frequency words.

C *Classic Letterland Resource*

Further materials

In addition to the products listed above, Letterland also has a wide range of pupil materials and *Advanced* materials for explaining all the remaining spelling patterns not covered in this teacher's guide.

For our complete product range, please visit www.letterland.com.

a–z
Phonemic Awareness
Fast Track

The Fast Track is a dynamic way to develop sensitivity to sounds in spoken language. It is also a fast-paced introduction to the Letterland **a–z** cast, who re-appear throughout the year as children progress from individual letter sounds and simple word building to the Letterland phonic fables which explain more advanced sounds and spelling patterns.

Phonemic Awareness Fast Track

Why use the Fast Track?

It is now widely accepted that phonemic awareness (identifying phonemes in *spoken* language) is a crucial first step in learning to read, because it enables good progress in phonics (linking phonemes to *written* language).

This *Teacher's Guide* provides a new Letterland strategy for introducing all the alphabet sounds within the first two to three weeks of your phonics teaching – the Phonemic Awareness Fast Track. The Fast Track consists of a variety of alliterative activities that expose the whole class to an auditory bombardment of alphabet sounds.

Even though the focus of the Fast Track is on identifying spoken sounds in words, in practice the Letterland pictogram mnemonics enable children to link phonemes to letter shapes right from the beginning. In each powerful pictogram image, children can 'see' a letter's sound.

Research as early as 1984 provides a strong correlation between pictures bonded into letters and early success in learning letter/sound correspondences.[1] Teachers using Letterland pictograms have always enjoyed remarkable success. Now teachers are experiencing even greater success, with the Fast Track making it possible to advance their children's progress by a whole term or more.

Timing

When to use the Fast Track Use the Fast Track at the start of the year, as an introduction to **a–z** for younger children, or as a quick review of **a–z** for older or more advanced children.

After the Fast Track There are many ways to move on after the Fast Track:

- If you would like to incorporate **a–z**, **ss**, **ff**, **ll**, **ck**, **ng**, **sh**, **ch**, **th** and **long vowels** in a word-building strand, work through all the Lesson Plans in Section 1. (Includes a high-frequency sight words strand.)

- If your children are already familiar with all of the above, you could skip straight to Section 2 (Onsets and rimes), Section 3 (Initial, final and medial sounds in words) or Section 4 (Consonant blends).

- Think of Section 5 as a bank of story explanations that you can draw on whenever you need to. Even if you are following the PiPs teaching order (pages 214–215), feel free, for example, to introduce the Yo-yo Man's story (pages 75 and 109) when a child writes **vere** instead of **very**, or to introduce the **aw** story (page 137) if a child consistently misspells the word **saw**.

[1] Ehri, L.C., Deffner, N.D, and Wilce, L.S. (1984). *Pictorial mnemonics for phonics*. Journal of Educational Psychology, 76, 880–893. See also the **National Reading Panel Report** (2000) which describes Letterland's application of the principle of presenting letters bonded with familiar objects and its use of character names 'prompting the relevant sound.' It further points out the importance and 'motivational value of associating letters with interesting characters or hand motions and incorporating these into activities and games that are fun.' (2–117)

Assessment

Here are some suggested assessment outcomes for the Fast Track. We realise that every teaching situation is different, so it is not necessary to use all the outcomes we have listed. You will find assessment activity ideas and *Pupil Record Sheets* on pages 23–26 and *Fast Track Activity Sheet* copymasters in the Appendices section. Teachers who have used this Fast Track have had excellent results, with most children learning the **a–z** letter sounds within two to three weeks!

Assessment outcomes

- Say all 26 **a–z** letter sounds in response to plain letters.
- Say all 26 Letterland character names in response to pictograms.
- Sort words according to initial sounds.
- Sequence three spoken letter sounds into first, middle and last position.

Extension assessment outcomes

- Write initial letter (**a–z**) in response to a picture.
- Read Letterland character names (including over 35 common words).
- Write each **a–z** letter in response to letter sound.
- Match **Aa–Zz** upper and lower case letters.
- Read a selection of Letterland song lyrics containing NLS high-frequency words.

Materials

All you will need is:

- *Letterland Picture Code Cards*

- *Letterland Vocabulary Cards*

- *Fast Track Activity Sheets* (see Appendices).

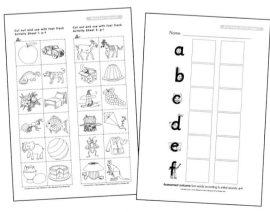

- Completely optional, but a lot of fun, is the addition of costumes or simple props for each character (see page 161).

Fast Track procedure

'Annie Apple'   'ă...'

1 Introduce the Letterlanders

- Introduce two or three letters in each lesson, using the *Picture Code Cards*. Show the picture side:
  This is Annie Apple. This is how she looks in Letterland.
  Now turn to the plain side:
  Most people only see her plain letter in words.

2 Discover the letter sound

- Use Letterland's fun and simple Child Strategy, the SOUNDS TRICK (page 143), for discovering each letter's sound: simply segment off the first sound of a character's name. 'Annie Apple, ă...'

- Be sure to turn to the **plain** letter side of the *Picture Code Card* when you say the letter sound, and always prompt children to give you *only* the letter sound when you show them the plain letter.

- From the second lesson, include a Quick Dash (page 155) to review all previously learned letter sounds. The Quick Dash prepares children for the assessment outcome: *Say letter sounds in response to plain letters.*

3 Word sort

- Choose some children to wear the *Picture Code Cards* (either in plastic pockets or in headbands).

- Hand out the relevant *Vocabulary Cards* to children seated in the class. Looking at the picture side only, they decide which Letterlander's sound starts the word on their card, then hand it over.

- This activity prepares children for the assessment outcome: *Sort words according to initial sound.*

4 Alphabet line

- The children at the front now have a chance to present themselves as the Letterland characters, holding up each *Vocabulary Card* in turn as they say:

  I'm Annie Apple. I say 'ă …' in words like **a**nt, **a**pple and **a**crobat.
  I'm Bouncy Ben. I say 'b …' in words like **b**ed, **b**lue and **b**all.
  I'm Clever Cat. I sat 'c…' in words like **c**at, **c**ar and **c**ake.

  Depending on the age and ability of the children, they could turn the cards over to the word side and invite the rest of the class to repeat the word with them.

- You may like to build the routine up, developing a rap-like speed through practice. With each new lesson, include a repeat of all the letters and words learned so far. (As the number of letters grows, you may wish to limit the previously learned letters to the latest five or ten, but continue to work through the alphabet order.)

- The aim is to build up a strong set of recall routes through this cummulative oral activity, strengthening both the **a–z** sequence and letter sound knowledge.

5 Order Please!

- Order Please! (see page 156) is a sequencing activity designed to prepare children for the assessment outcome: *Sequencing three letter sounds into first, middle and last position*. It also provides good preparation for word building. To play, you call out three letter sounds and three children holding *Picture Code Cards* line up in the same order.

6 Presenting a–z

- A great way to culminate the Fast Track is with a presentation of the whole alphabet, using the Alphabet Line routine (above). The children could share their routine with another class, at assembly or with their parents. They could even invite audience participation in reading out their words with them, or set the routine to music.

Fast Track extension activities

Here are some extension activities that you may like to build in to the Fast Track for children who already have some knowledge of **a–z**.

'mmm...'

'ĕ...'

Clever Cat

Annie Apple

Dippy Duck

Annie's Alphabet Song

Annie Apple, she says 'a...'
She says 'a...'
She says 'a...'
Annie Apple, she says 'a...'
She belongs to Mr A.

1 Increase the pace

Introduce five or six new characters in each lesson instead of two or three.

2 Actions

Teach an action for each character. (See **ACTIONS TRICK**, pages 148–149.)

3 Character names

Teach the **CHARACTER NAMES TRICK** for each character, helping children to read each Letterlander's name as a sight word (page 147).

4 Shared reading

Use the *Alphabet Songs* lyrics for a shared reading activity (see pages 188–190).
- Write up the words to an *Alphabet Song*.
- Point to each word as you teach the words to the song.
- Listen to the *Alphabet Song* together and point to the words.
- Sing the song together. You can really get the most out of the song by inviting a child to point to the character name each time they sing it, and the plain letter each time they sing the letter sound.

Note: This 'audio-visual' shared reading activity will reinforce the recognition of character names as sight words. It will also enable children to see the individual letter shape as they sing the individual letter sound – an excellent way to reinforce the sound/symbol link.

To make this a thoroughly multi-sensory activity, children can make the character's action each time they sing the letter sound.

5 Phonemic awareness games

- Children supply their own alliterative information for each character using the 'Alliteration Game' (page 150).
- For additional phonemic awareness games, see the Activity Bank (pages 162–170).

6 Writing letters

- Call out individual letter sounds for children to write down.
  (Prepares children for the assessment outcome: *Write a–z letters in response to letter sounds.*)

Assessment activity ideas

Here are some activity ideas for measuring the Fast Track assessment outcomes. If you plan to use these assessment activities for formal assessment, first demonstrate each activity to the whole class before children attempt it themselves.

For best results, wait until the children have had a few chances to review each group of five or six letters before measuring any of the assessment outcomes. For example, assess **a–f** a week or more after the children learn **f**, and build some review activities into your Fast Track lessons, such as the Quick Dash (page 155) and the Alphabet Line (page 21).

Say all the Letterland character names

Materials
● Use *Picture Code Cards* or the *Wall Frieze*.

Description
● Show the picture side of each *Picture Code Card*, and ask for the Letterlander's name.

Say the letter sound in response to plain letter

Description
● Write six letters (**a–f**; **g–l**; **m–r**, etc.) on a piece of paper.
● Ask a child to say each letter's *sound* as you point to it.

Sort words according to initial sounds

Materials
Word Sort Cut-outs
Fast Track Activity Sheet 1: **a–f**
Fast Track Activity Sheet 2: **g–l**
Fast Track Activity Sheet 3: **m–r**
Fast Track Activity Sheet 4: **s–w**
Fast Track Activity Sheet 5: **x–z**

Description
● On *Fast Track Activity Sheets 1–4*, children stick pictures next to the Letterlander with the same initial sound.
● On *Fast Track Activity Sheet 5* they circle objects that begin with the target sound.

Sequence three spoken letter sounds

Prepare for this activity by playing Order Please! (page 156) during Fast Track lessons.

Materials
Plain letter cards or *Picture Code Cards*

Description
● Give a child three plain letter cards or *Picture Code Cards*.
● Say three letter sounds aloud (e.g. 'a...', 'c...', 'd...').
● The child lines up the letter cards in the same order (in the Reading Direction).
● Repeat with a different sequence of the same letters.
● Repeat with a new set of three letters.

- *Variation:* If you prefer to do this activity with all the children at the same time (rather than as a one-on-one activity), you could provide each child in your class with sets of three letters at a time for them to sequence on paper before sticking them down.

Write initial letter in response to picture

Materials
Fast Track Activity Sheet 6: **a–f**   *Fast Track Activity Sheet 8:* **m–r**
Fast Track Activity Sheet 7: **g–l**   *Fast Track Activity Sheet 9:* **s–z**

Description
- Children write the matching initial letter next to each picture.

Read Letterland character names

Materials
Fast Track Activity Sheet 10: **a–g**   *Fast Track Activity Sheet 12:* **o–t**
Fast Track Activity Sheet 11: **h–n**   *Fast Track Activity Sheet 13:* **u–z**

Description
- Children cut out the pictograms and paste them next to the matching Letterland character name.

Write letter in response to letter sound

Description
- Call out six letter sounds, one by one. Ask: 'How can we write this sound?'
- Children write down the corresponding letter.

Match upper case and lower case letters

Administer these tests after children have heard the **CAPITAL LETTER TRICKS** (pages 145–146) and have had some classroom practice in matching capital and lower case letters, using the same groups of letters (**Aa–Ff**; **Gg–Ll**; **Mm–Rr**; **Ss–Zz**).

Description
- Write six lower case and six upper case letters on a piece of paper.
- Children join the matching letters.

Name: _____

Assessment outcome	a	b	c	d	e	f	g	h	i	j	k	l	m	n	o	p	q	r	s	t	u	v	w	x	y	z
Say all the Letterland character names																										
Say the letter sound in response to plain letter																										
Sort words according to initial sound																										

Sequence three spoken letter sounds	1		2		3		4		5	
	acd	edf	bed	ghi	klg	mno	pqr	mop	xyz	zxy
				ijl			stu	vwx	sut	zyx

Name: _____

Assessment outcome	a	b	c	d	e	f	g	h	i	j	k	l	m	n	o	p	q	r	s	t	u	v	w	x	y	z
Write initial letter in response to picture																										
Read Letterland character names																										
Write letter in response to letter sound																										
Match upper case and lower case letters																										

Section 1:
a–z Word Building

This section uses a variety of multi-sensory activities to consolidate **a–z**, or (if you have skipped the Fast Track) to introduce **a–z**, as well as **long vowels**, **ck**, **ng**, **ss**, **ff**, **ll**, **sh**, **ch** and **th**. Section 1 also contains a word-building strand and a systematic high-frequency sight words strand.

Section 1:
a-z Word Building

Assessment outcomes

- Say letter sound in response to plain letter.
- Write letter in response to sound (**a–z**; **ch**, **sh**, **th**).
- Match upper and lower case letters (**Aa–Zz**).
- Blend CVC / CCVC / CVCC words.
- Segment CVC / CCVC / CVCC words.
- Read a selection of high-frequency words.

Lesson Plans

Section 1 dedicates an entire Lesson Plan to each phoneme. In addition there is a separate, dedicated word-building strand. A systematic sight words strand is built in from the first lesson, in the form of a photocopiable reader, *My Letterland Reading Booklet*. For a free copy of this photocopiable booklet, visit **www.letterland.com**

Letter knowledge

a–z, **long vowels**, **sh**, **ch**, **th**, **ss**, **ff**, **ll**, **ng**, **ck**

Teaching order

c	ă/ā	d	h	m	t	s	ss	ĭ/ī	n	g
ŏ/ō	p	ĕ/ē	ŭ/ū	k	ck	ng	sh	ch	th/th	l	f
ff	ll	b	j	r	qu	v	w	x	y	z

This teaching order makes it possible to blend and segment a large number of decodable words after the sixth letter, and then to steadily increase the number of words children can sound out and spell. It also keeps potentially confusing shapes apart (like **b/d/p/q**; **m/n/u**; **s/z**).

Long vowels are introduced only very briefly. If your children are ready to use long vowels for blending and segmenting, you might like to introduce the 'Silent Magic e' concept early on (page 109).

Reading and spelling vocabulary

Children build up a large reading and spelling vocabulary using two main strategies:

1) Blending and segmenting regular words using letter sounds
2) Sight words recognition

Key reading materials are:

- *Take-home Reading and Spelling Lists* (pages 172–176): one photocopiable list per three or four letters.

- *My Letterland Reading Booklet* (page 158): This photocopiable reader incorporates NLS high-frequency words (List 1a), the Letterland character names and some decodable words into one or two simple sentences per page. Children complete one new page every lesson and **re-read all previous pages**. For a free download of this booklet, visit www.letterland.com

- The *Alliterative Words Grid* (page 171) features the 78 large words on the backs of the *Vocabulary Cards*. Use for a memorable additional sight words vocabulary.

Teacher strategies for Section 1

1) Quick Dash revision
- To ensure that children develop the skill of linking letter sounds to letter shapes, start each lesson with a Quick Dash (page 155) through all the letters you have taught so far.

2) Phonemic awareness throughout the day
- Be sure to emphasise words that begin with the target sound throughout the day. You could challenge the children to catch you saying everyday words that begin with the target sound, for example: **c**ount, **c**olour, **c**rayons, **c**up, **c**upboard, **c**lass, **c**lassroom, **c**oats, **c**ar...etc.
- You could keep a Word Bank on the board of words with the target sound that come up during the day.

3) Cross-curricular planning
For those of you who follow a cross-curricular approach, there are many options for extending your study of letter sounds into other curriculum areas. Taking Clever Cat as an example, you could:

- Introduce other topics with the target sound, for example: **c**olours, **c**ounting, **c**ats, **c**ollages, **C**anada, **c**aterpillars and **c**ostumes.
- Make the links explicit. Talk about the link between the target sound and what you are doing. For example, 'Why are we making **c**ollages in art today?' (Because **c**ollages begins with **C**lever **C**at's sound.)

4) Picture-code labels for objects that begin with the target sound
- Before each lesson, prepare labels for classroom objects that begin with the target sound and picture-code the initial letter. During the 'Phonemic awareness and language development' section in each lesson, let the children spot objects in the classroom that begin with the character's sound. Then bring out the labels you have prepared and stick them up.

5) Ideas for ending the day
For example, when teaching Clever Cat:

- Children line up to leave the classroom at the end of the day. Each child says, a 'Clever Cat word' as a password to be allowed out of the door.
- Each child writes down as many 'c...' words as they can. Alternatively, do this as an oral class activity.
- Ask children to bring something from home that begins with Clever Cat's sound for a 'Clever Cat's Words Collection'.

Materials for Section 1

You will need the following materials for every lesson in Section 1. Additional materials and preparations that are specific to each lesson are listed at the top of each Lesson Plan.

1) Letterland ABC Book
- Use only the picture to present the new Letterland character at the start of each lesson. Save the text and scene for later in the lesson.
- Read the text and explore the alliterative objects in the scene together during the 'Phonemic awareness and language development' section in each lesson.
- If you do not have an *ABC Book*, use a *Picture Code Card* to introduce the character.

2) Picture Code Cards (PCC)
- Gather together cards for all the letters you have introduced so far.
- Use them for Quick Dash revision, introducing the letter, *Alphabet Song*, finger tracing, etc.

> NOTE Always flip over to the plain letter side of the card to refer to the character's letter sound ('ă...'). This is important preparation for one of the main assessment outcomes: *Say the letter sound in response to the plain letter.*

3) Letterland Vocabulary Cards
- Use the three *Vocabulary Cards* that begin the target sound for the 'Phonemic awareness and language development' section in each lesson.
- You can also use the words on the back of the cards as additional sight vocabulary. (See page 171 for a photocopiable list of these words.)
- If you don't have *Letterland Vocabulary Cards*, you can use a sound bag or other picture cards.

4) Alphabet Songs and Handwriting Songs
- These are available on cassette or CD.
- Depending on the age and ability of your children, you may like to write out the lyrics (pages 186–190) to use as a shared reading text for the children as they learn the song.

5) Character name flashcards
- Enlarge and photocopy the cards on *Copymaster 8*.
- You will need one for each Lesson Plan.

6) NLS High-frequency Words List 1a
- Enlarge and photocopy the words on page 183.
- In each lesson, use any NLS words that *start* with the target sound.

7) Reading materials
- *My Letterland Reading Booklet* (page 158)
- *Take-home Reading and Spelling Lists* (pages 172–176)
- *Letterland Early Readers* (page 16)

8) Handwriting and other individual activities
- Choose suitable Copymasters or Workbooks from our range of Letterland support materials (page 16).

My Letterland Reading Booklet

Clever Cat

Materials
See the list on page 30.

Preparations
Write and picture-code classroom labels: **c**ups, **c**rayons, **c**upboard, **c**lock, **c**lassroom.

Note: The other lessons in Section 1 are a lot shorter. Refer back to this more detailed lesson whenever you need to.

Action (page 148)

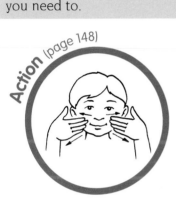

crayons

cupboard

can **cat**

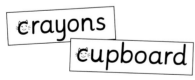

Clever Cat, her sound, action and song

- **Clever Cat** Introduce Clever Cat using the picture in the *ABC Book*. At this point, don't spend any time looking closely at the scene or reading the text. Save these for a 'Phonemic awareness' activity, below. Simply show children what this **c**olourful and **c**lever **c**at **c**alled **C**lever **C**at looks like when she is in Letterland. Talk about how her face and body relate to her letter, e.g. how her letter shape curves under her chin.

- **Sound** To see what Clever Cat looks like in words, show the *plain letter* side of her *Picture Code Card* (PCC). Clever Cat loves to make her sound in words, but she doesn't miaow or purr like ordinary cats. She's a Letterland cat so she whispers her own special sound instead. Then use the **SOUNDS TRICK** (page 143) to discover the *sound* she makes in words. Simply separate her letter sound from the start of her name: Clever Cat, 'c...'. (Whisper 'c...' to avoid adding an unwanted 'uh' sound: 'cuh'.)

- **Prepare for assessment outcome** To help children develop the link between the *plain letter* and the letter sound, ask for the *letter sound* in response to the plain letter side of the *PCC*. Praise correct answers with: **C**lever! or **C**orrect!

- **Action** For a memorable action to reinforce Clever Cat's sound, see page 148.

- **Song** Sing Clever Cat's *Alphabet Song* (words, page 188). Show the *picture side* of her *PCC* when you sing her name. Turn to the *plain* letter every time you sing her sound. You may like to write up the lyrics to use as a shared reading text.

Phonemic awareness and language development

Listen

- Read about Clever Cat in the *ABC Book*. Emphasise her sound as you read the text and explore the picture together.

- Introduce three **c** words using both sides of Clever Cat's *Vocabulary Cards*. Children say each big word, exaggerating the initial sound (e.g. **c**...at / **c**at, **c**...ar / **c**ar, **c**...ake / **c**ake). Make up a sentence to link each object to Clever Cat, e.g. **C**an you imagine **C**lever **C**at eating **c**ream **c**ake?

- Use any classroom labels you have prepared (e.g. **c**rayons, **c**upboard, **c**lock, **c**ups) and labels for NLS high-frequency words (**c**an, **c**ome, **c**at) to draw attention to Clever Cat's sound in words.

- Ask some questions to encourage children to think in an alliterative way, and to present some new and challenging language in a friendly context. Encourage discussion of each of these scenarios, and praise answers with, **C**ongratulations! or **C**lever!
  Can you imagine **C**lever **C**at playing tennis or **c**omputer games? Do you think she might like to **c**onduct our next **c**oncert? What instrument might she play, drums or **c**astanets? When she goes to stay in the **c**ountry in her **c**aravan, what do you think she likes to do: ride horses or **c**limb **c**liffs?

Note: If children spot exceptions to the hard 'c ...' sound (ni**c**e, **C**harlie, s**c**hool), put a wavy line underneath the letter and promise an explanation. (See page 160: Dealing with exceptions.)

Games

- Choose a game from the Activity Bank (pages 162–170) or play the Alliteration Game (below).

  The Alliteration Game (page 150). Help children to think up their own alliterative information about Clever Cat. For example:

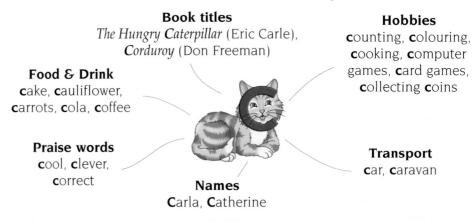

Book titles
The Hungry Caterpillar (Eric Carle),
Corduroy (Don Freeman)

Hobbies
counting, colouring, cooking, computer games, card games, collecting coins

Food & Drink
cake, cauliflower, carrots, cola, coffee

Praise words
cool, clever, correct

Transport
car, caravan

Names
Carla, Catherine

Letter shapes: c and C

Lower case c

- Some animals love it when you stroke them. Clever Cat likes you to stroke her letter like this. Finger trace the letter only, first on the picture-coded side and then the plain letter side of Clever Cat's *Picture Code Card*, while you say her Handwriting Verse: Curve round Clever Cat's face to begin.
  Then gently tickle her under her chin.

- Write a huge **c** on the board for children to air-trace while they sing or chant Clever Cat's *Handwriting Song*. Make sure you are facing the board as well, so that you are all forming the letter in the Reading Direction (to the right).

- Follow up with a handwriting activity*. (Choose a suitable product from the Letterland range of handwriting materials: page 16.)

Upper case C

- Introduce the concept of upper case letters with the **CAPITAL LETTER TRICK** (page 145): Whenever Clever Cat starts important words such as names, she takes a deep breath and gets bigger.

- Introduce the **CHARACTER NAMES TRICK** (page 147) to help children recognise the character names as sight words: Clever Cat appears as her capital letter TWICE in her own name.

- Show the Clever Cat name flashcard you have prepared, or write her name on the board and picture-code the two upper case **C**'s. Read her name together.

Picture-coding

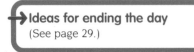

Clever Cat

Individual activity ideas

- *My Letterland Reading Booklet* (page 158) Page 1: This is Clever Cat.
- *See Letterland Materials* (pages 14–16) for Copymasters or Workbooks.

→ **Ideas for ending the day**
(See page 29.)

Annie Apple

Annie Apple, her sound, action and song

- **Annie Apple** Use the *ABC Book* (just the picture) to see what this talking **a**pple looks like when she is in Letterland.

- **Sound** Show the *plain letter* side of the *Picture Code Card* (PCC) to see what she looks like in words. Then use the **SOUNDS TRICK** (page 143) to discover the sound she makes in words: Annie Apple, 'ă …'. Ask for the *letter sound* in response to the plain letter.

- **Song** Sing Annie's *Alphabet Song*. Show the picture side of her *PCC* when you sing her name. Turn to the plain letter every time you sing her sound. (Words on page 188.)

Phonemic awareness and language development

Listen
- Read about Annie Apple in the *ABC Book*. Emphasise her sound and explore the picture together.

- Use *Vocabulary Cards* (page 30), your classroom labels (e.g. **arrow**) and NLS high-frequency words (**at**, **am**, **and**, **an**) without picture-coding to draw attention to Annie Apple's sound.

- Ask questions and encourage discussion. Praise answers with: '**A**bsolutely!' or '**A**dmirable answer!' For example: Is **A**nnie **A**pple the first letter in the **a**lphabet? Do you think she is **an a**dventurous **a**pple? Which of these might she like to become (**a**ctress, teacher, **a**crobat, bus driver, **a**mbulance driver, **a**stronaut). **A**nnie has visited **A**frica. Let's look for **A**frica in the **a**tlas.

Games
- Choose a game from the Activity Bank (pages 162–170) or play the Alliteration Game (page 150).

Letter shapes: a and A

- **Song** Sing or chant the **a** *Handwriting Song* (page 186) while children slowly finger trace or air trace the letter. Follow up with a handwriting activity.*

- **Storyline** Annie Apple always hops up on a nice big applestand to start important words like people's names or the first word in a sentence. Show the Annie Apple name flashcard you have prepared, or write it on the board and picture-code the two A's. See **CHARACTER NAMES TRICK** (page 147).

Individual activity ideas

- *My Letterland Reading Booklet* (page 158) Page 2: This is Annie Apple.

- *See *Letterland Materials* (pages 14–16) for Copymasters or Workbooks.

Materials
See the list on page 30.

Preparations
Write out and picture-code classroom labels: **a**rrow; **a**lphabet; **a**tlas.

Action (page 148)

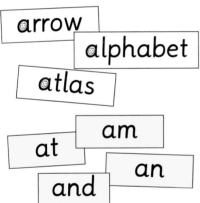

arrow
alphabet
atlas
am
at
an
and

Picture-coding

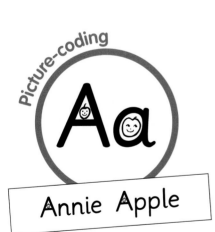

→ Ideas for ending the day
(See page 29.)

Mr A, the Apron Man

New concept

Alphabet names vs letter sounds

- Talk about the difference between *alphabet names* and *letter sounds*. In Letterland, there are only five people who say their alphabet names instead of a letter sound. They are the five Vowel Men.

Materials
See the list on page 30.

Preparations
Write out and picture-code classroom labels: **a**pron, **a**ge, **a**pe; prepare 'Vowel Flip-overs' (*Copymaster 1*).

Action (page 149)

April ape

Asia

Mr A's sound, action and song

- **Mr A** Annie Apple belongs to Mr A, who has come a long way from Asia to look after the apples in Letterland. He collects them in his apron – that's why he is called Mr A the Apron Man. Mr A appears in words that need his name 'ay...' like **apron**, **April**, **age** and **alien**!

- **Sound** Turn to the plain side of his *Picture Code Card*. Mr A's letter shape is the same as Annie Apple's, but when Mr A appears in words, he says his name, 'A!' and he shoots his hand up in the air to let everyone know he is there. Ask for Mr A's name (ay) in response to the plain letter.

- **Song** Sing Mr A's verse in the *Vowel Men Song*. Show the plain letter side of his *PCC* when you sing his name, 'A!'. (Words on page 190.)

Phonemic awareness and language development

Games

- Play the Listen and Jump Game (page 162) with a small variation. Children jump towards the Annie Apple or Mr A *Picture Code Card* depending on which sound they hear at the start of these words: **age**, **alien**, acrobat, **ape**, animal, Africa, **Asia**, **acorn**, appetite, **apron**. Extension: Use words that feature the target sounds inside: c**a**p, c**a**ke, etc.

- Create 'Vowel Flip-overs' (*Copymaster 1*). Read out the above list of words. Children flip to Annie Apple or Mr A.

Picture-coding

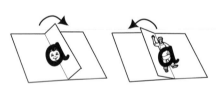

Letter shapes: a and A

- **Same shapes** Picture-code lower case and capital letters for Annie Apple and Mr A on the board. Use the picture-coding to show how they share exactly the same letter shapes – it is only their sounds that are different.

- **Sounds** Which two sounds can these letters make? Aa: (ă and ā). **Note:** Although Mr A spells his name with a capital letter, don't let the children confuse the capital letter shape with the long **a** sound. Both Annie Apple and Mr A have a lower case and a capital letter shape: **A**pple, **a**pple, **A**ge, **a**ge, ...etc.

Individual activity ideas

- *My Letterland Reading Booklet* (page 158). Page 3: **This is Mr A.**
- See *Letterland Materials* (pages 14–16) for Copymasters or Workbooks.

Dippy Duck

Materials
See the list on page 30.
Preparations
Write out and picture-code classroom labels: **d**oor, **d**esk, **d**rawer.

Action (page 148)

Dippy Duck, her sound, action and song

- **Dippy Duck** Use the *ABC Book* picture to see what this **d**elightful **d**uck looks like when she is in Letterland.

- **Sound** Show her *plain letter* to see what she looks like in words. Then discover the sound she makes in words using the **SOUNDS TRICK** (page 143): Dippy Duck, 'd…'. Ask for the *letter sound* in response to the plain letter.

- **Song** Sing Dippy's *Alphabet Song*. Show the picture side of her *PCC* when you sing her name. Turn to the plain letter every time you sing her sound. (Words on page 188.)

Phonemic awareness and language development

Listen
- Read about Dippy Duck in the *ABC Book*. Emphasise her sound and explore the picture together.

- Use *Vocabulary Cards* (page 30), classroom labels (e.g. **d**oor) and NLS words (**d**og, **d**ay, **d**ad) to draw attention to Dippy Duck's sound in words.

- Ask questions and discuss. Praise with: '**D**elightful!' or 'Well **d**one!' For example: What would **D**ippy **D**uck like for **d**inner, green grass or **d**elicious **d**uckweed? **D**oes **D**ippy's **d**uck **d**oor into her **d**en look like our **d**oors, or is it **d**ifferent? Is **D**ippy better at **d**rawing **d**inosaurs or painting people? Which **d**ay is **D**ippy **D**uck's favourite **d**ay? We**d**nes**d**ay – because her letter appears in it twice… (even though we only hear it once!)

Games
- Choose a game from the Activity Bank (pages 162–170) or play the Alliteration Game (page 150).

Letter shapes: d and D

- **Song** Sing or chant the **d** *Handwriting Song* (page 186) while children slowly finger trace or air trace the letter. Follow up with a handwriting activity.*

- **Storyline** Dippy Duck lives in a duck den at the edge of her duck pond. Her capital letter shape is the shape of her duck door. Dippy looks out of her duck door in the Reading Direction, as she makes her usual sound, 'd…' Show the Dippy Duck name flashcard you have prepared. Revise the **CHARACTER NAMES TRICK** (page 147).

Picture-coding

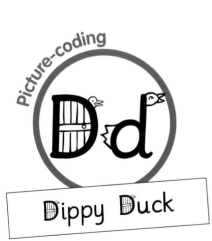

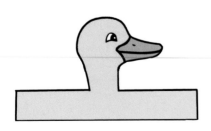

Individual activity ideas

- *My Letterland Reading Booklet* (page 158) Page 4: I am Dippy Duck. This is my mum. This is my dad.

- *See *Letterland Materials* (pages 14–16) for Copymasters or Workbooks.

- Make paper duck heads. Avoid **b**/**d** confusions with the activity on page 66.

Harry Hat Man

Harry Hat Man, his sound, action and song

- **Harry Hat Man** Use the *ABC Book* picture to see what this **h**appy and **h**elpful **H**at Man looks like when he is in Letterland.

- **Sound** Show the *plain letter* to see what he looks like in words. Then discover his letter sound using the **SOUNDS TRICK** (page 143): Harry Hat Man, 'hhh…'. Ask for the *letter sound* in response to the plain letter.

- **Song** Sing Harry's *Alphabet Song*. Show the picture side of his *PCC* when you sing his name. Turn to the plain letter every time you sing his sound. (Words on page 188.)

Phonemic awareness and language development

Listen

- Read about Harry Hat Man in the *ABC Book*. Emphasise his sound and explore the picture together.

- Use *Vocabulary Cards* (page 30), your classroom labels (e.g. **hat**) and NLS high-frequency words (**he**) to draw attention to Harry's sound.

- Ask questions and discuss: **H**ave you noticed that **H**arry **H**at Man doesn't wear shoes? It's because **h**e **h**ates noise – even the sound of his own footsteps! That's why you can **h**ardly **h**ear **h**im in words. Do you think noise gives him a **h**orrible **h**eadache? What do you think makes **H**arry **H**at Man **h**appiest, when you are noisy or when you are **h**elpful? Can you think of some ways of being **h**elpful that might make **h**im **h**appy?

Games

- Choose a game from the Activity Bank (pages 162–170) or play the Alliteration Game (page 150).

Letter shapes: h and H

- **Song** Sing or chant the **h** *Handwriting Song* (page 186) while children slowly finger trace or air trace the letter. Follow up with a handwriting activity.*

- **Storyline** Whenever the Hat Man can do something as important as starting a name or sentence, he is so happy that he does a handstand with his hat on. Show the Harry Hat Man name flashcard you have prepared. Revise the **CHARACTER NAMES TRICK** (page 147).

Individual activity ideas

- *My Letterland Reading Booklet* (page 158) Page 5: I am Harry Hat Man. This is my hand.

- *See *Letterland Materials* (pages 14–16) for Copymasters or Workbooks.

Materials
See the list on page 30.
Preparations
Write out and picture-code classroom labels: **h**ats, (Wash your) **h**ands.

Action (page 148)

Picture-coding

→ **Ideas for ending the day**
(See page 29.)

Munching Mike

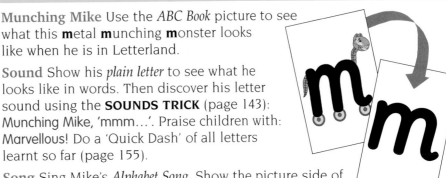

Munching Mike, his sound, action and song

- **Munching Mike** Use the *ABC Book* picture to see what this **m**etal **m**unching **m**onster looks like when he is in Letterland.

- **Sound** Show his *plain letter* to see what he looks like in words. Then discover his letter sound using the **SOUNDS TRICK** (page 143): Munching Mike, 'mmm…'. Praise children with: Marvellous! Do a 'Quick Dash' of all letters learnt so far (page 155).

- **Song** Sing Mike's *Alphabet Song*. Show the picture side of his *PCC* when you sing his name. Turn to the plain letter every time you sing his sound. (Words on page 189.)

Phonemic awareness and language development

Listen

- Read about Munching Mike in the *ABC Book*. Emphasise his sound and explore the picture together.

- Use *Vocabulary Cards* (page 30), classroom labels (e.g. **magnet**), and NLS words (**mum, me**) to draw attention to Munching Mike's sound in words.

- Ask questions and discuss. Praise answers with: '**M**arvellous!' '**M**agnificent!' or '**M**uch better!' You have **m**any, **m**any of these in your body beginning with '**mmm**…' what are they? (**m**uscles). Up in the sky, what would **M**unching **M**ike **m**unch if he could reach it? (**m**oon, **m**ilky way) What school subject **m**ight **M**unching **M**ike like **m**ost? (**m**aths)

Games

- Choose a game from the Activity Bank (pages 162–170) or play the Alliteration Game (page 150).

Letter shapes: m and M

- **Song** Sing or chant the **m** *Handwriting Song* (page 186) while children slowly finger trace or air trace the letter. Follow up with a handwriting activity.*

- **Storyline** Munching Mike is just a little monster, so he calls his Mum to do the job of starting important words like names, since Mike's Mum is much bigger than him. Show children the Munching Mike name flashcard. Revise the **CHARACTER NAMES TRICK** (page 147).

Individual activity ideas

- *My Letterland Reading Booklet* (page 158) Page 6: I like Munching Mike.

- *See *Letterland Materials* (pages 14–16) for Copymasters or Workbooks.

Materials
See the list on page 30.
Preparations
Write out and picture-code classroom labels: **m**agnet, **m**etal, **m**agazines, **m**ats.

Action (page 149)

magnet

mum   me

Picture-coding

Mm

Munching Mike

Ideas for ending the day (See page 29.)

Talking Tess

Talking Tess, her sound, action and song

Materials
See the list on page 30.

Preparations
Write out and picture-code classroom labels: **t**elephone, **t**able, **t**en, **t**wo, **t**oys, **t**eacher, **t**elevision.

- **Talking Tess** Use the *ABC Book* picture to see what this **t**all **t**echnically **t**alented woman looks like when she is in Letterland.
- **Sound** Show her *plain letter* to see what she looks like in words. Then discover her letter sound (page 143): Talking Tess, 't…'. Praise children with Terrific! Ask for all previously learnt *letter sounds* in response to the plain letters.
- **Song** Sing Tess's *Alphabet Song*. Show the picture side of her *PCC* when you sing her name. Turn to the plain letter every time you sing her sound. (Words on page 189.)

Phonemic awareness and language development

Listen

- Read about Talking Tess in the *ABC Book*. Emphasise her sound and explore the picture together.
- Use *Vocabulary Cards* (page 30), your coded classroom labels (e.g. **t**elephone), and NLS high-frequency words (**to, too, two**) to draw attention to Talking Tess's sound.
- Ask questions and discuss. **T**alking **T**ess has a **t**elescope. Do you know what it's for? She also has a **t**ank of **t**en **t**adpoles. What happens to **t**adpoles when they get bigger? Is **T**alking **T**ess **t**aller than Munching Mike! Yes! Remember to make her look **t**aller when you write her letter. Start at the **t**op! Can you find some other **t**all letters on the Wall Frieze? Praise word: **T**errific!

Games

- Choose a game from the Activity Bank (pages 162–170) or play the Alliteration Game (page 150).

Letter shapes: t and T

- **Song** Sing or chant the **t** *Handwriting Song* (page 187) while children slowly finger trace or air trace the letter. Follow up with a handwriting activity.*
- **Storyline** When Tess starts a name she takes a deep breath and grows so tall that her head disappears in the clouds! We still know it's Tess, because we can still see her arms. Show the Talking Tess name flashcard. Revise the **CHARACTER NAMES TRICK** (page 147).

Individual activity ideas

- *My Letterland Reading Booklet* (page 158) Page 7: This is for Talking Tess.
- *See Letterland Materials* (pages 14–16) for Copymasters or Workbooks.

Action (page 149)

telephone

two   too
  to

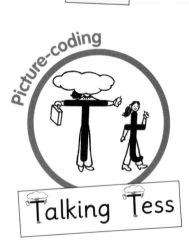

Picture-coding

Talking Tess

Ideas for ending the day
(See page 29.)

First blends

Objectives
- To revise all the letter sounds and shapes taught so far.
- To introduce the concept of blending.
- To introduce the **ROLLERCOASTER TRICK**.
- To blend words with **c**, **a**, **d**, **h**, **m** and **t**.

Quick Dash revision

- Use the Quick Dash (page 155) routine to revise all the letter sounds you have taught so far.

Teacher	Pupils
1. Who is this?	Clever Cat
2. What sound does she make in words?	'c...'

1. Who is this?	Annie Apple
2. What sound does she make in words?	'ă...'

- After you have reviewed **c**, **a**, **d**, **h**, **m** and **t** do a dash through the plain letter side of each card and ask for the letter sound only.

Reading Direction

Live Reading

- Place a Reading Direction arrow on the wall behind your Live Reading and Spelling area. Another on the floor can be useful, too.
- Help three children (holding the pictogram sides of the *Picture Code Cards*) to line up in this order: **c a t** (but don't say the word yet!)
- Invite children to imagine that the wall behind them is a great big page in a book, and that they are building a word for the children who are sitting down to read. That means they need to build the word in the Reading Direction.

The 'Store and release' technique

- Share 'Clever Cat's secret':

  I always sound better beside another letter,
  so don't make my sound all alone.
  Put a nice round apple beside me,
  so I don't have to be on my own.

Blend 'ca…' then add 't…'

● Ask the letter children to turn the cards around to reveal the plain letters.

● The whole class makes the sound that each letter makes in words.

● We are going to make Clever Cat and Annie Apple's sounds together. First, just get ready to say Clever Cat's sound, but don't say it. Then get ready to say Annie Apple's sound, but don't say it. Now, we are going to let both sounds burst out together. Are you ready? 'ca…!'

● Now blend all three sounds together: ca…t, cat.

Introduce the ROLLERCOASTER TRICK

● Introduce this blending strategy as set out on page 151.

● Tell the children that from now on, they can use this 'trick' whenever they need it – either for themselves or to help a partner read a word.

● In pairs, children blend the words **hat**, **mat**, **had** and **ham**, using the **ROLLERCOASTER TRICK**.

Individual activity ideas

● *My Letterland Reading Booklet* (page 158) Page 8: This cat is in a hat. Children read the sentence in pairs (blending the words **hat** and **cat**), and draw a cat in a hat.

Rollercoaster trick

This cat is in a hat.

My Letterland Reading Booklet   **8**

Sammy Snake

Materials
See the list on page 30.

Preparations
Write out and picture-code classroom labels: **s**cissors, **s**ix, **s**even, **s**tars.

Action (page 149)

Picture-coding

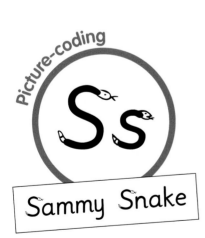

Sammy Snake, his sound, action and song

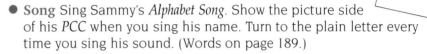

- **Sammy Snake** Use the *ABC Book* picture to see what this **s**weet, **s**miling snake looks like when he is in Letterland.

- **Sound** Show the *plain letter side* of the *Picture Code Card (PCC)* to see what his letter looks like in words. Then discover the sound he makes in words using the **SOUNDS TRICK** (page 143): Sammy Snake, 'sss…'. Ask for the *letter sound* in response to the plain letter. Praise with: Super!

- **Song** Sing Sammy's *Alphabet Song*. Show the picture side of his *PCC* when you sing his name. Turn to the plain letter every time you sing his sound. (Words on page 189.)

Phonemic awareness and language development

Listen
- Read about Sammy Snake in the *ABC Book*. Emphasise his sound and explore the picture together.

- Use *Vocabulary Cards* (page 30), your classroom labels (e.g. **sun**) and NLS high-frequency words (**said**, **see**) to draw attention to Sammy Snake's sound.

- Ask questions and discuss. **S**ammy **S**nake loves to hi**ss** his '**sss**…' **s**ound in words. Can you hear it **s**ix times in this **s**entence? Li**sss**ten… "**S**ammy **S**nake loves to **s**it in the **s**un on the **s**and by the **s**ea." What might **S**ammy like to eat - **s**ixty-**s**ix **s**izzling **s**ausages, or mashed potatoes and macaroni? Which of these might he like to become? (**s**ongwriter and **s**inger, carpenter, **s**urfer) Praise word: **S**uper!

Games
- Choose a game from the Activity Bank (pages 162–170) or play the Alliteration Game (page 150).

Letter shapes: s and S

- **Song** Sing or chant the **s** *Handwriting Song* (page 187) while children slowly finger trace or air trace the letter. Follow up with a handwriting activity.*

- **Storyline** Whenever Sammy can do something as important as starting a name or sentence, he takes a deep breath and gets bigger. He says, 'Now I'm a **sss**uper-**sss**ized **sss**nake!' Show the Sammy Snake name flashcard. Revise the **CHARACTER NAMES TRICK**: (page 147).

Individual activity ideas

- *My Letterland Reading Booklet* (page 158) Page 9: This is for Sammy Snake.

- *See Letterland Materials* (pages 14–16) for Copymasters or Workbooks.

→ **Ideas for ending the day**
(See page 29.)

Blending with endings: s, s & ss

Quick Dash revision

- Use the Quick Dash routine (page 155) to revise all the letter sounds you have taught so far.

Blending: Sammy at the end of words (plurals)

- Write **cat** on the board.
- Add Sammy Snake's *PCC* to the end of the word and ask children to make Sammy's sound at the end of the word **cats**.
- Repeat with the words **hats** and **mats**.
- What is Sammy doing? (He's adding his sound to the end of a word to change the meaning of the word from one to 'ssseveral of sssomething'.)

Sleeping Sammy
Sammy is needed in **so** many words that sometimes he has a quick snooze to catch up on lost sleep. Then, instead of his wide-awake 'sss…', you'll hear him snoozing 'zzz…' in words like **is**, **was**, **his**, **goes**, **boys** and **girls**.

Live Spelling: choose an ending (d, t or s)

- Hand out *Picture Code Cards* **a**, **d**, **h**, **m**, **t**, **s**, **s**, **i**. Use the plain letter sides.
- Ask the **h** and **a** children to stand at the front of the class. Children blend the sounds 'ha…'.
- Stretch out the word **had**, 'ha…d' to help children to hear the sounds, without distorting the sound of the whole word.
- Children repeat the word in the same stretched-out manner, and decide which letter child needs to come up to *end* the word **had**.
- Repeat with **ha(s)**, **ha(m)**, **hi(s)**, **hi(t)**, **ha(t)** and **hat(s)**.
- For words ending in **s**, children choose between Sammy's hissing sound (as in cat**s**) and his sleeping sound (as in hi**s**). (See back of sleeping **s** card.)

Sammy Snake's best friend Sally

- Build the word **hiss** by giving a line of four children the appropriate *PCCs* Sammy Snake's best friend – his sister Sally – sometimes joins him at the end of short words. Then they both love to hiss exactly the same sound at exactly the same time, so you only hear their sound once – like in the word **hiss**.
- Repeat with the words **miss**, **kiss** and **mess** to reinforce the point.

Individual activity ideas

- *My Letterland Reading Booklet* (page 158) Page 10: I can see the cat. I can see the cats. Children read each sentence (in pairs) and then illustrate them in the boxes provided.
- See page 92 for additional activities.

First segmenting words

Objectives
- To revise all the letter sounds taught so far.
- To segment words with **c**, **a**, **d**, **h**, **m**, **t** and **s**.
- To introduce the SLOW-SPEAK TRICK.

h a t s

Can you see the _ _ _?

Can you see the _ _ _ _?

My Letterland Reading Booklet ⑪

Revision

- Use the Quick Dash routine (page 155) to revise all the letter sounds you have taught so far.
- Choose an activity from the Activity Bank to revise all letters you have taught so far (pages 162–170).

First segmenting activity

- Introduce the **SLOW-SPEAK TRICK** (page 152).
- Tell children that from now on, they can use this **SLOW-SPEAK TRICK** when they want to work out which letters to write in a word.
- Give out *Picture Code Cards* for **c**, **a**, **d**, **h**, **m**, **t** and both **s**'s (Sammy Snake and Sleeping Sammy).
- Say the word **sad**, followed up by a **SLOW-SPEAK** version of the word ('sssad'). Children repeat the word in **SLOW-SPEAK**. Ask the children which Letterlanders are needed to build the word. Children holding those letter cards come up and make sad faces as they spell the word.
- Now say the word **sat**. Children **SLOW-SPEAK** the word and decide who should come up to change the word **sad** into **sat**.
- Repeat with these words: **mat** → **mats** → **cats** → **cat** → **hat** → **hats**.

SLOW-SPEAK dictation

- Make this **SLOW-SPEAK** dictation a group activity at this stage. Say some or all of these words several times, both normally and in **SLOW-SPEAK**: **had**, **ham**, **hat**, **hats**, **mat**, **mats**, **sad**, **dad**, **cat**, **cats**, **has**.
- Children do the same.
- Ask them to tell you which letter sound they hear (in the order they occur in the word) as you write them on the board.
- If you think the children are ready, you could follow up by dictating the same words for children to write down.
- After each word, put it on the board so every child can check their own work.

Individual activity ideas

- *My Letterland Reading Booklet* (page 158) Page 11: Children write the words cat and cats.

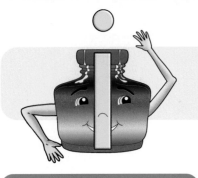

Impy Ink

Materials
See the list on page 30.

Preparations
Write out and picture-code classroom labels: **i**nk, **i**nsects.

Action (page 149)

Picture-coding
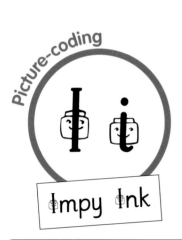

→ **Ideas for ending the day**
(See page 29.)

Impy Ink, his sound, action and song

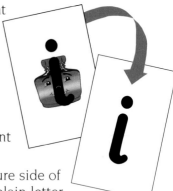

- **Impy Ink** Use the *ABC Book* picture to see what this **i**ncredible and **i**nteresting **i**nk bottle looks like when he is in Letterland.

- **Sound** Show Impy's *plain letter (PCC)* to see what he looks like in words. Then discover his letter sound using the **SOUNDS TRICK** (page 143): Impy Ink, 'i…'.

- For revision do a Quick Dash of all letters learnt so far (page 155).

- **Song** Sing Impy's *Alphabet Song*. Show the picture side of his *PCC* when you sing his name. Turn to the plain letter every time you sing his sound. (Words on page 188.)

Phonemic awareness and language development

Listen

- Read about Impy Ink in the *ABC Book*. Emphasise his sound and explore the picture together.

- Use *Vocabulary Cards* (page 30), your classroom labels (e.g. **i**nk) and NLS high-frequency words (**is, in, it**) to draw attention to Impy Ink's sound.

- Ask questions and discuss. **I**mpy **I**nk has an **i**ncredible **i**magination. He th**i**nks of lots of **i**nteresting things. For example, why do you think he always puts a spot of **i**nk above h**i**s head? Discuss possible reasons. Lead the children to decide that maybe this is Impy's way of helping children to recognise him in words, because his letter is so thin and little without the dot. Praise words: **I**ncredible! or **I**nteresting!

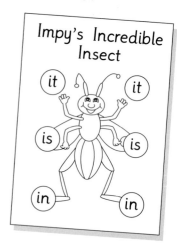
Impy's Incredible Insect

Games

- Choose a game from the Activity Bank (pages 162–170) or play the Alliteration Game (page 150).

Letter shapes: i and I

- **Song** Sing or chant the **i** *Handwriting Song* (page 186) while children slowly finger trace or air trace the letter. Follow up with a handwriting activity.*

- **Storyline** When Impy takes a deep breath, his letter gets so tall and thin that you can't see his ink spot anymore. His capital letter looks like his incredible ink pen that writes in rainbow ink! Show the Impy Ink name flashcard you have prepared. Revise the **CHARACTER NAME TRICK** (page 147).

Individual activity ideas

- *My Letterland Reading Booklet* (page 158) Page 12: It is Impy Ink's insect.

- *See *Letterland Materials* (pages 14–16) for Copymasters or Workbooks.

Mr I, the Ice Cream Man

Materials
See the list on page 30.

Preparations
Write out and picture-code classroom labels: **i**ce-cream, **i**sland, **i**vy; prepare 'Vowel Flip-overs' (*Copymaster 1*).

Action *(page 149)*

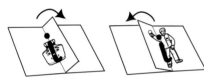

Picture-coding

Mr I's sound, action and song

- **Mr I** Mr I sells two products in Letterland: ink and ice-cream. Mr I puts his talking ink bottles in words like insect and interesting. But *he himself* appears in words that need his name: **island**, **ivy**, **idea** and **ice-cream**.

- **Sound** Turn to the plain side of his *Picture Code Card*. Mr I's letter shape is the same as Impy Ink's, but when Mr I appears in words, he says his name, 'I!' (eye) and he shoots his hand up in the air to let everyone know he is there. Ask for Mr I's name (eye) in response to the plain letter.

- **Song** Sing Mr I's verse in the *Vowel Men Song*. Show the plain letter side of his *PCC* when you sing his name, 'I!'. (Words on page 190.)

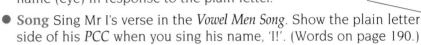

Phonemic awareness and language development

Games

- Play the Listen and Jump Game (page 162) with a small variation. Children jump towards the Impy Ink or Mr I *Picture Code Card* depending on which sound they hear at the start of these words: insect, **island**, **ice-cream**, interesting, **iron**, in, **ivy**, ink. Extension: Use words that feature the target sound inside: b**i**t, b**i**te, etc.

- Create 'Vowel Flip-overs' (*Copymaster 1*): Read out the above list of words. Children flip to Impy Ink or Mr I.

NLS words

- Write **I like** on the board. Invite a child to think of a way to end the sentence. Ask some children to add a stick man Mr I to the words **I** and **like**. Point out that the important word **I** is always a capital letter.

- Revise all letter sounds with the 'I like…Game' (page 150).

Letter shapes: i and I

- **Same shapes** Picture-code lower case and capital letters for Impy Ink and Mr I on the board. They share exactly the same letter shapes – it is only their sounds that are different.

- **Sounds** Which two sounds can these letters make? Ii: (ĭ and ī)
  Note: Although Mr I spells his name with a capital letter, don't let the children confuse the capital letter shape with the long **i** sound: **i**sland, **I**sland, **i**nsect, **I**nsect, etc.

Individual activity ideas

- *My Letterland Reading Booklet* (page 158). Page 13: I like Mr I.
- See *Letterland Materials* (pages 14–16) for Copymasters or Workbooks.

Noisy Nick

Materials
See the list on page 30.

Preparations
Write out and picture-code classroom labels: **n**ine, **n**umbers, **n**ames.

Noisy Nick, his sound, action and song

- **Noisy Nick** Use the *ABC Book* picture to see what this **n**ice but very **n**oisy boy looks like when he is in Letterland.
- **Sound** Show his plain letter *(PCC)* then discover his letter sound using the **SOUNDS TRICK** (page 143): Noisy Nick, 'nnn...'. Ask for the *letter sound* in response to the plain letter.
- **Song** Sing Nick's *Alphabet Song*. Show the picture side of his *PCC* when you sing his name. Turn to the plain letter every time you sing his sound. (Words on page 189.)

Phonemic awareness and language development

Listen
- Read about Noisy Nick in the *ABC Book*. Emphasise his sound and explore the picture together.
- Use *Vocabulary Cards* (page 30), your classroom labels (e.g. **n**ine), and NLS high-frequency words (**n**o) to draw attention to Noisy Nick's sound.
- Ask questions and discuss. Do you know how **N**ick got his **n**ickname, **N**oisy **N**ick? He has a very **n**oisy hobby. He likes to make things with wood, so he is always banging **n**ails and making a **n**asty **n**oise! **N**ow... which parts of our bodies start with **N**ick's 'nnn...' sound? (eyes, **n**ose, mouth, **n**eck, arms, hand, fingers, [finger]**n**ails) Praise word: **N**ice!

> **kn-**: Kicking King appears in words like **knee** and **know**, but he never kicks when he is **n**ext to **N**ick. That's why he is silent in these words.

Action (page 149)

nine

no

Games
- Choose a game from the Activity Bank (pages 162–170) or play the Alliteration Game (page 150).

Letter shapes: n and N

- **Song** Sing or chant the **n** *Handwriting Song* (page 186) while children slowly finger trace or air trace the letter. Follow up with a handwriting activity.*
- **Storyline** Nick starts important words by using his three nice, new nails. You can see them in Noisy Nick's name. To write his big letter shape you need to go down the first nail, back up again, down the sloping nail and up the last nail. Show the Noisy Nick name flashcard you have prepared. Revise the **CHARACTER NAME TRICK** (page 147).

Individual activity ideas

- *My Letterland Reading Booklet* (page 158) Page 14: I can see Noisy Nick.
- *See *Letterland Materials* (pages 14–16) for Copymasters or Workbooks.

Picture-coding

Noisy Nick

→ **Ideas for ending the day**
(See page 29.)

Golden Girl

Golden Girl, her sound, action and song

- **Golden Girl** Use the *ABC Book* picture to meet this **g**ood **g**irl in **g**reen.
- **Sound** Show her *plain letter* to see what she looks like in words. Then discover the sound she makes in words using the **SOUNDS TRICK** (page 143): Golden Girl, 'g...'. Ask for the *letter sound* in response to the plain letter. Praise with **G**ood! or **G**reat!
- **Song** Sing Golden Girl's *Alphabet Song*. Show the picture side of her *PCC* when you sing her name. Turn to the plain letter every time you sing her sound. (Words on page 188.)

Phonemic awareness and language development

Listen

- Read about Golden Girl in the *ABC Book*. Emphasise her sound and explore the picture together.
- Use *Vocabulary Cards* (page 30), your classroom labels (e.g. **glue**), and NLS high-frequency words (**go, going, get**) to draw attention to Golden Girl's sound.
- Ask questions and discuss. Is **G**olden **G**irl facing the Reading Direction, like all the other Letterlanders? No! Do you know why? Let's play a **g**uessing **g**ame to find out. Listen carefully: do you think its because she 'feels funny' or because she 'gets giddy'? **G**ood! She **g**ets **g**iddy unless she turns around and looks back instead of looking in the Reading Direction. Praise words: **G**reat! or **G**ood girl!

Games

- Choose a game from the Activity Bank (pages 162–170) or play the Alliteration Game (page 150).

Letter shapes: g and G

- **Song** Sing or chant the **g** *Handwriting Song* (page 186) while children slowly finger trace or air trace the letter. Follow up with a handwriting activity.*
- **Storyline** When Golden Girl is needed to start an important word, she gets into her go-cart. On her swing she is not looking in the Reading Direction. When she is in her go-cart she has to look where she is going, so that she does not bump into the other Letterlanders. Show the Golden Girl name flashcard you have prepared. Revise the **CHARACTER NAMES TRICK** (page 147).

Individual activity ideas

- *My Letterland Reading Booklet* (page 158) Page 15: I am Golden Girl. I am going to see my mum and dad.
- *See *Letterland Materials* (pages 14–16) for Copymasters or Workbooks.

Materials
See the list on page 30.

Preparations
Write out and picture-code classroom labels: **g**lue, **g**love, **g**reen.

Action (page 148)

glue

going   get

go

Picture-coding

Gg

Golden Girl

➤ **Ideas for ending the day**
(See page 29.)

Segmenting

Objectives
- To revise all the letter sounds taught so far.
- To segment words with **c**, **a**, **d**, **h**, **m**, **t**, **s**, **ss**, **i**, **n** and **g**.

h i m

Revision

- Use the Quick Dash routine (page 155) to revise all the letter sounds you have taught so far.
- Choose an activity from the Activity Bank (pages 162–170). Use any and all of the letter sounds you have taught so far.

Live Spelling

- Give out *Picture Code Cards*: **c**, **a**, **d**, **h**, **m**, **t**, **s**, **ss**, **i**, **n**, and **g**.
- Call out the word **it** both normally and in **SLOW-SPEAK** (page 152). Ask the children who think they are needed to build the word to come up and make the word at the front of the class.
- Now say the word **is**. Children **SLOW-SPEAK** the word and decide who should come up to change the word **it** into **is**. Will Sammy Snake be awake or having a quick snooze?
- Continue with these words:
  it → is → his → him → hit → hid → did → dig
  an → can → man → and → hand → handstand
  in → tin
  hiss → kiss → miss → mess → less

SLOW-SPEAK dictation

- Use the blackboard and do this as a group activity.
- Say some or all of the above Live Spelling words several times, both normally and in **SLOW-SPEAK**.
- Children repeat each word in the same **SLOW-SPEAK** manner.
- Ask them to tell you which letter sound they hear in the initial position; in the final position; in the middle position.
- If you think the children are ready, you could follow up by dictating the same words for children to write down.

Individual activity ideas

- *My Letterland Reading Booklet* (page 158) Page 16: Munching Mike is going to see his mum.
- Children draw Munching Mike's mum (capital letter) in the foreground and Munching Mike in the background with a winding path connecting them. They might enjoy drawing in some mountains in the background.

Oscar Orange

Oscar Orange, his sound, action and song

- **Oscar Orange** Use the *ABC Book* picture to see what this nice round talking **o**range looks like when he is in Letterland.

- **Sound** Show his round *plain letter* to see what he looks like in words. Then discover his special sound using the **SOUNDS TRICK** (page 143): Oscar Orange, 'ŏ …'. Ask for the *letter sound* in response to the plain letter.

- **Song** Sing Oscar's *Alphabet Song*. Show the picture side of his *PCC* when you sing his name. Turn to the plain letter every time you sing his sound. (Words page 189.)

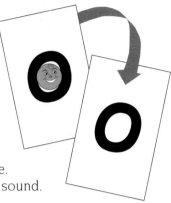

Phonemic awareness and language development

Listen

- Read about Oscar Orange in the *ABC Book*. Emphasise his sound and explore the picture together.

- Use *Vocabulary Cards* (page 30), your classroom labels (e.g. **o**range) and NLS high-frequency words (**o**n, **o**ff) to draw attention to Oscar's sound.

- Ask questions and discuss. Which of these do you think **O**scar **O**range would prefer as a pet: **o**strich/horse; monkey/**o**ctopus? What do you think he would prefer to eat: **o**melette/scrambled eggs? Play Oscar's favourite game, **O**scar's **O**pposites: Say a word and ask children to give its **o**pposite, e.g. day/night; little/big; short/tall; up/down; **o**n/**o**ff.

Games

- Choose a game from the Activity Bank (pages 162–170).

Letter shapes: o and O

- **Song** Sing or chant the **o** *Handwriting Song* (page 187) while children slowly air trace the letter. Follow up with a handwriting activity.*

- **Storyline** When Oscar Orange is needed to start an important word, he takes a deep breath and gets bigger. Show the Oscar Orange name flashcard you have prepared. Revise the **CHARACTER NAMES TRICK** (page 147).

Individual activity ideas

- *My Letterland Reading Booklet* (page 158) Page 17: Oscar Orange is on a box.

- *See *Letterland Materials* (pages 14–16) for Copymasters or Workbooks.

Oscar's Bothersome Little Brother

To explain the many irregular o's in words like c**o**me, d**o**es, d**o**ne, l**o**ve, **o**ther, m**o**ther, s**o**me, w**o**n and M**o**nday, your *Picture Code Card* set includes Oscar's Bothersome Little Br**o**ther who can't say 'ŏ…' properly. Instead he just says 'uh…'. Luckily everyone l**o**ves him in spite of the trouble he causes.

Materials
See the list on page 30.

Preparations
Write out and picture-code classroom labels: **O**ctober, **o**n, **o**range, **o**range **o**bjects.

Action (page 149)

orange

off   on

Picture-coding

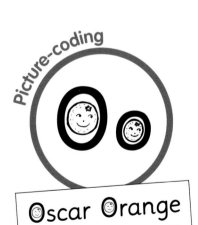

Oscar **O**range

→ **Ideas for ending the day**
(See page 29.)

Mr O, the Old Man

Materials
See the list on page 30.

Preparations
Write out and picture-code classroom labels: **o**ld, **o**pen, **o**nly; prepare 'Vowel Flip-overs' (*Copymaster 1*).

Mr O's sound, action and song

- **Mr O** Mr O, the Old Man is the oldest Vowel Man in Letterland. He brings in whole boat-loads of oranges from over the ocean. (He also brings over special talking oranges that he pops in words like **on**, **off** and **orange**.) But Mr O himself appears in words that need his name, like **old**, **ocean** and **over**.

- **Sound** Turn to the plain side of his *Picture Code Card*. Mr O's letter shape is the same as Oscar Orange's, but when Mr O appears in words, he says his name, 'O!' (oh) and he shoots his hand up in the air to let everyone know he is there. Ask for Mr O's name (oh) in response to the plain letter.

- **Song** Sing Mr O's verse in the *Vowel Men Song*. Show the plain letter side of his *PCC* when you sing his name, 'O!'. (Words on page 190.)

Action (page 149)

Phonemic awareness and language development

Games

- Play the Listen and Jump Game (page 162) with a small variation; Children jump towards the Oscar Orange or Mr O *Picture Code Card* depending on which sound they hear at the start of these words: **ocean**, on, **open**, **old**, office, **only**, ostrich, octopus. Extension: Use words that feature the target sound inside: h**o**p, h**o**pe, etc.

- Alternatively, create 'Vowel Flip-overs' (*Copymaster 1*). Read out the above list of words. Children flip to Oscar Orange or Mr O.

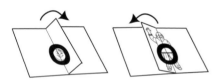

NLS words

- Can children hear and see Mr O inside these words: n**o**, g**o**, g**o**ing?

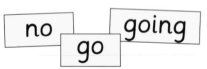

Letter shapes: o and O

Picture-coding

- **Same shapes** Picture-code lower case and capital letters for Oscar Orange and Mr O on the board. They share exactly the same letter shapes – its only their sounds that are different.

- **Sounds** Which two sounds can these letters make? Oo: (ŏ and ō)
  Note: Although Mr O spells his name with a capital letter, don't let the children assume the capital letter shape is always a long **o** sound. It's both: **O**ffice, **o**ffice, **O**cean, **o**cean, etc.

Individual activity ideas

- *My Letterland Reading Booklet* (page 158) Page 18: Hello Mr O! (no) (go)
- See *Letterland Materials* (pages 14–16) for Copymasters or Workbooks.

Peter Puppy

Peter Puppy, his sound, action and song

- **Peter Puppy** Use the *ABC Book* picture to see what this **p**layful little **p**uppy with long ears looks like when he is in Letterland.
- **Sound** Show his *plain letter* to see what he looks like in words. Then discover his letter sound (page 143): Peter Puppy, 'p...'. Ask for the *letter sound* in response to the plain letter and praise with Perfect!
- **Song** Sing Peter Puppy's *Alphabet Song*. Show the picture side of his *PCC* when you sing his name. Turn to the plain letter every time you sing his sound. (Words on page 189.)

Phonemic awareness and language development

Listen

- Read about Peter Puppy in the *ABC Book*. Emphasise his sound and explore the picture together.
- Use *Vocabulary Cards* (page 30), your classroom labels (e.g. **paper**) and NLS high-frequency words (**play**) to draw attention to Peter Puppy's sound.
- Ask questions and discuss. Can you finish this sentence? **P**eter **P**uppy **p**ut his **p**aw in his **p**ocket and **p**ulled out ...? (a **p**encil, a **p**ony, **p**izza, a **p**ear, **p**aint, **p**aper, **p**enguin, etc.) **P**eter **P**uppy always feels **p**leased and **p**roud when **p**eople are **p**olite. What **p**olite things can we say to make him **p**roud of us? (**p**lease and thank you) Remind children of Oscar's Opposites. What is the opposite of **p**ush? (**p**ull) Praise word: **P**erfect!

Games

- Choose a game from the Activity Bank (pages 162–170) or play the Alliteration Game (page 150).

Letter shapes: p and P

- **Song** Sing or chant the **p** *Handwriting Song* (page 187) while children slowly finger trace or air trace the letter. Follow up with a handwriting activity.*
- **Storyline** When Peter Puppy has a chance to start an important word, he is so pleased that he pops up so that everyone can see him better. He hopes his ears will pop up too, but they still droop. Show children the Peter Puppy name flashcard. Revise the **CHARACTER NAMES TRICK** (page 147).

Individual activity ideas

- *My Letterland Reading Booklet* (page 158) Page 19: "Can I play?" said Peter Puppy.
- *See *Letterland Materials* (pages 14–16) for Copymasters or Workbooks.

Materials
See the list on page 30.

Preparations
Write out and picture-code classroom labels: **p**aper, **p**encils, **p**ictures, **p**ink, **p**urple, **p**aints, **p**lants, **p**oster.

Action (page 149)

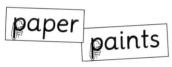

paper paints

play

Picture-coding

Peter Puppy

Ideas for ending the day
(See page 29.)

Segmenting

Objectives
- To revise all letter sounds you have taught so far.
- To segment words with **c**, **a**, **d**, **h**, **t**, **s**, **i**, **n**, **g**, **o** and **p**.
- To focus on short vowel sounds: **a**, **i** and **o**.

Revision

- Use the Quick Dash routine (page 155) to revise all the letter sounds you have taught so far.
- Choose an activity from the Activity Bank (pages 162–170) focusing on the letter sounds you will use in this segmenting lesson.

Live Spelling

- Give out *Picture Code Cards*: **c**, **a**, **d**, **h**, **t**, **s**, **i**, **n**, **g**, **o** and **p**.
- Call out the word **hot** both normally and in **SLOW-SPEAK**.
- Ask the children who think they are needed to build the word to come up and make the word at the front of the class.
- Now say the word **hat**. Children **SLOW-SPEAK** the word and decide who should come up to change the word **hot** into **hat**.
- Continue with these words:
  hot → hat → hit → it → in → on
  cat → cot
  dig → dog → dogs → dot → dots
  pat → pot → pots → stop → spot → spots → dots
  pit → pin → pop

SLOW-SPEAK dictation

- Use the blackboard and do this as a group activity.
- Say some or all of the above Live Spelling words several times, both normally and in **SLOW-SPEAK**.
- Children repeat the words in the same **SLOW-SPEAK** manner.
- Ask them to tell you which letter sound they hear in the initial position; in the final position; in the middle position.
- If you think the children are ready, you could follow up by dictating the same words for them to write down on paper.

Individual activity ideas

- *My Letterland Reading Booklet* (page 158) Page 20: Children complete the words hot and hat.

h o t

Harry the Hat Man is
h _ t in his h _ t.

My Letterland Reading Booklet ⑳

Eddy Elephant

Materials
See the list on page 30.

Preparations
Write out and picture-code classroom labels: **EXIT**, **e**leven, **e**mpty.

Action (page 148)

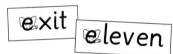

Picture-coding

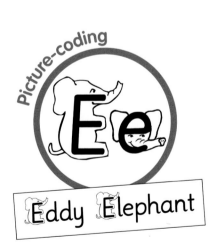

Eddy Elephant, his sound, action and song

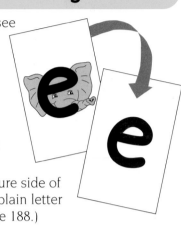

- **Eddy Elephant** Use the *ABC Book* picture to see what this **e**nergetic **e**lephant looks like when he is in Letterland.

- **Sound** Show his *plain letter* to see what he looks like in words. Then use the **SOUNDS TRICK** (page 143) to discover the sound he makes in words: Eddy Elephant, 'ĕ …'. Ask for the *letter sound* in response to the plain letter. Praise children's efforts with **Excellent!**

- **Song** Sing Eddy's *Alphabet Song*. Show the picture side of his *PCC* when you sing his name. Turn to the plain letter every time you sing his sound. (Words on page 188.)

Phonemic awareness and language development

Listen

- Read about Eddy Elephant in the *ABC Book*. Emphasise his sound and explore the picture together.

- Use *Vocabulary Cards* (page 30), your classroom labels (e.g. **EXIT**) and NLS high-frequency words (**yes**, **get**, **went**) to draw attention to Eddy Elephant's sound.

- Ask questions and discuss. Do you think **E**ddy does **e**xercises **e**very day? He must be very **e**nergetic. Could **E**ddy fit in an **e**mpty **e**nvelope? Can you think of a part of your body that starts with **E**ddy's sound? (**e**lbow) **E**ddy sometimes goes to schools and **e**ncourages **e**veryone to make an **e**xtra special **e**ffort to make his sound just right, and to get a good **e**ducation. Praise word: **E**xcellent!

Games

- Choose a game from the Activity Bank (pages 162–170) or play the Alliteration Game (page 150).

Letter shapes: e and E

- **Song** Sing or chant the **e** *Handwriting Song* (page 186) while children slowly finger trace or air trace the letter. Follow up with a handwriting activity.*

- **Storyline** Eddy Elephant is very proud of his 'elephant on end' trick. He sits down and points everything - his trunk and all his feet - in the Reading Direction whenever he starts an important word. Show the Eddy Elephant name flashcard you have prepared. Revise the **CHARACTER NAMES TRICK** (page 147).

Individual activity ideas

- *My Letterland Reading Booklet* (page 158) Page 21: We all like Eddy Elephant.

- *See Letterland Materials* (pages 14–16) for Copymasters or Workbooks.

→ **Ideas for ending the day**
(See page 29.)

Mr E, the Easy Magic Man

Materials
See the list on page 30.

Preparations
Write out and picture-code classroom labels: **e**qual; prepare 'Vowel Flip-overs' (*Copymaster 1*).

Action (page 149)

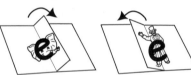

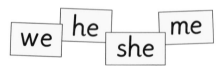

we he she me

Picture-coding

Mr E's sound, action and song

- **Mr E** Mr E, the Easy Magic Man is the man who has Eddy Elephant for a pet. Mr E does a lot of magic tricks in words. His tricks make is eeeasy for us to read. That's why he is called the Easy Magic Man! He loves to say his name, 'E!' (ee) in words, just like the other Vowel Men. (Revise other Vowel Men briefly.)

- **Sound** Show his *plain letter*. Mr E's letter shape is the same as Eddy Elephant's, but when Mr E appears in words, he says his name, 'E!' (ee) and he shoots his hand up in the air to let everyone know he is there. Ask for Mr E's name (ee) in response to the plain letter.

- **Song** Sing Mr E's verse in the *Vowel Men Song*. Show the plain letter side of his *PCC* when you sing his name, 'E!'. (Words on page 190.)

Phonemic awareness and language development

Games
- Play the Listen and Jump Game (page 162) with a small variation. Children jump towards the Eddy Elephant or Mr E *Picture Code Card* depending on which sound they hear *inside* these words: bet, **beat**, fed, **feed**, get, jet, **keep**, **sheep**, let, **leap**, met, **meat**.

- Create 'Vowel Flip-overs' (*Copymaster 1*). Read out the above list of words. Children flip to Eddy Elephant or Mr E.

NLS words
- Can children hear and see Mr E inside these words: h**e**, w**e**, m**e**, sh**e**, s**ee**?

Letter shapes: e and E

- **Same shapes** Picture-code lower case and capital letters for Eddy Elephant and Mr E on the board. They share exactly the same letter shapes – it's only their sounds that are different.

- **Sounds** Which two sounds can these letters make? Ee: (ĕ and ē)
  Note: Although Mr E spells his name with a capital letter, don't let the children confuse the capital letter shape with the long ē sound: **E**ggs, **e**ggs, **E**at, **e**at, etc.

Individual activity ideas

- *My Letterland Reading Booklet* (page 158) Page 22: "Can you see me?" said Mr E.

- See *Letterland Materials* (pages 14–16) for Copymasters or Workbooks.

Blending and segmenting

Objectives
- To revise all the letter sounds taught so far.
- To segment words with **c**, **a**, **d**, **h**, **m**, **t**, **s**, **i**, **n**, **g**, **o** and **p**.
- To focus on short vowel sounds: **a**, **e**, **i** and **o**.

My Letterland Reading Booklet (23)

Revision

- Use the Quick Dash routine (page 155) to revise all the letter sounds you have learned so far.
- Choose an activity from the Activity Bank (pages 162–170) with a focus on the short vowel sounds **a**, **e**, **i** and **o**.

Blending: Vowels-go-round

- Choose four children to be the short vowel characters Annie Apple, Eddy Elephant, Impy Ink and Oscar Orange.
- Hand out the short vowel *Picture Code Cards* for **a**, **e**, **i** and **o**.
- Hand out additional *Picture Code Cards*: **c**, **d**, **h**, **m**, **t**, **s**, **n**, **g** and **p**.
- The **p** and **t** letter children stand at the front of the class, leaving a space for a third child to stand in between them.
- The vowel children stand in a circle and take turns to appear in the middle of the word.
- The class blends the word and decides if it is a real word or not.
- Repeat with **d__g** and **h__t**.

SLOW-SPEAK dictation

- Use the blackboard and do this as a group activity.
- Say some or all of the above blending words several times, both normally and in **SLOW-SPEAK**.
- Children repeat the words in the same **SLOW-SPEAK** manner.
- Ask them to tell you which letter sound they hear in the beginning position; in the final position; in the middle position.
- If you think the children are ready, you could follow up by dictating the same words for them to write down.

Individual activity ideas

- *My Letterland Reading Booklet* (page 158) Page 23: Children complete the words **pan**, **pin** and **pen**.
- See page 93 for additional activities.

Uppy Umbrella

Uppy Umbrella, her sound, action and song

- **Uppy Umbrella** Use the *ABC Book* picture to see what this **u**pbeat and **u**nusual **u**mbrella looks like when she is in Letterland.

- **Sound** Show her *plain letter* to see what she looks like in words. Then discover her letter sound using the **SOUNDS TRICK** (page 143): Uppy Umbrella, 'ŭ ...'. Ask for the *letter sound* in response to the plain letter.

- **Song** Sing Uppy's *Alphabet Song*. Show the picture side of her *PCC* when you sing her name. Turn to the plain letter every time you sing her sound. (Words on page 189.)

Phonemic awareness and language development

Listen

- Read about Uppy Umbrella in the *ABC Book*. Emphasise her sound and explore the picture together.

- Use *Vocabulary Cards* (page 30), your classroom labels (e.g. **under**) and NLS high-frequency words (**up**) to draw attention to Uppy Umbrella's sound.

- Ask questions and discuss. Do you think **U**ppy **U**mbrella sleeps downstairs or **u**pstairs? Where do you sleep? Can you think of some creatures that live **u**nderwater? Do you think **U**ppy likes being **u**pside down? **U**ppy **U**mbrella does something that other **u**mbrellas don't do. What **u**nusual thing does **U**ppy **U**mbrella do? (She talks!) What is the opposite of over? (**u**nder)

Games

- Choose a game from the Activity Bank (pages 162–170) or play the Alliteration Game (page 150).

Letter shapes: u and U

- **Song** Sing or chant the **u** *Handwriting Song* (page 187) while children slowly finger trace or air trace the letter. Follow up with a handwriting activity.*

- **Storyline** When Uppy Umbrella starts an important word all she has to do to make her letter bigger is take a deep breath. Show the Uppy Umbrella name flashcard you have prepared. Revise the **CHARACTER NAMES TRICK** (page 147).

Individual activity ideas

- *My Letterland Reading Booklet* (page 158) Page 24: Uppy Umbrella is going up, up and away.

- *See *Letterland Materials* (pages 14–16) for Copymasters or Workbooks.

Materials
See the list on page 30.

Preparations
Write out and picture-code classroom labels: **u**nder, **u**mbrellas.

Action (page 149)

under

up

Picture-coding

Uppy Umbrella

→ Ideas for ending the day
(See page 29.)

Mr U, the Uniform Man

Materials
See the list on page 30.

Preparations
Write out and picture-code classroom labels: **u**niform; prepare 'Vowel Flip-overs' *(Copymaster 1)*.

Action (page 149)

Picture-coding

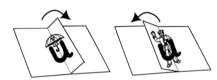

uniform

you

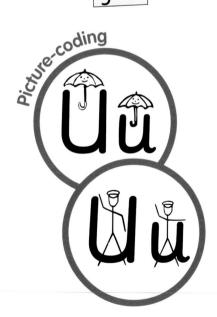

Mr U's sound, action and song

- **Mr U** Mr U has the important job of looking after all the umbrellas in Letterland. In fact, Uppy Umbrella is one of Mr U's special talking umbrellas. You can tell Mr U has an important job because he is wearing a **u**niform. What do you think he says in words? His name of course: 'U!' (you). (Revise other Vowel Men briefly.)

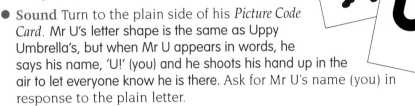

- **Sound** Turn to the plain side of his *Picture Code Card*. Mr U's letter shape is the same as Uppy Umbrella's, but when Mr U appears in words, he says his name, 'U!' (you) and he shoots his hand up in the air to let everyone know he is there. Ask for Mr U's name (you) in response to the plain letter.

- **Song** Sing Mr U's verse in the *Vowel Men Song*. Show the plain letter side of his *PCC* when you sing his name, 'U!'. (Words on page 190.)

Phonemic awareness and language development

Games
- Play the Listen and Jump Game (page 162) with a small variation: children jump towards the Uppy Umbrella or Mr U *Picture Code Card* depending on which sound they hear at the start: us, **uniform**, **united**, umbrella, **use**, **useful**, up, under.
  Extension: Use words that contain the target sound *inside* them, e.g. c**u**p, c**u**be, h**u**t, m**u**sic, sh**u**t, c**u**te, etc.
- Create 'Vowel Flip-overs' *(Copymaster 1)*: Read out the above list of words. Children flip to Uppy Umbrella or Mr U.

NLS words
- Can children hear Mr U's name inside the word: yo**u**?

Letter shapes: u and U

- **Same shapes** Picture-code lower case and capital letters for Uppy Umbrella and Mr U on the board. Explain how they share exactly the same letter shapes – it is only their sounds that are different.

- **Sounds** Which two sounds can these letters make? Uu: (ŭ and ū)
  Note: Although Mr U spells his name with a capital letter, don't let the children confuse the capital letter shape with the long **u** sound: **U**p, **u**p, **U**niform, **u**niform, etc.

Individual activity ideas

- *My Letterland Reading Booklet* (page 158) Page 25: "How are you?" said Mr U.
- See *Letterland Materials* (pages 14–16) for Copymasters or Workbooks.

Kicking King

Kicking King, his sound, action and song

- **Kicking King** Use the *ABC Book* picture to meet this **k**ind **k**ing.
- **Sound** Discover his letter sound using the **SOUNDS TRICK** (page 143): Kicking King, 'k...'. Clever Cat is very proud to share the same sound as Kicking King. But she prefers to curl up at the beginning of words, so Kicking King usually says their sound at the end of words – where there is plenty of room to kick!
- **Song** Sing Kicking King's *Alphabet Song*. Show the picture side of his *PCC* when you sing his name. Turn to the plain letter every time you sing his sound. (Words on page 188.)

Phonemic awareness and language development

Listen

- Read about Kicking King in the *ABC Book*. Emphasise his sound and explore the picture together.
- Use *Vocabulary Cards* (page 30) and your classroom labels (e.g. **key**), to draw attention to Kicking King's sound.
- Ask questions and discuss. Not every country has a **k**ing. Does our country have a **k**ing? Do you think **K**icking **K**ing is a nasty king or a **k**ind **k**ing? Kicking **K**ing loves to practise his **k**ick in words. Can you hear him **k**icking in these words? (**k**itchen, bedroom, **k**ettle, chair, **k**eys, **k**eep, **k**etchup) How many times can you hear **K**icking **K**ing's sound in his name? **K**ic**k**ing **K**ing (3 times)

Games

- Choose a game from the Activity Bank (pages 162–170) or play the Alliteration Game (page 150).

Letter shapes: k and K

- **Song** Sing or chant the **k** *Handwriting Song* (page 186) while children slowly finger trace or air trace the letter. Follow up with a handwriting activity.*
- **Storyline** When Kicking King starts an important word, he takes a deep breath. Then, amazingly, his arm and kicking leg get longer so he can look more important in a word. Show the Kicking King name flashcard you have prepared. Revise the **CHARACTER NAMES TRICK** (page 147).

Individual activity ideas

- *My Letterland Reading Booklet* (page 158) Page 26: "Can I play?" said Kicking King.
- *See Letterland Materials* (pages 14–16) for Copymasters or Workbooks.

Materials
See the list on page 30.
Preparations
Write out and picture-code classroom labels: **k**eys.

Action (page 149)

keys

Picture-coding

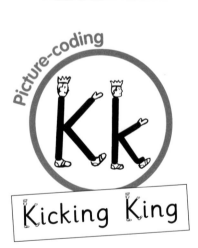

Kicking King

Ideas for ending the day
(See page 29.)

Blending and segmenting: -ck & -ng

Objectives
- To revise all the letter sounds taught so far.
- To introduce endings **ck** and **ng**
- Blending and segmenting

Clever Cat or Kicking King?

Remind children that Clever Cat and Kicking King make the same sound. But how will they know which letter to use? Explain that Clever Cat is proud to *begin* far more words than Kicking King. Kicking King finds it too cramped at the start of words. He prefers, when he can, to be at the end of words where there is more space to kick. (The proof is in the dictionary – have a look!)

Introducing -ck

- Show the **-ck** *PCC* and tell the **-ck** story:
  Clever Cat loves watching Kicking King practise his kicks at the end of short quick words like **back**, **duck**, **pack**, **quick**, **rock**, **sick**, **sock**, and **trick**. Kicking King tells Clever Cat to stay safely behind him each time he does a **quick kick!**

Live Reading and Spelling

- Hand out *PCCs* **ck**, **k**, **i**, **s** and **t** and help children build the word **kick**.
- **SLOW-SPEAK** the word **sick**. Children repeat the word in the same stretched-out manner.
- Who should sit down and who should come up to make the word **sick**?
- Insert the **t** child to build the word **stick**. Children blend the word aloud.

Introducing -ng

- Write **Kicking King** on the board, and ask the children to read it.
- Underline the **ing** in both words. Ask the children to read the sound.
- Show the **-ng** *PCC* and tell the **-ng** story:

  Noisy Nick and Golden Girl are making a singing sound. Why? Golden Girl thinks that when they make their sounds together, they sound like singing bells. She has even written a song about the **ng** sound they make in words. So now, whenever they are next to each other in a word, Noisy Nick and Golden Girl si**ng** their own special si**ng**ing **ng** sound.

Live Spelling

- Hand out *PCCs* for **k**, **i** and **ng**, and help children to build the word **king**.
- All together, say the word **king** but hold on to the end sound **-ng**.
- Say the **-ng** sound together a few times, pointing out that it sounds like a singing sound.
- Listen to the Letterland Bells Song on the *Blends and Digraphs Songs* cassette or CD.
- Next, hand out *Picture Code Cards* **s**, **o** and **u**.
- Call out the words **sing**, then **song**, then **sung**. The children decide who should sit down or come up to complete each word.

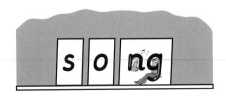

Note: See pages 92 and 93 for additional activities.

Sounds only: sh, ch & th

Objectives
- To revise all the letter sounds you have taught so far.
- To introduce **sh**, **ch**, **th** (as SOUNDS only).

Introducing three new sounds: sh, ch and th

- Teach the sound **sh** along with an action: children put an index finger in front of their mouths and make a 'shushing' action.
- Teach the **ch** sound along with an action: children put an index finger under their noses and pretend to sneeze – (not achoo! but a polite ch!)
- Teach the unvoiced **th** sound (as in **th**ree and **th**ink) along with an action: children hold their **th**umbs in front of their mouths to feel the breath escaping. Teach the children to stick out their tongues a little bit as they make this sound.

Activity ideas

Linking action and sound
- In random order, make the three sounds (**sh**, **ch** and **th**). Children repeat the sound and make the corresponding action.
- In random order, make the **sh**, **ch** and **th** actions. Children supply the corresponding sound as they repeat the action.

Activity Bank
- Choose some activities from the Activity Bank (pages 162–170). You could practise each sound individually or choose activities where children use all three sounds.

Words with sh, ch and th
- Can the children think of any words that start with each sound?
- Read out this list of words. Pause after each word. Children repeat the target sound and make the action: **ship**, **chip**, **three**, **cheese**, **she**, **chipmunk**, **shower**, **think**, **chin**, **thank you**, **show**.

Sounds and spellings: sh & ch

Objectives
- To revise all the letter sounds taught so far.
- To introduce **sh** and **ch** stories.

hush

much

Introducing sh

The '**sh**-story' is a great opportunity for role-play and to use some simple props (the Hat Man's Hat and a Sammy Snake headband).

- Choose two children to be Sammy Snake and the Hat Man. Sammy stands a few paces off to the left of the Hat Man as they stand facing the class.

  Which sound does Sammy usually make in words? Yes, he like to hiss 'sss…' very loudly. How does the Hat Man feel about noise? That's right, he **h**ates it! So what do you think happens when Sammy comes slithering and sliding up behind the Hat Man in a word? (Sammy Snake should start slithering up to the Hat Man, making his loud 'sss…' sound.) Do you think he will put up with all that noise? What do you think he does? He turns back and says '**sh**…!' to hush Sammy up.

- Show both sides of the **sh** *Picture Code Card*.

  So, whenever you see Sammy and the Hat Man side by side in a word, don't expect Sammy's usual 'sss…' sound, or the Hat Man's usual 'hhh…' sound. Expect one big 'sh…!' instead.

Introducing ch

- Again, role-play this simple story with or without props.

  Clever Cat belongs to the Hairy Hat Man. He looks after her well and she loves him. But she has one problem. As soon as she finds herself next to him in a word, his hairy hat makes her nose tickle. So whenever they come together in a word, all you can hear is her sneeze, '**ch**…'

  (To picture-code: Clever Cat's paw is politely raised to cover her sneeze and her eyes are closed. Point out that it's impossible to keep your eyes open when you really sneeze.)

Activity ideas

- Divide the class into Sammy Snakes and Hat Men. Each makes their single sound until you give the signal telling them to pair up. Immediately the children should fill the room with 'sh…' sounds as the Hat Men use the hushing action to act out the new sound. Repeat with Clever Cat and the Hat Man for 'ch…'.
- Listen to the 'Sh Song' and 'Ch Song' on the *Blends and Digraphs Songs*.

Live Reading and Spelling

- Hand out *Picture Code Cards* for **sh** and **ch**, as well as **i**, **n**, **p** and **o**.
- **SLOW-SPEAK** the word **ship**. Children repeat the word and decide who is needed to build the word.
- Continue with **chip** → **chop** → **shop** → **ship** → **shin** → **chin**.

Individual activities

- *My Letterland Reading Booklet* (page 158) Page 27: Children draw the **sh** pictogram and a **ship** as well as the **ch** pictogram and some **children**.
- See pages 89–90 for additional activities.

Sounds and spellings: th & th

Objectives
• To introduce voiced and unvoiced 'th...' sounds.

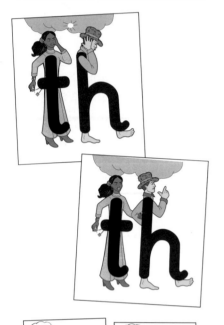

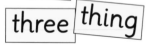

Introducing th (both sounds)

● The following story covers both **th** sounds: voiced (as in **the**, **this**, **that** and **they**); and unvoiced (as in **three**, **thunder**, **think** and **thin**). Role-play the story with or without props (a Hat Man hat and some thunder clouds).

Talking Tess spends a lot of time making her tiny 't...' sound in many, many words. But have you ever noticed that Tess and the Hat Man make a completely different sound whenever they meet up in a word? Talking Tess blames it on the weather – especially thunderstorms. Talking Tess loves to listen to thunderstorms, but the Hat Man hates the thunder – it's so loud! So Talking Tess always hurries up to the Hat Man to comfort him as she says, 'There, **th**ere. It's only **th**e **th**under!'

● The last phrase (**the thunder**) contains both the voiced and the unvoiced **th** sounds. Get everyone to say **the** out loud and then to whisper the unvoiced **th** sound in the word **thunder**. Hold up the voiced and unvoiced **th** *Picture Code Cards* in turn. Help the children to realise that the **th** sound appears in some words voiced (as in **there**, **the** and **this**) and in some words as a whispered sound (as in **thunder**, **three** and **thing**).

● If children are having difficulty saying the sound, teach them to wet their thumbs four times as they say 'There, **th**ere. It's only **th**e **th**under'. If they don't stick out their tongues just a little bit, they may end up sounding like Dippy Duck ('dere') or Firefighter Fred ('funder') instead of Tess and the Hat Man!

Activity ideas

Word wall

● If you have a word wall of high-frequency words, ask children to point out all the words with **th**: **the**, **there**, **this**, **that**, **these** as well as **three** and **thing**.

Word hunt

● Ask children to hunt for **th** words in their books and write them down.

Live Spelling

● Hand out *Picture Code Cards* for **sh**, **ch** and **th/th**, **a**, **t**, **s**, **i**, **n**, **o** and **p**.
● Line up the children in the word **that**. (Use the **th** as in **there** card.)
● Children blend the word aloud.
● Continue with the following word string: **thin*** → **chin** → **chip** → **chips** → **chip** → **chop** → **shop** → **shops** → **ships** → **ship**

(*Use the **th** as in **thunder** card.)

Individual activity ideas

● *My Letterland Reading Booklet* (page 158) Page 28: Children draw the **th** pictogram and a number **three**.
● See page 90 for additional activities.

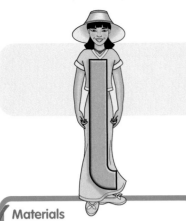

Lucy Lamp Light

Materials
See the list on page 30.

Preparations
Write out and picture-code classroom labels: leaf, lamp, light, letters.

Action (page 149)

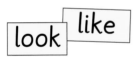
lamp

look like

Picture-coding

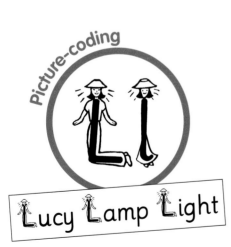

Lucy Lamp Light

→ **Ideas for ending the day**
(See page 29.)

Lucy Lamp Light, her sound, action and song

- **Lucy Lamp Light** Use the *ABC Book* picture to see what this long and lovely lady looks like when she is in Letterland.

- **Sound** Show her *plain letter* to see what she looks like in words. Then discover the sound she makes in words (page 143): Lucy Lamp Light, 'lll…'. Ask for the *letter sound* in response to the plain letter, keeping mouths almost shut to avoid 'llluh'. Praise children's efforts with Lovely!

- **Song** Sing Lucy's *Alphabet Song*. Show the picture side of her *PCC* when you sing her name. Turn to the plain letter every time you sing her sound. (Words on page 188.)

Phonemic awareness and language development

Listen

- Read about Lucy in the *ABC Book*. Emphasise her sound and explore the picture together.

- Use *Vocabulary Cards* (page 30), your classroom labels (e.g. **lamp**) and NLS words (**look**, **like**) to draw attention to Lucy Lamp Light's sound.

- Ask questions and discuss. What do we call Lucy Lamp Light's long house with a lovely light on top? (lighthouse) How many times can you hear her sound at the start of these words? (little lambs leaping down the lane). When we go to the library, does the librarian lend us books or give us books? There are 26 of them in the alphabet: (letters). A place that starts with Lucy's sound: (Letterland). Praise word: Lovely !

Games

- Choose a game from the Activity Bank (pages 162–170) or play the Alliteration Game (page 150).

Letter shapes: l and L

- **Song** Sing or chant the l *Handwriting Song* (page 186) while children slowly finger trace or air trace the letter. Follow up with a handwriting activity.*

- **Storyline** Whenever Lucy Lamp Light starts important words, she takes a deep breath and gets bigger. In her case, however, her legs also grow longer, so long, in fact, that she has to sit down with her legs on the line. Show the name flashcard you have prepared. Revise the **CHARACTER NAMES TRICK** (page 147).

Individual activity ideas

- *My Letterland Reading Booklet* (page 158) Page 29: Look! Can you see Lucy Lamp Light's light?

- *See *Letterland Materials* (pages 14–16) for Copymasters or Workbooks.

Firefighter Fred

Firefighter Fred, his sound, action and song

- **Firefighter Fred** Use the *ABC Book* picture to see what this **f**amous, **f**earless **f**irefighter looks like when he is in Letterland.

- **Sound** Show his *plain letter side* to see what he looks like when he makes his special sound in words. Then discover his letter sound (page 143): Firefighter Fred, 'fff…'. Ask for the *letter sound* in response to the plain letter. Praise with: Fabulous!

- **Song** Sing Fred's **f**abulous *Alphabet Song*. Show the picture side of his *PCC* when you sing his name. Turn to the plain letter every time you sing his sound. (Words on page 188.)

Phonemic awareness and language development

Listen

- Read about Firefighter Fred in the *ABC Book*. Emphasise his sound and explore the picture together.

- Use *Vocabulary Cards* (page 30), your classroom labels (e.g. **flowers**) and NLS high-frequency words (**for**) to draw attention to Fred's sound.

- Ask questions and discuss. What **f**ive things have you all got in your hands right now, just like **F**irefighter **F**red? (**f**ive **f**ingers) What comes out of his **f**ire hose? (**f**oam) Which do you think **F**irefighter **F**red would prefer, **b**read and **b**utter **or f**resh **f**ruit… going sailing at sea or going **f**ishing in his **f**avourite **f**orest lake? Can we think of a **f**ew **f**amous people? Praise words: **F**abulous! and **F**antastic!

Games

- Choose a game from the Activity Bank (pages 162–170) or play the Alliteration Game (page 150).

Letter shapes: f and F

- **Song** Sing or chant the **f** *Handwriting Song* (page 186) while children slowly finger trace or air trace the letter. Follow up with a handwriting activity.*

- **Storyline** Whenever Firefighter Fred can do something as important as starting a name or sentence, he takes a deep breath and becomes a bit bigger and sharper as well. Show the Firefighter Fred name flashcard you have prepared. Revise the **CHARACTER NAMES TRICK** (page 147).

Individual activity ideas

- *My Letterland Reading Booklet* (page 158) Page 30: This is for Firefighter Fred.
- *See *Letterland Materials* (pages 14–16) for Copymasters or Workbooks.

Materials
See the list on page 30.
Preparations
Write out and picture-code classroom labels: **f**our, **f**ive, **f**ifteen, **f**ifty, **f**ifty-**f**ive, **f**lowers.

Action (page 148)

flowers

for

Picture-coding

Firefighter Fred

Ideas for ending the day
(See page 29.)

Blending and segmenting: ff & ll

Objectives
- Live Spelling with short vowels **a**, **e**, **i**, **o** and **u**; **f**, **l**, **t**, **g**, **s** and **p**.
- To introduce endings **ff** and **ll**.

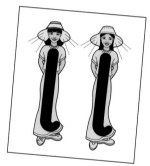

Note: See page 92 for additional activities.

Live Spelling

● Hand out *Picture Code Cards* for the letters below and use the following Live Spelling chains. Include both **s** cards.

fit → lit → lift

legs → logs → log → lot → lots → lot → let → lit → lip → lap

Best friends: ff and ll

● Write up the words **hiss**, **kiss** and **miss** on the board.

● Remind children of Sammy Snake's best friend Sally, and how they both make exactly the same sound at exactly the same time.

● Introduce **ff** and **ll**:

Firefighter Fred's 's best friend is Firefighter Frank. One of their favourite spots in words is at the end. For example, Firefighter Fred never sets **off** to fight a fire without his best friend Frank. That is why you always see two firefighters in the word **off**.

ff words: **cliff, cuff, fluff, huff, muff, off, puff, scoff, scruff, sniff, snuff, staff, stiff, stuff**

You will usually see two Lamp Ladies at the end of short words. Why? Well, Lucy feels a bit lonely at the end of little words. So she calls in her best friend Linda for company. They share their sound, and light up lots of little words very well.

ll words: **all, ball, bell, bill, call, doll, fall, fell, fill, full, hall, hill, kill, pull, sell, shall, shell, small, smell, spell, still, tall, tell, till, wall, well, will**

Live Spelling

● Hand out *Picture Code Cards* **ss**, **ff** and **ll** as well as **h, m, t, s, i, n, o, p, e, u, k, l** and **f**.

● Prepare children by telling them that there will be best friends in all of these Live Spelling words:

spell → sell → sill → fill → fell → hill

huff → puff → sniff → stiff → off

hiss → kiss → miss → mess → less

Bouncy Ben

Materials
See the list on page 30.

Preparations
Write out and picture-code classroom labels: **b**all, **b**at, **b**lue, **b**rown, **b**lack.

Action (page 148)

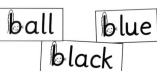

Picture-coding

b & d letter shapes

Bouncy Ben, his sound, action and song

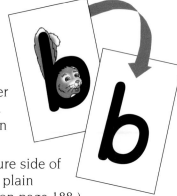

- **Bouncy Ben** Use the *ABC Book* picture to see what this **b**right **b**ouncing **b**unny with **b**ig **b**rown ears looks like when he is in Letterland.

- **Sound** Show the *plain letter side* of the PCC to see what he looks like in words. Then discover his letter sound (page 143): Bouncy Ben, 'b...'. Ask for the *letter sound* in response to the plain letter. Praise with Brilliant!

- **Song** Sing Ben's *Alphabet Song*. Show the picture side of his *PCC* when you sing his name. Turn to the plain letter every time you sing his sound. (Words on page 188.)

Phonemic awareness and language development

Listen
- Read about Bouncy Ben in the *ABC Book*. Emphasise his sound and explore the picture together.

- Use *Vocabulary Cards* (page 30), your classroom labels (e.g. **ball**) and NLS high-frequency words (**big**) to draw attention to Bouncy Ben's sound.

- Ask questions and discuss. Does **B**ouncy **B**en live in a house halfway up a hill or in a **b**urrow under a **b**ridge? What does Ben like **b**est; walking, hopping or **b**ouncing along in the Reading Direction? **B**reakfast – fresh fruit or **b**rown **b**read, **b**utter and **b**lueberries? What might **B**en **b**uild? (**b**ridge, house, **b**oat, **b**ookcase) Do you think he **b**oasts about his **b**eautiful **b**ig **b**rown ears? Praise word: '**B**rilliant!'

Games
- Choose a game from the Activity Bank (pages 162–170) or play the Alliteration Game (page 150).

Letter shapes: b and B

- **Song** Sing or chant the **b** *Handwriting Song* (page 186) while children slowly finger trace or air trace the letter. Follow up with a handwriting activity.*

- **Storyline** Whenever Bouncy Ben can do something as important as starting a name or a sentence, he balances his 'best, blue ball' between his 'big, brown ears'! Show the Bouncy Ben name flashcard you have prepared. Revise the **CHARACTER NAMES TRICK** (page 147).

Individual activity ideas

- *My Letterland Reading Booklet* (page 158) Page 31: This is for Bouncy Ben.

- *See *Letterland Materials* (pages 14–16) for Copymasters or Workbooks.

- Show children how to find Dippy Duck and/or Bouncy Ben in their own hands (see left). Make a duck head (page 35) for their right index fingers and ears and wiskers for their left hands.

Jumping Jim

Jumping Jim, his sound, action and song

- **Jumping Jim** Use the *ABC Book* picture to see what this **j**umping and **j**uggling boy looks like when he is in Letterland.
- **Sound** Show the *plain letter side* of the *PCC* to see what he looks like in words. Then find out what sound he makes in words (page 143): Jumping Jim, 'j...' Ask for the *letter sound* in response to the plain letter.
- **Song** Sing Jumping Jim's *Alphabet Song*. Show the picture side of his *PCC* when you sing his name. Turn to the plain letter every time you sing his sound. (Words on page 189.)

Phonemic awareness and language development

Listen

- Read about Jim in the *ABC Book*. Emphasise his sound and explore the picture together.
- Use *Vocabulary Cards* (page 30) and your classroom labels (e.g. **jigsaw**), to draw attention to Jumping Jim's sound.
- Ask questions and discuss. What kind of shoes does **J**umping **J**im wear, boots or **j**ogging shoes? Remember – he always **j**umps in the Reading Direction, so always make sure his **j**ogging shoes are behind him! A healthy drink that begins with his sound? (**j**uice) He's a very **j**olly fellow, so which emotion do you think he feels most? (anger, sadness or **j**oy)
- Follow-up: Listen to some **j**azz and practice a short 'skat'.

Games

- Choose a game from the Activity Bank (pages 162–170) or play the Alliteration Game (page 150).

Letter shapes: j and J

- **Song** Sing or chant the **j** *Handwriting Song* (page 186) while children slowly finger trace or air trace the letter. Follow up with a handwriting activity.*
- **Storyline** Whenever Jumping Jim can start an important word, he is so pleased that he does a big jump and his head disappears in the clouds. We can no longer see even one of his juggling balls. Show the Jumping Jim name flashcard you have prepared. Revise the **CHARACTER NAMES TRICK** (page 147).

Individual activity ideas

- *My Letterland Reading Booklet* (page 158) Page 32: Look up! It's Jumping Jim.
- *See Letterland Materials* (pages 14–16) for Copymasters or Workbooks.

Materials
See the list on page 30.

Preparations
Write out and picture-code classroom labels: **j**igsaw, January, June, July, **j**ars, **j**ug, **j**uice.

Action (page 149)

Picture-coding

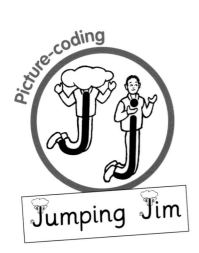

→ **Ideas for ending the day**
(See page 29.)

Blending and segmenting

Objectives
- To revise all letter sounds.
- To focus on **b**, **j** and short vowels **a**, **e**, **i**, **o** and **u**.

Note: See page 93 for additional activities.

Revision

- Use the Quick Dash routine (page 155) to revise all the letter sounds you have taught so far.
- Choose an activity from the Activity Bank (pages 162–70). Use any and all letter sounds you have taught so far.

Blending: Vowels-go-round

- Choose two children to hold *Picture Code Cards* **b** and **t**, leaving space for a third child to stand between them.
- Hand out the short vowel *Picture Code Cards* **a**, **e**, **i**, **o** and **u**.
- The vowel children form a circle and take turns appearing between the **b** and **t**.
- The class blends the sounds to read each word, deciding in each case whether it is a real word or not: **bat → bet → bit → bot → but**

Live Spelling

- Hand out *Picture Code Cards* for **a**, **d**, **m**, **t**, **i**, **g**, **p**, **e**, **u**, **b** and **j**.
- Live Spell the following words:
  bet → bed → bad → bid → bud
  jump → jet → jig → jam → Jim
- Alternatively, use these words for a **SLOW-SPEAK** dictation.

Red Robot

Materials
See the list on page 30.

Preparations
Write out and picture-code classroom labels: **r**ed, **r**ead, **r**ecycle.

Action (page 149)

Picture-coding

→ **Ideas for ending the day**
(See page 29.)

Red Robot, his sound, action and song

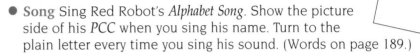

- **Red Robot** Use the *ABC Book* picture to see what this **r**oller-skating **r**ascal looks like when he is in Letterland.

- **Sound** Show the *plain letter side* of the *PCC* to see what he looks like in words. Then discover the sound he makes in words (page 143): Red Robot, 'rrr…'. Ask for the *letter sound* in response to the plain letter and praise children with That's right!

- **Song** Sing Red Robot's *Alphabet Song*. Show the picture side of his *PCC* when you sing his name. Turn to the plain letter every time you sing his sound. (Words on page 189.)

Phonemic awareness and language development

Listen
- Read about Red Robot in the *ABC Book*. Emphasise his sound and explore the picture together.

- Use *Vocabulary Cards* (page 30) and your classroom labels (e.g. **r**ed) to draw attention to Red Robot's sound.

- Ask questions and discuss. **R**ed **R**obot is always **r**ushing around. Does he like to walk, bounce or **r**un in the **R**eading Direction? What sorts of things might he **r**un off with? (**r**ed **r**oses, **r**ings, watches, **r**eading books, money, cakes, **r**ice with **r**aisins, puzzles, **r**ecipes, **r**are **r**eptiles, cameras, **r**ocks) **R**ed **R**obot's **r**iddle: What **r**uns all over our school but never moves? (**r**oof) Praise with: **R**ight! or **R**eally good!

Games
- Choose a game from the Activity Bank (pages 162–170) or play the Alliteration Game (page 150).

Letter shapes: r and R

- **Song** Sing or chant the **r** *Handwriting Song* (page 187) while children slowly finger trace or air trace the letter. Follow up with a handwriting activity.*

- **Storyline** Whenever Red Robot starts somebody's name or a sentence, he takes a big breath, changes shape and gets bigger. Can the children still recognise him? Show the Red Robot name flashcard you have prepared. Revise the **CHARACTER NAMES TRICK** (page 147).

Individual activity ideas

- *My Letterland Reading Booklet* (page 158) Page 33: Red Robot is running away.

- *See Letterland Materials* (pages 14–16) for Copymasters or Workbooks.

Quarrelsome Queen

Quarrelsome Queen, her sound, action and song

- **Quarrelsome Queen** Use the *ABC Book* picture to see what this **qu**ick and **qu**arrelsome **qu**een looks like when she is in Letterland.

- **Sound** Show her *plain letter* to discover what she looks like in words. Then discover the sound she makes in words: (page 143). Quarrelsome Queen, 'qu...' Ask for the *letter sound* in response to the plain letter, and praise with Quite right!

- **Song** Sing her *Alphabet Song*. Show the picture side of her *PCC* when you sing her name. Turn to the plain letter every time you sing her sound. (Words on page 189.)

Phonemic awareness and language development

Listen

- Read about Quarrelsome Queen in the *ABC Book*. Emphasise her sound and explore the picture together.

- Use *Vocabulary Cards* (page 30) and your classroom labels (e.g. **question**) to draw attention to her sound.

- Ask questions and discuss. **Qu**arrelsome **Qu**een is very **qu**ick to **qu**arrel. Discuss the term 'quarrelsome'. Normally she has no less than 9 **qu**arrels a day, which explains why her letter looks like the number 9. She is even too **qu**arrelsome to face the Reading Direction! And please don't ever try to take her royal umbrella away from her in a word. Always write an **u**mbrella letter next to her in words – if you want to avoid a **qu**arrel! What **qu**estions would you like to ask **Qu**arrelsome **Qu**een? Praise with: **Qu**ite right!

Games

- Choose a game from the Activity Bank (page 162–170) or play the Alliteration Game (page 150).

Letter shapes: q and Q

- **Song** Sing or chant the **q** *Handwriting Song* (page 187) while children slowly finger trace or air trace the letter. Follow up with a handwriting activity.*

- **Storyline** Whenever Quarrelsome Queen starts a name or a sentence, she goes to her Quiet Room to recover from all her quarrelling. Show the Quarrelsome Queen name flashcard you have prepared. Revise the **CHARACTER NAMES TRICK** (page 147).

Individual activity ideas

- *My Letterland Reading Booklet* (page 158) Page 34: This quilt is for Quarrelsome Queen.

- *See *Letterland Materials* (pages 14–16) for Copymasters or Workbooks.

Sidebar

✓ **Materials**
See the list on page 30.

✓ **Preparations**
Write out and picture-code classroom labels: **Q**uiet Corner, **q**uestion, 'Please be **q**uiet.

Action (page 149)

Quiet Corner
question

Picture-coding

Quarrelsome Queen

→ **Ideas for ending the day**
(See page 29.)

Vicky Violet

Materials
See the list on page 30.

Preparations
Write out and picture-code classroom labels: **v**ase, **v**iolin.

Action (page 149)

vase

Picture-coding

Vicky **V**iolet

Vicky Violet, her sound, action and song

- **Vicky Violet** Use the *ABC Book* picture to see what this **v**ery lovely girl and her **v**ase of **v**iolets look like in Letterland.

- **Sound** Show the *plain letter side* of the *PCC* to see what her **v**ery special **v**ase looks like in words. Then use the **SOUNDS TRICK** to discover the letter sound (page 143): Vicky Violet, 'vvv...'. Ask for the *letter sound* in response to the plain letter. Praise with: Very good!

- **Song** Sing Vicky Violet's *Alphabet Song*. Show the picture side of her *PCC* when you sing her name. Turn to the plain letter every time you sing her sound. (Words on page 189.)

Phonemic awareness and language development

Listen
- Read about Vicky Violet in the *ABC Book*. Emphasise her sound and explore the picture together.

- Use *Vocabulary Cards* (page 30) and your classroom labels (e.g. **vase**) to draw attention to Vicky's sound.

- Ask questions and discuss. Where in Letterland would you go to find **v**ery lovely **v**iolets like the ones in **V**icky's **v**ase, the Letterland Library or **V**olcano **V**alley? What is a **v**ery healthy group of foods beginning with 'vvv...'? (**v**egetables) Why are **v**egetables so healthy for us? (**v**itamins) What are the fi**v**e **v**owels? What is **V**icky **V**iolet's fa**v**ourite fla**v**our of ice-cream? (strawberry, chocolate or **v**anilla) Praise with: **V**ery good!

Games
- Choose a game from the Activity Bank (pages 162–170) or play the Alliteration Game (page 150).

Letter shapes: v and V

- **Song** Sing or chant the **v** *Handwriting Song* (page 187) while children slowly finger trace or air trace the letter. Follow up with a handwriting activity.*

- **Storyline** Whenever Vicky starts a name or a sentence she uses a very valuable, very big vase. Show the Vicky Violet name flashcard you have prepared. Revise the **CHARACTER NAMES TRICK** (page 147).

Individual Activity Ideas

- *My Letterland Reading Booklet* (page 158) Page 35: Vicky Violet went to visit a volcano.

- *See *Letterland Materials* (pages 14–16) for Copymasters or Workbooks.

→ **Ideas for ending the day**
(See page 29.)

Blending and segmenting: -ve

Objectives
- To revise all letter sounds.
- To introduce silent **e** in words like **give** and **live**.

Revision

- Use the Quick Dash routine (page 155) to revise all the letter sounds you have taught so far.
- Choose an activity from the Activity Bank (pages 162–170). Use any and all letter sounds you have taught so far.

Live Spelling

- Help children to Live Spell these words:

  red → rid → rip → rib → rub → rug → run → ran

  quick → quilt → liquid

Introducing Vase-Prop e

- No English words end in **v**. The Letterland explanation for why we need to add an **e** to the end of words that end with a 'vvv…' sound is as follows:
- Show the **-ve** *Picture Code Card* and tell the Vase-Prop **e** story:

  All of Vicky Violet's vases have a pointy base, so the slightest breeze can blow them over! Because the winds in words always blow in the Reading Direction, the risk is always that a vase will tip over this way (→) unless it is propped up by a Vase-Prop **e**. The vases are safe from the wind *inside* words, but they always need a Vase-Prop **e** at the end of words like: **give, live, love, have** and **above**.

Live Spelling

- Help children to Live Spell these words:

  have → give → live → love → above

Why 'of' is not spelt 'ov'

Violets are Firefighter Fred's favourite flowers, so he can't resist bringing one of Vicky Violet's smaller vases with him every time he goes into the word **of**. Even though the vase is small, it's 'vvv…' is louder than Fireman Fred's 'fff…' sound.

Walter Walrus

Materials
See the list on page 30.

Preparations
Write out and picture-code classroom labels: **w**indow, **w**ater, **w**inter, **w**eather.

Walter Walrus, his sound, action and song

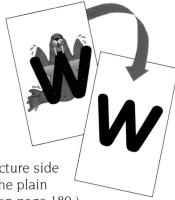

- **Walter Walrus** Use the *ABC Book* picture to introduce this **w**et and **w**ily **w**alrus and his **w**ater **w**ells.
- **Sound** Show the *plain letter side* of the *PCC* to see what his **w**ells look like in words. Then discover his letter sound (page 143): Walter Walrus, 'www…'. Ask for the *letter sound* in response to the plain letter and praise with: Wonderful!.
- **Song** Sing Walter's *Alphabet Song*. Show the picture side of his *PCC* when you sing his name. Turn to the plain letter every time you sing his sound. (Words on page 189.)

Phonemic awareness and language development

Listen
- Read about Walter Walrus in the *ABC Book*. Emphasise his sound and explore the picture together.
- Use *Vocabulary Cards* (page 30), your classroom labels (e.g. **window**) and NLS high-frequency words (**was**, **went**, **we**) to draw attention to Walter Walrus's sound.
- Ask questions and discuss. **W**alter **W**alrus is one of the two main trouble-makers in Letterland. He often causes trouble for letters next to him in a word. **W**hat do you think he does? He teases and splashes them and gets them **w**et with **w**ater from his **w**ells. (See, for example, **ow**, **aw** and **ew** lessons.) Do you think he **w**alks or **w**addles in the Reading Direction? **W**ould you all **w**ave like **W**alter? Praise with: **W**onderful! **W**hat a **w**inner! or **W**ell done!

Games
- Choose a game from the Activity Bank (pages 162–170) or play the Alliteration Game (page 150).

Letter shapes: w and W

- **Song** Sing or chant the **w** *Handwriting Song* (page 186) while children slowly finger trace or air trace the letter. Follow up with a handwriting activity.*
- **Storyline** Whenever Walter Walrus starts a name or a sentence, he takes a deep breath and gets bigger. Show the Walter Walrus name flashcard you have prepared. Revise the **CHARACTER NAMES TRICK** (page 147).

Individual activity ideas

- *My Letterland Reading Booklet* (page 158) Page 36: Go away Walter Walrus! I am getting wet!
- *See *Letterland Materials* (pages 14–16) for Copymasters or Workbooks.

Action (page 149)

window

was   went

we

Picture-coding

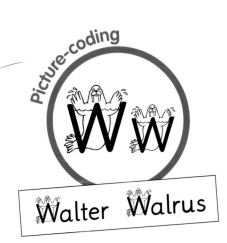

Walter Walrus

→ **Ideas for ending the day**
(See page 29.)

Fix-it Max

Materials
See the list on page 30.

Preparations
Write out and picture-code classroom labels: si**x**, bo**x**, si**x**teen, E**X**IT.

Action (page 149)

Picture-coding

Fix-it Max, his sound, action and song

- **Fix-it Max** Use the *ABC Book* picture to see what this e**x**cellent fi**x**er and his letter look like in Letterland.

- **Sound** Show the *plain letter* to see what his letter looks like in words. Then discover his letter sound by separating off the LAST sound of his name: Ma**x**, 'k-ss...'. Ask for the *letter sound* in response to the plain letter. Praise with: E...**x**cellent!

- **Song** Sing Fix-it Max's *Alphabet Song*. Show the picture side of his *PCC* when you sing his name. Turn to the plain letter every time you sing his sound. (Words on page 190.)

Phonemic awareness and language development

Listen

- Read about Fix-it Max in the *ABC Book*. Emphasise his sound and explore the picture together.

- Use *Vocabulary Cards* (page 30) and your classroom labels (e.g. si**x**) to draw attention to Fix-it Max's sound.

- Ask questions and discuss. Do you think Ma**x** ever whispers his '**k-ss**' sound at the start of a word? (No, when he starts the words 'xmas' and 'x-ray', he makes an 'eh' sound, and in 'xylophone' he has a quick snooze and makes a 'zzz...' sound.) How old do you think he is, five or si**x**? Ma**x** makes his '**k-ss**' sound in only a few words, because another two or three Letterlanders often do the job instead (-ks or - cks).

Games

- Choose a game from the Activity Bank (pages 162–170) or play the Alliteration Game (page 150).

Letter shapes: x and X

- **Song** Sing or chant the **x** *Handwriting Song* (page 187) while children slowly finger trace or air trace the letter. Follow up with a handwriting activity.*

- **Storyline** To make his letter bigger, Max takes a deep breath and gets bigger. Show children an EXIT label – one of the only words where his capital letter makes his 'k-ss...' sound. Revise the **CHARACTER NAMES TRICK** (page 147).

Individual activity ideas

- *My Letterland Reading Booklet* (page 158) Page 37: Fix-it Max can fix it.

- *See Letterland Materials* (pages 14–16) for Copymasters or Workbooks.

➜ **Ideas for ending the day**
(See page 29.)

Yellow Yo-yo Man

Yellow Yo-yo Man, his sound, action and song

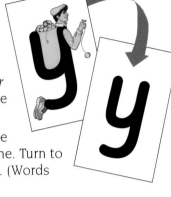

- **Yellow Yo-yo Man** Use the *ABC Book* picture to see what this **y**oung **y**o-**y**o seller looks like when he is in Letterland.

- **Sound** Show his *plain letter* to see what he looks like in words. Then discover his letter sound: Yellow Yo-yo Man, 'y…'. Ask for the *letter sound* in response to the plain letter and praise with: Yes!

- **Song** Sing Yo-yo Man's *Alphabet Song*. Show the picture side of his *PCC* when you sing his name. Turn to the plain letter every time you sing his sound. (Words on page 190.)

Phonemic awareness and language development

Listen

- Read about Yellow Yo-yo Man in the *ABC Book*. Emphasise his sound and explore the picture together.

- Use *Vocabulary Cards* (page 30), your classroom labels (e.g. **yellow**) and NLS high-frequency words (**yes**, **you**) to draw attention to Yellow Yo-yo Man's sound.

- Ask questions and discuss. **Y**o-**y**o Man has only a few chances to make his 'yyy…' sound in words. The best place to hear him is in words like **y**o-**y**o, **y**ellow, **y**ou, **y**et, **y**esterday, **y**ear, **y**oung, **y**awn and **yyyy**esss! The rest of the time he takes the **y**o-**y**o's out of his sack and works for Mr E or Mr I. (See pages 75, 109 and 117 as well as the Vowels Chart on page 107.) If he is at the end of your name, he is probably working for Mr E! (Jenn**y** and Am**y**. Also: ver**y**, bab**y**, etc.) Sometimes he works for Mr I (m**y**, tr**y**, bu**y**, etc.)

Games

- Choose a game from the Activity Bank (pages 162–170) or play the Alliteration Game (page 150).

Letter shapes: y and Y

- **Song** Sing or chant the **y** *Handwriting Song* (page 187) while children slowly finger trace or air trace the letter. Follow up with a handwriting activity.*

- **Storyline** Whenever Yellow Yo-yo Man starts a name or a sentence, he quickly empties out some of his yo-yos (which are heavy) so that he can step lightly up onto the line to show how important that word is. Show the Yellow Yo-yo Man name flashcard. Revise the **CHARACTER NAMES TRICK** (page 147).

Individual activity ideas

- *My Letterland Reading Booklet* (page 158) Page 38: Is it you, Yellow Yo-yo Man? Yes it is!

- *See *Letterland Materials* (pages 14–16) for Copymasters or Workbooks.

Materials
See the list on page 30.

Preparations
Write out and picture-code classroom labels: **y**ellow, **y**o-**y**o.

Action (page 149)

yellow

yes you

Picture-coding

Yo-Yo Man

→ **Ideas for ending the day**
(See page 29.)

Zig Zag Zebra

Zig Zag Zebra, her sound, action and song

- **Zig Zag Zebra** Use the *ABC Book* picture to see what this **z**ipping and **z**ooming **z**ebra looks like when she is in Letterland.

- **Sound** Show the *plain letter side* of the PCC to see what she looks like in words. Then use the **SOUNDS TRICK** to discover her sound: Zig Zag Zebra, 'zzz...'. Ask for the *letter sound* in response to the plain letter.

- **Song** Sing Zig Zag Zebra's *Alphabet Song*. Show the picture side of her *PCC* when you sing her name. Turn to the plain letter every time you sing her sound. (Words on page 190.)

Phonemic awareness and language development

Listen

- Read about Zig Zag Zebra in the *ABC Book*. Emphasise her sound and explore the picture together.

- Use *Vocabulary Cards* (page 30) and your classroom labels (e.g. **zip**) to draw attention to Zig Zag Zebra's sound.

- Ask questions and discuss. **Z**ig **Z**ag **Z**ebra is very quiet and shy, so you won't see her letter in a lot of words. In fact she's so shy she doesn't even face in the Reading Direction. (Can children remember why Golden Girl and Quarrelsome Queen don't either?) Do you remember who makes her '**zzz**...' sound at the end of lots more words? (Sammy Snake snoozing - see page 42.) What do you think **Z**ig **Z**ag **Z**ebra's favourite words might be? (**z**ebra and **z**oo)

Games

- Choose a game from the Activity Bank (pages 162–170) or play the Alliteration Game (page 150).

Letter shapes: z and Z

- **Song** Sing or chant the **z** *Handwriting Song* (page 187) while children slowly finger trace or air trace the letter. Follow up with a handwriting activity.*

- **Storyline** Whenever Zig Zag Zebra starts a name or a sentence, she takes a deep breath and gets bigger. Show the Zig Zag Zebra name flashcard. Revise the **CHARACTER NAMES TRICK** (page 147).

Individual activity ideas

- *My Letterland Reading Booklet* (page 158) Page 39: Come and play Zig Zag Zebra!

- *See Letterland Materials* (pages 14–16) for Copymasters or Workbooks.

✔ **Materials**
See the list on page 30.

✔ **Preparations**
Write out and picture-code classroom labels: pu**zz**le, **z**ero, **z**ip.

Action (page 149)

zip

Picture-coding

Zig Zag Zebra

➔ **Ideas for ending the day**
(See page 29.)

Section 2:
Onsets and Rimes:
Reading and Spelling
by Analogy

In this section, children learn to apply the knowledge that certain letter patterns are repeated in words. "If I can read **cat** I can also read **at, bat, fat, hat, mat, pat, rat, sat,** and **that.**"

Section 2:
Onsets and Rimes:
Reading and Spelling by Analogy

Assessment outcomes

- To hear onsets and rimes in CVC words.
- To blend and segment CVC words in rhyming sets.
- To blend rhyming words on the *Letterland Vocabulary Cards* (e.g. b**all**, c**all**, f**all**, h**all**, t**all**).
- To blend words that rhyme with Letterland character names (e.g. M**ike**: b**ike**, h**ike**, l**ike**).

Lesson Plans

Section 2 provides **one sample lesson** followed by a selection of activity ideas and resources for focusing on rhyming words. There is material for between 10 and 15 lessons, all of which will develop the skill of reading and spelling by analogy.

Section 2 covers the following areas:

- phonological awareness using onsets and rimes*
- the skill of reading and spelling by analogy
- the fifth Letterland child strategy: the **RHYMING WORDS TRICK**.

  * see Glossary (page 217).

Letter knowledge

1) Take-home Reading and Spelling Lists (page 177)
These lists feature the following rimes:

–at –an –and –am –ad –ap

–ed –eg –en –et –ell

–in –ip –ig –it –ill

–op –ot –og

–ug –un

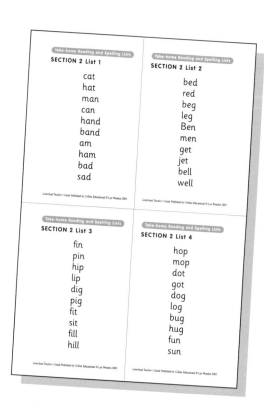

Take-home Reading and Spelling Lists
SECTION 2 List 1

cat
hat
man
can
hand
band
am
ham
bad
sad

Letterland Teacher's Guide Published by Collins Educational © Lyn Wendon 2003

Take-home Reading and Spelling Lists
SECTION 2 List 2

bed
red
beg
leg
Ben
men
get
jet
bell
well

Letterland Teacher's Guide Published by Collins Educational © Lyn Wendon 2003

Take-home Reading and Spelling Lists
SECTION 2 List 3

fin
pin
hip
lip
dig
pig
fit
sit
fill
hill

Letterland Teacher's Guide Published by Collins Educational © Lyn Wendon 2003

Take-home Reading and Spelling Lists
SECTION 2 List 4

hop
mop
dot
got
dog
log
bug
hug
fun
sun

Letterland Teacher's Guide Published by Collins Educational © Lyn Wendon 2003

2) Letterland Vocabulary Cards

The *Letterland Vocabulary Cards* pack contains 78 picture cards and 6 photocopiable *Rhyming Words Lists* that feature all the words on the backs of the cards. Children can use these lists in a variety of activities (see pages 83, 152–153 and 162–170 for details).

bed	ball	blue	cake	car	cat
red	tall	blue	bake	bar	at
bed	call	glue	cake	car	bat
fed	ball	true	fake	far	mat
ted	wall	clue	lake	hard	hat
led	fall	flue	snake	dark	sat
sled	small	rescue	awake	park	that
	all				

Rhyming Words Lists

3) Letterland character names

You can also use character names to introduce hundreds of rhyming words by analogy. For more details see page 147.

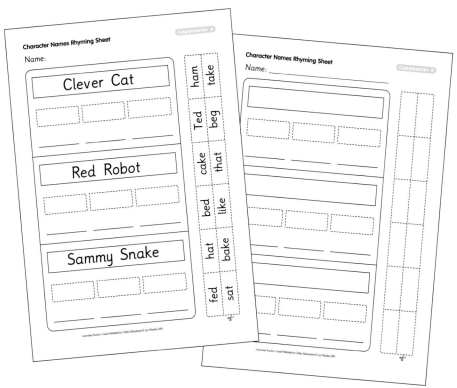

Assessment activities

Use any of the *Reading and Spelling Lists* (pages 171–184), for dictation or reading activities, as well as any of the word lists and activities in the Lesson Plans to assess the Section 2 outcomes listed on the previous page. You can download *Pupil Record Sheets* for Section 2 from www.letterland.com.

Rhyming Chants: -at, -an, -am

✓ **Materials**
Picture Code Cards

✓ **Preparations**
Write up Rhyming Chants; letter cards for each child: **-at**, **-an**, **-am**, **b**, **c**, **d**, **f**, **h**, **j**, **m**, **p**, **r**, **s**, **t**, **v** and **y**.

Listen first: Rhyming Chants

- Write out the **-at** Rhyming Chant then practise saying or chanting it together.
- Picture-code Annie Apple in **a**m, h**a**ppy, **a**t, b**a**t, c**a**t and th**a**t, but *not* in the word **saying** which features Mr A. You could add a stick man for Mr A.
- Underline the rhyming **-at** words. Ask the children which two Letterlanders make their sounds together in each of the rhyming words.
- Picture-code Talking Tess at the end of each rhyming word.
- Ask the children to think of more words that rhyme with **at**, **bat**, **cat** and **that**.

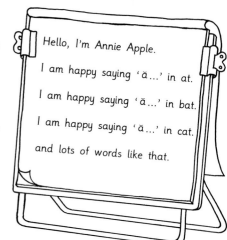

Hello, I'm Annie Apple.

I am happy saying 'ă...' in at.

I am happy saying 'ă...' in bat.

I am happy saying 'ă...' in cat.

and lots of words like that.

Live Reading and Spelling

- Hand out the following *Picture Code Cards*: **a**, **t**, **c**, **h**, **m**, **p**, **b**, **f**, **r** and **s**.
- Two children stand at the front of the class and make the word **at**, showing the picture-coded sides of the *Picture Code Cards*.
- Teach the children the following **'store and release'** technique. Let's turn the cards over and look at the plain letters. What sound does this letter make in words? 'a...'. And this one? 't...'. We are going to make Annie Apple's and Talking Tess's sounds together. Get ready to say Annie Apple's sound, but don't say it yet. Get ready to say Talking Tess's sound, but don't say it yet. Now, we are going to let both sounds burst out together... 'at...!'
- Ask a third child to come up and hold Clever Cat's letter at the front of the word.
- What word do we get when we blend these sounds together? 'c...at', 'cat'
- Call out each of the following words as an onset and rime: b...at; fff...at; hhh...at; mmm...at; p...at; rrr...at and sss...at. The child holding the matching initial sound comes up with their card and completes the word. The rest of the children blend the sounds together to discover the word.
- Repeat the above process with **–an** and **–am**.

I am happy saying 'ă...' in can.
I am happy saying 'ă...' in fan.
I am happy saying 'ă...' in man.
and happy saying 'ă...' in pan.
and than!

I am happy saying 'ă...' in am.
I am happy saying 'ă...' in jam.
I am happy saying 'ă...' in ham.
and happy in a traffic jam.

Individual activity ideas

- Hand out letter cards for rimes: **at**, **an** and **am** and onsets: **b**, **c**, **d**, **f**, **h**, **j**, **m**, **p**, **r**, **s**, **t**, **v** and **y**. Children build as many words as they can, and write them down.
- Children write their own rhymes using the words they have created.

Onsets and rimes activities

Pick and choose from the following six activities for teaching the remaining rimes.

PiPs Step 2.1, 4.1, 4.3, 4.4

Materials
Picture Code Cards
Preparations
Write up Rhyming Chants and the letter cards as in the previous lesson.

1 Rhyming Chants and Live Spelling

Procedure

Use the same procedure as outlined in the Rhyming Chants Lesson Plan on the previous page, i.e.

- Learn a rhyming verse.
- Use the rhyming words in a Live Reading and Spelling activity.
- Use the rimes in a word-building activity.

Below are suggestions for creating your own rhyming verses.

Here are two more examples of rhyming verses you could use:

I am happy saying 'ă...' in bad.
I am happy saying 'ă...' in sad.
I am happy saying 'ă...' in mad.
and happy saying 'ă...' in dad.

I am happy saying 'ă...' in cap.
I am happy saying 'ă...' in gap.
I am happy saying 'ă...' in map.
and happy saying 'ă...' in nap.

Goodnight

For rhyming verses with Eddy Elephant:

I very much like saying 'ĕ ...' in words like…
(**–ed; –eg; –en; –et; –ell**)
e.g. **bed, fed, red, Ted, beg, leg, peg**…

For rhyming verses with Impy Ink:

Listen to my 'ĭ ...' sound in…
(**–in; –ip; –ig; –it; –ill**)
e.g. **pin, tin, zip, pig, fit, till**…

For rhyming verses with Oscar Orange:

Can you spot my 'ŏ ...' sound in…
(**–op; –ot; –og**)
e.g. **pop, top, spot, fog, log**…

For rhyming verses with Uppy Umbrella:

It's fun saying 'ŭ ...' in words like…
(**–ug; –un**)
e.g. **mug, dug, hug, bun, sun**…

Materials
Copymaster 2

Preparations
Prepare a Word Sort Sheet for each child (see below).

2 Word sort: –og, –at, –un, –en, –in, –ip, –op, –ell

Procedure

Whole-class activity

- Write all these rimes on the blackboard or display them on cards: **-og**, **-at**, **-un**, **-en**, **-in**, **-ip**, **-op**, **-ell**.
- Place a pocket or bag underneath each rime.
- Place all the *Copymaster 2* pictures in a hat.
- Children take turns to pick out one of the pictures and decide which rime it belongs to.
- The child places their picture in the appropriate pocket/bag.

Individual activity

- Give each child a sheet of paper with eight squares large enough to fit two pictures and two words in each (see left).
- Also give each child the sheet of *Copymaster 2* pictures.
- Children cut out the picture and stick two rhyming words in each box.
- Optional: Children write the rime underneath each picture.

3 Rhyming bingo

Procedure

Whole-class activity

- Hand out one Bingo Board to each child. (Use *Copymaster 3*.)
- Place the *Copymaster 2* pictures in a hat.
- Choose one picture at a time and call out the word.
- If children have the matching rime on their board, they cover it with a counter or cross it off.
- The first child/children to cover all the squares on their board wins.

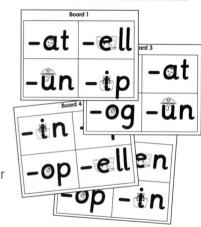

4 Word challenge

Procedure

Whole-class activity

- Choose a rime. Write it on the board and say it together.
- Ask the children to write as many words as they can think of that contain the same rime.
- Whoever has the most words reads out their list.
- The other children cross off any word on their list that the first child reads out.
- If anyone still has any words left, they read them out, and so on, until there are no more new words.
- Count the total number of words the children can now read and spell by analogy.

5 Using the Letterland Vocabulary Cards

Procedure

- Help children to read the large words on the backs of the 78 *Vocabulary Cards*, simply by saying the name of each picture. From there, it is a short step to reading all the remaining rhyming words on each card.

- These rhyming words are also available as photocopiable *Rhyming Words Lists* on the insert accompanying the *Vocabulary Cards*.

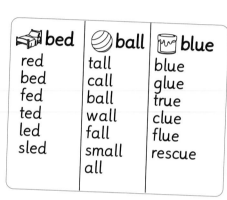

Photocopiable Rhyming Words List

bed	ball	blue
red	tall	blue
bed	call	glue
fed	ball	true
ted	wall	clue
led	fall	flue
sled	small	rescue
	all	

You can use the rhyming word clusters on the *Vocabulary Cards* in many different ways:

- children create rhyming stories, sentences or poems
- paired reading practice
- formal reading assessment.

6 Using the Letterland character names

By the end of Section 2, children will be familiar with the concept of reading and spelling simple CVC words by analogy. As an extension, you could show the children how to apply the **RHYMING WORDS TRICK** (page 152) to the character names that they have learnt to read. For example, if they can read M**unch**ing M**ike**, they can read b**unch**, h**unch**, l**unch**, m**unch**, p**unch**, b**ike**, h**ike**, l**ike** and str**ike**.

Whole-class activities

- Write the following words on pieces of card: **Bouncy**, **Ben**, **ten**, **men**, **man** and **bed**. (Keep the **Bouncy** and **Ben** cards together so that it reads as a name.)

- Ask a child to find Bouncy Ben's name. Take away the card that says **Bouncy**. Ask which word is left.

- Ask which words on the board have the same ending (rime) as the name **Ben**. Place the rhyming cards (**ten** and **men**) under the name **Ben**.

- Ask for volunteers to blend the sounds to read the rhyming words.

More rhyming words: *(including an odd-one-out!)*

Clever, **Cat**	bat, hat, *ham*, sat, mat, that
Firefighter, **Fred**	bed, fed, red, Ted, *beg*
Harry, **Hat**, **Man**	can, fan, pan, *pen* / cat, mat, bat, *ham*
Impy, **Ink**	link, pink, rink, sink, *sank*
Kicking, **King**	ring, sing, wing, string, *rang*
Munching, **Mike**	bike, hike, like, *make*
Red, **Robot**	bed, fed, led, *pen*
Sammy Snake	bake, cake, hake, lake, make, *like*

Individual activities

- Use the *Character Names Rhyming Sheet* (Copymaster 4) to create cut and paste worksheets by inserting a selection of the rhyming words above.

- Include one non-rhyming word per set.

- Children cut out the words and paste them under the rhyming character name. Then they write the word underneath.

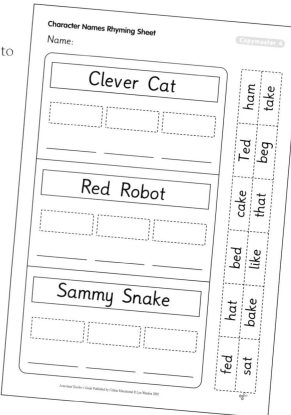

Section 3:
Beginnings, Middles and Endings

Children's listening skills are refined in this section, as they learn to listen for the first, the final and then the middle sound in spoken words. These activities make excellent preparation for Section 5, when children learn about middle sounds that are made up of two and three letters (e.g. r**ai**n, c**a**rd, g**oa**l, be**a**rd).

Section 3: Beginnings, Middles and Endings

Assessment outcomes

- To identify and write letter sounds in the initial position.
- To identify and write letter sounds in the final position.
- To identify and write letter sounds in the medial position.
- To blend and segment CVC words.
- To blend and segment words with double consonants and consonant digraphs.

If your class has already covered these objectives, move on to Section 4.

Lesson Plans

In Section 3, Lessons 1–5 are provided in detail. Ideas for the remaining lessons (Lessons 6–11) are provided in a shorter format.

The focus is on hearing, spelling and writing *initial*, *final* and then *medial* letter sounds in simple words, in preparation for the more advanced spelling patterns that children will encounter in Sections 4 and 5.

Letter knowledge

a–z, **sh**, **ch**, **th**, **ss**, **ff**, **ll**, **ck**, **ng**

Reading and spelling vocabulary

1) Take-home Reading and Spelling Lists (page 170)
- Send home roughly one list each week.

2) NLS High-frequency Words List 1b (page 184)
- Children continue to work through this list, using the 'Look/say/write/cover/check' strategy (page 159).

Assessment activities

Use any of the *Reading and Spelling Lists* for Sections 2 and 3 (pages 177–178), for dictation activities (where children write down beginning sounds, final sounds or middle sounds only), or for blending. You can download *Pupil Record Sheets* for Section 3 word lists from www.letterland.com. You can also use any of the Copymasters listed below for informal or formal assessment activities.

Copymasters for use in Section 3

1) *Copymasters* 5 and 6
2) You could also re-use *Fast Track Activity Sheets 1–9*

Introduction to initial sounds

Listen first

- Remind children of the Letterlanders' **ALLITERATION TRICK** (page 150).
- Draw Bouncy Ben, Golden Girl, Red Robot, Yo–yo Man, Oscar Orange and Peter Puppy in a mindmap around the word **colours**.

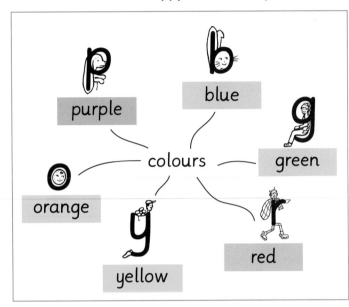

- Ask the children to guess each Letterlander's favourite colour. (Any colour that begins with the same sound: **B**ouncy **B**en/ **b**lue, etc.)
- Repeat the above alliteration activity with **foods**. Use any characters you like.
- Show a selection of *Vocabulary Cards*. Ask the children to suggest which Letterlander each object might belong to by creating a sentence. (e.g. Annie Apple loves to act like an **acrobat**. Bouncy Ben loves to bounce on his **bed**. Clever Cat has a shiny red **car**.)

Show me

Letter cards
- Give each child a selection of letter cards you have prepared. (Use any letters you would like to review.)
- Read out a selection of words.
- Children hold up the letter that matches the first sound of the word.

Activity Bank (pages 162–70)
- Choose any of the activities that focus on initial sounds.

Individual activity ideas

- Using *Copymaster 5*, children name each picture and then fill in the missing first letter.
- Write out the word **colours** at the top of a page. In feint print, write the word for each colour (**red**, **orange**, **yellow**, **green**, **blue**, **pink**). Copy one for each child. Children picture-code the first letter of each word and write over the feint letters in the matching colour. Send the list home so that children can learn to read these words as sight words.

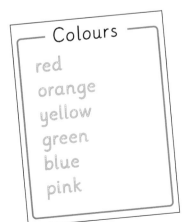

Segmenting initial sounds

Demonstration

Live Spelling and Reading

- Hand out *Picture Code Cards*: **b**, **d**, **f**, **h**, **j**, **m**, **n**, **p**, **r**, **s**, **t**, **w** and **u**.

- Use the Quick Dash routine (page 155) to review each character's letter sound.

- Ask two children to build the rime **–un** with *Picture Code Cards*, as they stand facing the class.

- Slowly say each of the following words: **b**un, **f**un, **g**un, **n**un, **p**un, **r**un and **s**un.

- Build the first word together. Each time you say a new word, the child holding the old initial sound sits down, and the child holding the new initial sound comes up and completes the word. The whole class checks the word by blending it aloud.

- Repeat with rimes **–en** and **–ig**.

Show me

Activity Bank (pages 162–70)

- Choose some activities that focus on initial sounds.

Individual activity ideas

- Give each child a sheet of paper with three columns. Write in one of the three rimes (**–un**; **–en**; **–ig**) at the top of each column. Children try to build as many words as they can in each column.

- Independent writing: Children write and illustrate a four-page booklet. On each page they should show a Letterland character with an object that begins with their letter sound.

- Fill in the missing letter: *Fast Track Activity Sheets 6–9*.

-un	-en	-ig

Initial sounds: sh & ch

Demonstration

- Say the word **sh…i…p**, slowly.
- Ask the children to repeat the first sound of the word **ship**.
- Write the word **ship** on the board, explaining that we write the sound 'sh…' with two letters. Even though there are two letters, it is still one sound. Ask the children:

  Is Sammy Snake making his usual 'sss…' sound? Is the Hat Man whispering his usual 'hhh…' sound?

  We have already learnt each Letterlander's usual sound. Now we are going to learn some of the other sounds that Letterlanders make in words. Whenever the Letterlanders do not make their usual sound in a word, there is usually a story to explain why.
- Review the **sh** story (page 61) by getting two children to act it out as you provide the story explanation. Use props if you have a costume box.
- Listen to and sing the **sh** song on the *Blends and Digraphs Songs Cassette* or *CD*.
- Review the **ch** story (page 61).
- Listen to and sing the **ch** song on the *Blends and Digraphs Songs Cassette* or *CD*. Children can all make the sneeze gesture (paw to nose) at each 'ch…' sound.

Show me

Listen and point
- Ask two pairs of children to stand far apart, holding *Picture Code Cards* **sh** and **ch**.
- Read out the following words and ask the seated children to point to the correct phoneme, saying 'sh…' or 'ch…':
  ship, **sh**in, **ch**in, **sh**op, **sh**eep, **ch**op, **ch**eese, **sh**ower, **ch**ain, **sh**ow

Find a Hat Man
- Divide the class into Harry Hat Men and Sammy Snakes. The snakes make slithering hand movements and the Hat Men hop. Each makes their individual sound until you say 'Find a Hat Man'. Then all the Hat Men stand still. Children pair up and act out the 'sh…' action, filling the room with 'sh…' sounds.
- Repeat with Harry Hat Men and Clever Cats, ending with lots of quiet sneezes, without any voice: 'ch…'.

Live Spelling
- Hand out the following *Picture Code Cards*: **i**, **o**, **p**, **n** and **sh**, **ch**.
- Slowly read out the word **ship** and ask the children holding the appropriate cards to come up and build the word, with the child holding the **h** card miming the hushing gesture.
- The rest of the class blends the sounds to read the word.
- Continue word building with the following words:
  ship → chip → chop → shop → chop → chip → chin → shin → ship

Initial sounds: th, th, sh & ch

Demonstration

Listen first!
- Ask children to say the word **thunder**, exaggerating the initial sound.
- Help them to notice that their tongues stick out slightly when they say these words, (prolonging 'th…'): **thin**, **think**, **thank you** and **thirsty**.
- Next say the word **this**, exaggerating the initial sound.
- Repeat the voiced **th** sound in the words **the**, **this**, **they**, **them**, **these**, **those**, **there**, **than** and **that**.
- Help children to notice their throats vibrating when they make the voiced 'th…' as in **this**.

The th story
- Review the **th** story (page 62).
- Listen to and sing the **th** song on the *Blends and Digraphs Songs Cassette* or *CD*.

Show me

- On the board or flipchart, stick up the *Picture Code Cards*: **ch**, **sh** and one **th** card. Use the plain **th** side to avoid having to distinguish between voiced and unvoiced **th**.
- Stick a pocket or bag under each card.
- Photocopy the pictures on *Copymaster 6* and cut them out. Put them in a hat or box.
- Give each child a chance to pick a picture from the hat or box. The child says the word, exaggerating the initial sound, and then sticks it in the appropriate pocket or bag. The rest of the class comments on the decision.

Individual activity ideas

- Use the same pictures on *Copymaster 6* to make a flapchart with three flaps.
- Stick a different phoneme (**ch**, **sh** and **th**) on the front of each flap.
- Children cut out the pictures and stick them under the appropriate flap.
- You may wish to use this as an assessment activity.

Endings: -t and -g

Listen first

- Not so long ago we used the Letterlanders' **ALLITERATION TRICK** (page 150) to discover what things each Letterlander might like best. We listened very carefully to the first sound in words. Now we are going to listen very carefully again, but this time we are going to listen for the **last** sound in words. Let's start with two Letterlanders who like to be at the end of words: Talking Tess and Golden Girl.

- Display the *Picture Code Cards* for Talking Tess and Golden Girl.

- Read out the following words slowly: **bug**, **big**, **but**, **bit**, **bag**, **bat**, **hug**, **bet**, **hut**, **beg**. After each word, ask children which of the two Letterlanders they can hear at the end of the word. Turn to the plain side of the *Picture Code Cards* to confirm their choice and make the sound again.

Show me

- Play the Listen and Jump Game (page 162) with words ending in **g**.

- Play the Tray Game (page 166) with words ending in **t**.

- Hand out two small cards to each child. Children write a **t** on one and a **g** on the other. Read out the words from the above games again. This time, children hold up the card that matches the final sound.

Individual activity ideas

- Give each child a piece of paper with two columns. Write a large **t** at the top of one column and a large **g** at the top of the other.

- Children picture-code each big letter at the top of the columns.

- Children draw things *ending* in **t** and **g**, for example, **dog**, **pig**, **bag**, **hat**, **cat**, **bat**, or any other words ending in these sounds.

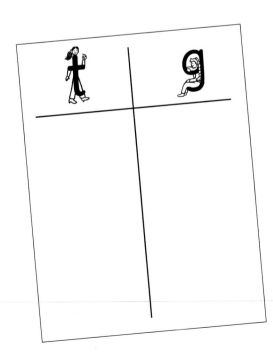

Endings and medial sounds

Here are some activity ideas and short format Lesson Plans for teaching the remaining endings and middle sounds in this Section.

PiPs Step 3.2, 5.3, 5.4

Lesson 6: -ck

Materials
Blends and Digraph Songs Cassette or CD

Preparations
Prepare and photocopy the *Word-building Sheet*.

- Review the **-ck** story (page 59).
- Live Spelling: **back → sack → sock → rock → lock → lick → kick → chick**
- Give each pair of children a *Word-building Sheet*, laid out as follows:

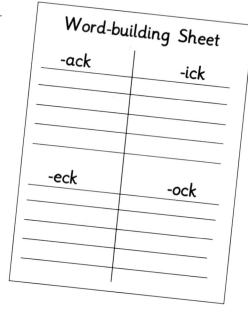

Word-building Sheet

-ack	-ick

-eck	-ock

- Ask them to see how many real words they can build using these endings, by trying to blend aloud each letter of the alphabet in the initial position. Remind them to try the **h** digraphs **sh**, **ch**, and **th**, too, as well as **qu**. If the resulting word is a real word, they write it down.
- The pair that has the most words reads out their list. If the other children hear a word on their own list, they cross it off. If anyone still has words left over, they read them out. Count up the total number of words the class has managed to build.

PiPs Step 3.2, 5.3

Lesson 7: -ff, -ll, -ss

Preparations
Prepare cards of the words in bold.

- Review the 'Best friends at the end' stories (pages 42 and 65).
- Write the following words in large print on large pieces of card: **off, puff, huff, bell, bill, doll, fill, hill, sell, shall, shell, tell, fuss, hiss, kiss, less, loss, mess, miss**.
- Give each child a different word to picture-code the ending. Then display the coded words under the heading: 'Best friends at the end'.

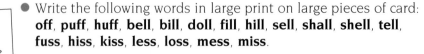

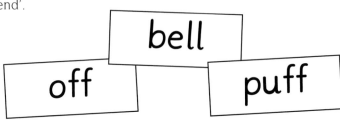

Materials
ng *Picture Code Card; Blends and Digraphs Songs Cassette or CD*

Preparations
Write up the song lyrics.

Lesson 8: -ng

- Review the **–ng Bells Story** (page 59).
- Write up the lyrics for the Letterland Bells Song with its **-ing**, **-ang**, **-ong**, **-ung** refrain. All sing the song with the cassette or CD as you point to each word.

Lesson 9: Blending medial sounds

Materials
Picture Code Cards; Alphabet Songs Cassette or CD

Preparations
Write up the song lyrics; **Optional:** Prepare Bingo Boards (page 168).

The importance of vowels
- Hand out all the *Picture Code Cards* except for the vowels and **r**, **y** and **w**. Ask the children to make a few words with these 18 cards. They will soon discover that they cannot make even one! Nobody can make a single word without at least one vowel in it.

Activities
- Review short vowel sounds using the **SOUNDS TRICK** (page 143).
- Use the lyrics for the 'Vowel Sounds Song' (page 190).
- All sing the song with the cassette or CD as you point to each word.
- Play **VOWELS–GO–ROUND** (Activity Bank, page 167).
- Play **SHORT VOWELS BINGO** (Activity Bank, page 168).

Vowel Sounds Song

I am Annie Apple.
I am a talking apple,
I say 'ă, ă, ă,'
I say 'ă..., ă..., ă...'.

We are the vowel sounds.
There are lots of us around.
In fact, have you heard:
We're in almost every word.

Vowels-Go-Round

Lesson 10: Blending CVC words

Materials
Picture Code Cards

- Play **SILLY QUESTIONS** (Activity Bank, page 170).

Lesson 11: Segmenting CVC words

- Hand out all the *Picture Code Cards*. Call out any regular short vowel word. If a child thinks they are holding a relevant card, they stand up, go to the front and build the word.
- The rest of the class checks the word by blending it aloud.
- Play the **FULL CIRCLE GAME** (Activity Bank, page 168).

Section 4: Consonant Blends

Consonant blends don't usually cause problems for children who have a solid grounding in the **a–z** letter sounds. This section focuses on listening for these subtle consonant blends at the beginning of words, and using consonant blend words in oral activities.

Section 4: Consonant Blends

Assessment outcomes

- To blend CCVC/CVCC words.
- To segment CCVC/CVCC words.
- To read a selection of high-frequency words.

Lesson Plans

There are seven Lesson Plans in Section 4, all provided in step-by-step detail.

This Section provides a series of fun interactive activities for familiarising children's ears and eyes with consonant blends.

Since the consonants continue to make their usual sounds in consonant blends, there are no new stories in this Section. Remind the children of the characters and their usual sounds if necessary.

Letter knowledge

Consonant blends:
bl, cl, fl, pl, sl, gl / br, cr, dr, fr, gr, pr
sc, sk, sp, st, sm, sn, sw / scr, spr, spl, str

Endings:
ss, ff, ll, ck, ng

Reading and spelling vocabulary

1) Take-home Reading and Spelling Lists (page 179)
- Send home roughly one list each week.

2) NLS High-frequency Words List 1b (page 184)
- Children continue to work through the NLS *High-frequency Words List 1b*, using the 'Look/say/cover/write/check' strategy (page 159).

3) Song lyrics
- If time allows, write up the lyrics to some of the Consonant Blends Songs (in the booklet accompanying the CD) and use as a shared reading text as you learn the song.

Assessment activities

Use any of the *Reading and Spelling Lists* (pages 171–184), for dictation or reading activities, as well as any of the word lists and activities in the Lesson Plans to assess the Section 4 outcomes listed above. You can download *Pupil Record Sheets* for Section 4 assessment outcomes from www.letterland.com.

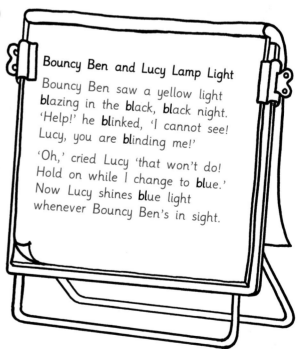

Bouncy Ben and Lucy Lamp Light

Bouncy Ben saw a yellow light
blazing in the **bl**ack, **bl**ack night.
'Help!' he **bl**inked, 'I cannot see!
Lucy, you are **bl**inding me!'

'Oh,' cried Lucy 'that won't do!
Hold on while I change to **bl**ue.'
Now Lucy shines **bl**ue light
whenever Bouncy Ben's in sight.

Teaching strategies for Section 4

Pronunciation guide

Correct pronunciation of the single letter sounds is the first key to reading and spelling consonant blends successfully. If a child has been taught the consonant sounds correctly, none of the consonant blends should cause difficulties in reading, and only a few may cause difficulties in spelling. For correct pronunciation:

- Always whisper the eight unvoiced consonants ('**c**…', '**fff**…', '**hhh**…', '**k**…', '**p**…', '**s**…', '**t**…', and '**k-ss**…').
- Keep your mouth *almost closed* when saying '**b**…', '**d**…', '**g**…', '**j**…' and '**yyy**…' to keep any added 'uh' sound to a minimum.
- Prolong the sounds: '**fff**…', '**hhh**…', '**sss**…', '**lll**…', '**mmm**…', '**nnn**…', '**rrr**…', '**vvv**…', '**www**…', '**yyy**…' and '**zzz**…'. Again, keep the mouth almost shut because as soon as the jaw drops it causes an 'uh' sound.

For more details on teaching letter sounds, see pages xx–xx.

The Slow-speak trick

The **SLOW-SPEAK TRICK** (stretching a word out so that you can hear each phoneme) works with phonically regular words. It will come in handy when children attempt to read and spell consonant blends, during Live Spelling and dictation activities or independent reading and spelling.

For **SLOW-SPEAK** dictation: first, you **SLOW-SPEAK** a word. Then children repeat the word in **SLOW-SPEAK** and write down the sounds they hear. After each word, model sounding out and writing the word on the board for children to self-check.

For more details on the **SLOW-SPEAK TRICK**, see page 152.

k-ss…

bl, cl, fl, gl, pl & sl

✓ **Materials**
Picture Code Cards; Blends and Digraphs Songs Cassette or CD

✓ **Preparation**
Letter cards for each child: **bl, cl, fl, gl, pl, sl**; Write up song lyrics.

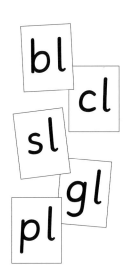

Listen first

- First go over the sounds: **/b/** and **/g/** (don't drop the jaw) and whisper **/c/, /f/, /g/, /p/** and **/s/**.

- As you read out the words beginning with **l** in the left hand column of the list below, prolong the initial 'lll...' sound.

- Children should store up then blend the first two sounds together quickly without a pause to discover the new word, i.e. not 'puhluh' but 'plllann'.

Add Fred's whispered 'fff...' sound	**Add Bouncy Ben's 'b...' sound**
lame → flame	lack → black
light → flight	low → blow
lip → flip	lock → block
lies → flies	loo → blue
Add Clever Cat's whispered 'c...' sound	**Add Sammy's whispered 'sss...' sound**
lump → clump	leap → sleep
lean → clean	lip → slip
lock → clock	lied → slide
lap → clap	low → slow
Add Golden Girl's 'g...' sound	**Add Peter Puppy's whispered 'p...' sound**
loo → glue	lace → place
love → glove	lane → plane
litter → glitter	late → plate
loom → gloom	lay → play

Show me

Which blend?

- Give each child your prepared letter cards for: **bl, cl, fl, gl, pl** and **sl**.

- Read out some words from the lists above. Children segment off and say just the *initial* consonant blend, then hold up the letters that match the sound.

Live Spelling/Slow-speak dictation

- Distribute the **a, b, c, ck, d, f, g, i, l, n, o, p, s, t** and **th** *Picture Code Cards* and help children to Live Spell these words. Alternatively, dictate them in **SLOW-SPEAK** for children to repeat and write down.

  black → **block** → **clock** → **cloth**
  flap → **flat** → **flag** → **glad** → **plan** → **plastic**

Shared reading and singing

- If time allows, learn one or more of the Consonant Blend Songs (on the *Blends and Digraphs Cassette* or CD), using the lyrics as a shared reading text.

br, cr, dr, fr, gr, pr & tr

Materials
Blends and Digraphs Songs Cassette or CD; Picture Code Cards

Listen first

● First review each of the consonant sounds: **/b/**, **/c/**, **/d/**, **/f/**, **/g/**, **/p/** and **/t/**.

● As you read out some of the words/non-words in the left-hand columns below, prolong the initial 'rrr…' sound.

● Children should blend the first two sounds together quickly without a pause to *discover* the new word, i.e. not 'buhruh' but: 'brrread'.

Add Bouncy Ben's 'b…' sound
ridge → bridge
ring → bring
rush → brush

Add Clever Cat's whispered 'c…' sound
rash → crash
'ross' → cross
'rowd' → crowd

Add Golden Girl's 'g…' sound
'rass' → grass
'randma' → grandma
'reen' → green

Add Talking Tess's whispered 't…' sound
rain → train
'ree' → tree
rip → trip

Add Fred's whispered 'fff…' sound
'rog' → frog
'rom' → from
'ront' → front

Add Dippy Duck's 'd…' sound
raw → draw
'ress' → dress
rink → drink

Add Peter Puppy's whispered 'p…' sound
rinse → prince
'rincess' → princess
resent → present

Other words:
brown, brother, brake, crunchy, crisps, crayons, drowsy, fresh, fruit, frill, grumpy, gravy, priceless, tricky, troll, try, truck

Show me

Sense or nonsense game
● Write down all the adjective-noun pairs you can think of using the above consonant blends. (Use the word lists above to think of additional adjectives and nouns.)

● Say an adjective-noun pair aloud. Children decide: "Sense or nonsense!", e.g. **crunchy cream; crunchy crayons; cross crayons, crazy cracker**, etc.

Live Spelling/Slow-speak dictation
● Distribute *Picture Code Cards* and help the children to Live Spell these words. Alternatively, dictate them in **SLOW-SPEAK** for children to repeat and write down:
bring → crash → cross → cress → dress → press → print → project → frog → from → grab → gran → grunt → drip → drink → trick → truck → track → trap → trust

Shared reading and singing
● If time allows, learn one or more of the Consonant Blend Songs (on the *Blends and Digraphs Cassette* or CD), using the lyrics as a shared reading text.

Firefighter Fred and Red Robot

Firefighter Fred is fond of frogs
but Red Robot is not.
He frankly hates the frisky things
and leaps back on the spot.

'Mind that friendly frog' laughs Fred,
but Red Robot takes fright.
He's so afraid of frogs you see,
he turns from red to white!

sc, sk, sp & st

Materials
Blends and Digraphs Songs Cassette or CD; Picture Code Cards

s k

Sammy Snake
and Kicking King

Who's that **sk**iing **sk**illfully?
It looks like Sammy Snake.
He's being careful not to **sk**id
onto the frozen lake.

He has seen Kicking King
skimming along on **sk**ates
who shows he's just as **sk**ilful
at putting on his brakes!

Listen first

- Slowly say a number of words or non-words beginning with **sc**, **sk**, **sp** or **st**, but do not make the 's…' sound. Children discover the new word by adding 's…', e.g. **poil/spoil**; **tick/stick**; **cribble/scribble**; **care/scare**; **pring/spring**; **kip/skip**; **tamp/stamp**. Avoid dropping the jaw between sounds, causing 'sssuh-c…' instead of the sound you want, 'sssc…'

Sorting game: differentiate between /s/ and /st/

- Three children hold *Picture Code Cards* and stand at the front of the class: **s** and **st** (two children hold the **st** card).
- Choose two more children. Say one word in each of the following word pairs to each child: **stand/sand**; **say/stay**; **steal/seal**; **stick/sick**; **sing/sting**; **stir/sir**; **store/sore**; **stuck/suck**.
- Each child decides who to join: the **s** child or the **st** child. The others decide if they are right.

Show me

Sense or nonsense game

- See previous lesson for details. Some suggestions for this lesson are: **spinning spider**; **spinning spaghetti**; **spiky sparrow**; **speckled sparrow**; **sprouting spinach**; **sprouting spacesuit**, etc.

Live Spelling/Slow-speak dictation

- Distribute the relevant *Picture Code Cards* and help the children to Live Spell the following words:
  skip → skin → spin → spot → stop → skid → disk → desk nest → pest → test → vest → west → rest → rust → just → gust → trust
- Alternatively, use the words for a **SLOW-SPEAK** dictation (page 152).

Shared reading and singing

- If time allows, learn one or more of the Consonant Blend Songs on the *Blends and Digraphs Songs Cassette* or *CD,* using the lyrics as a shared reading text.

Word bank

sc: scared, scooter, score, scout

sk: ski, skid, skin, skip, skipping, skirt, sky, skate

–sk: ask, basket, desk, disk, dusk, mask, risk, whiskers

sp: spell, spend, spent, spin, spoon, spot, spider

st: stairs, stand, star, start, station, stay, stick, still, stone, stood, stop, story, stove

–st: against, almost, artist, best, cost, dentist, fast, first, last, oldest, trust, youngest

–st–: monster, postman, rusty, sister, tasty, thirsty, yesterday

sm, sn & sw

Listen first

Saying the sounds

● Say the following words *without* the initial **s**. Children add the initial 'sss…' sound to discover the new words.

sm mall/small; mart/smart; mell/smell; mile/smile; moke/smoke; mooth/smooth; mash/smash

sn nack/snack; nail/snail; nake/snake; nap/snap; neeze/sneeze; niff/sniff; nip/snip; now/snow; nowball/snowball

sw wan/swan; weep/sweep; weet/sweet; well/swell; wift/swift; wim/swim; wing/swing

Tip: The **sm**, **sn** and **sw** blends all join a whispered sound, 'sss…', to a voiced one.

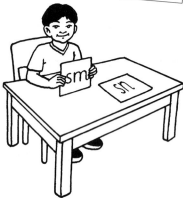

Show me

sm, sn or sw?

● Hand out prepared letter cards for **sm**, **sn** and **sw**.

● Read out a mixture of the above **sm**, **sn** and **sw** words.

● Children hold up the letters that match the initial sound.

Live Spelling/Slow-speak dictation

● Distribute the *Picture Code Cards* and help the children to Live Spell: **smell → smash → snack → snap → sniff → swim → swing**

● Alternatively, use the words for a **SLOW-SPEAK** dictation.

Shared reading and singing

● You will find songs to practice each of these consonant blends on the *Blends and Digraphs Songs Cassette* or *CD*. If time allows, write up the lyrics and use them as a shared reading text as you learn the song.

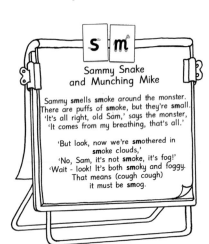

Sammy Snake and Munching Mike

Sammy **sm**ells **sm**oke around the monster.
There are puffs of **sm**oke, but they're **sm**all.
'It's all right, old Sam,' says the monster,
'It comes from my breathing, that's all.'

'But look, now we're **sm**othered in **sm**oke clouds,'
'No, Sam, it's not **sm**oke, it's fog!'
'Wait - look! It's both **sm**oky and foggy.
That means (cough cough)
it must be **sm**og.

scr, spl, spr, squ & str

Materials
Blends and Digraphs Songs Cassette or CD; Picture Code Cards

Preparation
Each child writes **scr** and **squ** on both sides of separate cards. They picture-code one side only.

Listen first

● First teach this sound: 'spr...'.

● Children add 'spr...' to discover these words: **ay/spray**; **out/sprout**; **inkle/sprinkle**; **ing/spring**.

Show me

scr or squ?

● Ask the children to have ready their prepared **scr** and **squ** cards. Then slowly say the following words:
squabble → scratch → squash → scream → scribble → squid → squeak → scrapbook

● After each word the children should repeat it and hold up the relevant card for the initial blend, so they learn to discriminate the small difference between the 'scr...' and 'sqr...' sounds.

str

● Write the initial consonant cluster **str** on the board. Ask the children to think of a word beginning with **str** that rhymes with **wrong (strong)**; **bring (string)**; **joke (stroke)** and **juggle (struggle)**.

Live Spelling/Slow-speak dictation

● Hand out **a**, **c**, **g**, **i**, **l**, **n**, **o**, **p**, **r**, **s**, and **t** *Picture Code Cards* to every child, so that everyone is ready in case his or her letter is needed.

● Ask the children to come forward if they think they are needed to form the words:
scrap → splash → split → sprint → spring → string → strong → strict

● Alternatively, use these words for a **SLOW-SPEAK** dictation.

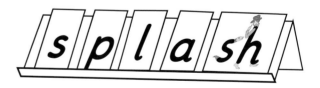

shr & thr

Materials
*Blends and Digraphs Songs Cassette
or CD; Picture Code Cards*

Preparation
Prepare letter cards for each child:
shr and **thr**.

Listen first

- Ask a volunteer to write up and picture-code the phoneme he or she hears at the start of these words: **ship**, **shark**, **she**.
- Let another child retell the **sh** story (page 61).
- Repeat with the **th** story (using the *whispered* **th** card) and these words: **thunder, thin** and **thumb**.

Show me

shr or thr?

- Add 'rrr…' to each digraph, and say each consonant blend together: 'shr…' and 'thr…'.
- Ask the children to have ready the **shr** and **thr** cards. They listen carefully to the initial blends of each of the following words, repeat the initial consonant blend, then hold up the card that matches the sound:
  thread → three → shred → through → shriek → thrill → throat → shrug → throne → thrush → shrimp
- Check that the children understand the meaning of each of these words.

Live Spelling/Slow-speak dictation

- Distribute the **g**, **h**, **i**, **m**, **p**, **r**, **s**, **t**, **ll**, **th** and **sh** *Picture Code Cards*. Ask the children to come forward as and when they are needed to build the following words:
  thrill → thrush → shrug → shrimp
- If any single card holders come forward to make the phonemes **th** or **sh**, ask if the pictogram on their card illustrates the sound needed.
- Alternatively, use these words for a **SLOW-SPEAK** dictation activity.

Extension

- Introduce Mr E's twin brother (page 114), a second Mr E, to build the high frequency word **three**. It helps to show the children that these two **e**'s are not two elephants saying ĕ but two Vowel Men saying their name, **E!**, together.

Section 5:
Digraphs and Trigraphs

Letterland phonic fables transform digraphs and trigraphs into memorable stories. For any children who have difficulty recognising letter patterns in words and linking them to new sounds, these recall routes are a lifeline! Reading takes on a new dimension as children become detectives on the look out for new letter patterns in the words all around them, and their reading vocabulary grows by leaps and bounds.

Section 5: Digraphs and Trigraphs

Assessment outcomes

- To blend and segment words with long vowel/silent final **e**.
- To blend and segment words with vowel digraphs.
- To blend and segment words with **r**-controlled vowels.
- To blend and segment words with **w**-controlled vowels.
- To read and spell a selection of high frequency words.

Lesson Plans

This Section sees the introduction of some simple but incredibly powerful stories that will unlock the thousands of words in which the **a–z** letters combine to make new sounds. They also provide easy answers to awkward questions like, "Why isn't Annie Apple making her usual sound in the word **aw**ful?"

Most lessons in Section 5 follow a simple pattern:

1 **Listen first** Play a short game to attune children's ears to the target sound.

2 **Deduce** the new spelling pattern from a known word (often one of the memorable Letterland character names).

3 **Learn** the brief Letterland story. This becomes the *recall route* for the new sound/spelling pattern.

4 **Consolidate** new letter knowledge through multi-sensory activities, including role-play, song, picture-coding, drawing, Live Spelling and more.

Letter knowledge

a–e / ai / ay	**o–e / oa / ow**	**ow / ou** (cow, ouch)	**oo / u** (foot, pull)
e–e / ee / ea	**u–e / oo / ew / ue**	**oi / oy**	**aw / au**
i–e / ie / y / igh	**ar / or / oor / our**	**er / ur / ir**	**air / ear**

Assessment activities

Tell your class that every new digraph they learn will open up 50–100 (or more!) new words for them to read and spell. To measure Section 5 assessment outcomes use:

- *Take-home Reading and Spelling Lists* (pages 180–82). Send home roughly one a week for children to learn before you test them in class.

- *NLS High-frequency Words List 1b* (page 184) together with the 'Look/say/cover/write/check' strategy (page 159).

- Downloadable *Pupil Record Sheets* for Section 5 from **www.letterland.com**.

- Also use any of the whole-class and individual activities in the Lesson Plans as informal, continuous assessment activities.

Teacher strategies for Section 5

1) Becoming word detectives

Here is a quick overview of four key concepts in Section 5 that will help children to read and spell thousands of new words. Encourage the children to become **word detectives**, using these fun concepts to spot silent final e's, Vowels Out Walking and the two big trouble makers in 1000's of words all around them!

The Silent Magic e concept

A silent **e** on the end of a word usually means the previous vowel will be a Vowel Man saying his name.

> The Silent Magic **e** concept accounts for the long vowel in **a–e**, **e–e**, **i–e**, **o–e** and **u–e** words.

The Vowels Out Walking concept

When two vowels go out walking, the FIRST one does the talking. The first one says his name, but his friend won't do the same.

> The second Vowel Man is quiet in **ai**, **ee**, **ea**, etc, because he is too busy looking out for vowel-stealing **r**obots!

The r-controlled vowels concept

Watch out when there's a robot about! If there is a vowel behind a robot's back, don't expect that vowel to be making its usual sound...

> Red Robot's band of five vowel-stealing robots accounts for **ar**, **or**, **er**, **ur**, **ir** plus **air**, **ear**, etc.

The w-controlled vowels concept

Watch out when Walter Walrus is about! He usually causes trouble for the vowel right next to him.

> Walter's wily ways account for **aw**, **ew**, **ow** and more.

2) Role-play, Live Spelling and dictation

Role-play Children can actually role-play each spelling pattern's sound by recreating the scene on the *Picture Code Card*. Props can strengthen associations and add motivation. (Ideas on page 185.)

Live Spelling Other children can join the role-play children to build whole words around them, with *Picture Code Cards* (e.g. add to **oa** to build **boat**, **goat** and **float**).

Dictation You can use the Live Spelling words in each lesson for a follow-up dictation (or instead of Live Spelling, if time is short). Write out each word immediately after dictating it, so children can self-correct.

Mr O shoots up his hand and says his name, 'O!', while Mr A silently looks out for Vowel Stealers.

3) Shared reading and singing

Each song on the *Blends and Digraph Songs Cassette* or *CD* contains many instances of the target sound and its spelling pattern.

You can turn any digraph song into a shared reading activity by writing up the lyrics (in the booklet accompanying the cassette). Use the text to:

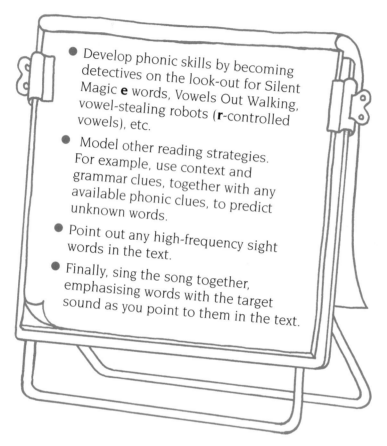

- Develop phonic skills by becoming detectives on the look-out for Silent Magic **e** words, Vowels Out Walking, vowel-stealing robots (**r**-controlled vowels), etc.

- Model other reading strategies. For example, use context and grammar clues, together with any available phonic clues, to predict unknown words.

- Point out any high-frequency sight words in the text.

- Finally, sing the song together, emphasising words with the target sound as you point to them in the text.

4) Review activity: Quick Dash

For a quick and effective review strategy, do a Quick Dash (page 155) through all the digraph *Picture Code Cards* you have presented so far. For a detailed review, children can retell each story in brief, and make the sound. For a real Quick Dash, children call out just the sound as you dash through each *Picture Code Card* in your pile.

Review long vowels

Materials
Letterland ABC Book; Picture Code Cards (Vowel Men); Alphabet Songs

Preparation
Provide paper for Vowel Charts.

Action (page 149)

NOTE: If you would like to go into more detail for each long vowel, see: Mr A (page 34), Mr E (page 54), Mr I (page 45), Mr O (page 50) and Mr U (page 57).

NOTE: Sometimes, when Mr U is inside a word, his name sounds less like 'you' and more like 'oo' (as in June, flute, rude, include, exclude and prune).

Demonstration

● Use the *ABC Book* and the *Picture Code Cards* to review The Vowel Men*.

● Remind children: The five Vowel Men are the only characters in Letterland who ever say their names in words.

● Review each Vowel Man's action: When Mr A says his name in a word, he has a special action. He shoots his arm up and shouts out his name to let everyone know that it's him and not Annie Apple in this word. (Repeat the same action for Mr E, Mr I, Mr O and Mr U.)

● Listen to the Vowel Men Song on the *Alphabet Songs Cassette* or CD (words page 190).

Show me

Picture-code

● Write these sentences on the board and ask the children to help with picture-coding both the short and long vowels.

Mr A has apples in his apron.
Mr E loves elephants and so do we.
Mr I sells ice-cream and ink.
Mr O sees an octopus in the ocean.
Mr U has useful umbrellas for us.

Individual activity ideas

Vowels Chart

● Help the children to make a short and long Vowels Chart. Add Yo-yo Man in the middle to show his role as a part-time Vowel Man, working at times for Mr E and at times for Mr I. Let the children know there will be stories to explain his part-time vowel work later on (pages 109 and 117, as well as page 75).

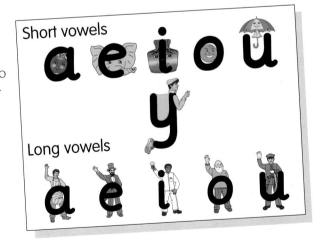

Short vowels
a e i o u
y
Long vowels
a e i o u

*Note: Why are all the long vowels men? This choice is prompted by a concern to counterbalance, at least slightly, the normal lack of any male presence in primary classrooms. Secondly, the use of one familiar word, 'Mr' unifies all five vowels in children's minds.

Long vowels in common words

✓ **Materials**
Picture Code Cards
✓ **Preparation**
Cards or paper for signs

The Vowel Men in little words

Reading tip
● When children come across vowels in unknown words, if pronouncing the vowel as short doesn't make a meaningful word, encourage them to try pronouncing it as a long vowel. In other words,

If the vowel sound does not make sense, try the Vowel Man saying his name!

Word search
● If you are looking for Vowel Men in words, here is a little tip: the Vowel Men have a habit of appearing in very little words. See if children can spot the words below in their reading books. As they find them, they can write out each word and picture-code the Vowel Men.

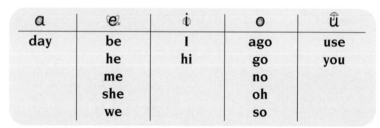

a	e	i	o	u
day	be	I	ago	use
	he	hi	go	you
	me		no	
	she		oh	
	we		so	

The Vowel Men in –ind and –old words

Reading tip
● When you see words ending in **–ind** or **–old**, expect to hear a Vowel Man.

Mr I has a habit of saying his name in 'kind words*', because he is such a kind man. And Mr O has a habit of saying his name in 'old words*', because he is such an old man (*words that rhyme with <u>kind</u> and <u>old</u>).

Live Spelling
● Help the children to Live Spell these words using *Picture Code Cards*.

kind → mind → remind → old → cold

Dictation
● Dictate any of these words and sentences for the children to write down.
behind, find, kind, mind, remind, cold, fold, hold, old, sold, told

I find Mr I is very kind.
Mr O sold me a pot of gold.

The Vowel Men on signs

● We all need to be able to read signs because they carry information for us. Let the children design their own signs, highlighting any long vowels by picture-coding them.

The Silent Magic e concept

New concept

Materials
Picture Code Cards; Blends and Digraphs Songs; props (page 161)

Preparation
Write sentences and photocopy (see Individual activity ideas).

Demonstration

Introducing silent final e
A final silent **e** has the power to make the Vowel Men appear and say their names.

Sammy Snake

- Use sight word **Sammy Snake** to introduce the Silent Magic **e** concept:

  Can you hear Annie Apple's sound or Mr A's name in the word **snake**?
  Can we hear Eddy Elephant making his usual 'ĕ …' sound? No! Why not?
  In Letterland there is nearly always a story to explain the new sound.

Show the card and tell the Silent Magic e story:

- **Introducing Silent Magic e**
  One day, Mr E decided to think up a new magic trick so that all the Vowel Men could appear in words more often. After a lot of experimenting, he came up with a very special new kind of **e**. He announced it like this:

  > Introducing the **e** you cannot hear,
  > with the power to make Vowel Men appear!

  The brand new Silent Magic **e** shoots magic sparks backwards over exactly one letter to make any Vowel Man appear and say his name.

Picture-code

- Write the word **tap** twice on the board. Picture code both **a**'s with a red apple to show Annie Apple's sound. Read **'tap, tap'** together.
- Ask a child to tiptoe up and very quietly write a big red Silent Magic **e** on the second version of **tap**. (Why quietly? Because Magic **e**'s are silent letters!)
- Add a top hat and wand on to the child's (red) **e** and draw a shower of magic (yellow) sparks back *over exactly one letter*.
- Wipe out Annie Apple's letter. Make Mr A appear by writing **a** again and adding a stick man right through it.
- Read the two words: **tap** and **tape**.

  Silent Magic **e**'s magic works in two ways:

  1) It makes Vowel Men appear.
  2) It completely changes the meaning of the word!

Common exceptions
have, **give**, **there**, **where**, **were**, **one**, **done**, etc. Congratulate children who spot these 'power failures' and make a list of them for a display.

y (as in ver**y** and 1000's of other words!)
To cure common spelling errors such as **vere** and **everebode**, explain that Mr E made almost all his final **e**'s into *Silent* Magic **e**'s, so now for words that *need his name*, **ē**, at the end, he has to ask Yellow Yo-yo Man to do the job for him. Yo-yo Man is ver**y** happ**y** about this because that gives him a chance to appear in roughl**y** 5000 words for Mr E!

Show me

Sing
● Sing the Magic **e** Song together. Demonstrate the picture-coding 'instructions' described in the song by picture-coding **game** on the board.

Picture-code
● plan → plane, spin → spine, hop → hope, cub → cube, pet → Pete
● For example: **hop → hope**
Add a Silent Magic **e** to **hop**. Then draw your top hat on the **e**, and Mr E's wand. Shoot yellow sparks back over exactly one letter so they land on Oscar Orange. Now make him disappear by rubbing him out. Who will take his place? His friend Mr O appears and says his name: O! So let's draw a stick man for Mr O. Has Magic **e** completely changed the meaning of the word? Yes!

Live Spelling
● Three children build the word **tap**, using *Picture Code Cards*.
● Another child holds Mr A's *Picture Code Card* and stands right behind Annie Apple, back-to-back.
● Give another child the Silent Magic **e** card and the wand to wave over Peter Puppy so the sparks land on Annie Apple.
● As soon as the sparks land, Annie Apple 'disappears' and Mr A appears in her place (both turn to their right) and says his name: 'A!'
● The class sounds out the new word: **tape**.
● Now or later, repeat with:
  spin → spine, hop → hope, cub → cube, pet → Pete
● For the best effect, use a wand and long vowel props (page 161).

Individual activity ideas

Picture-code
● Write the following sentences in large print, and photocopy one for each child to picture-code.

Mr A made a plane.

We hope Mr O is at home.

Can you use Mr U's flute?

Mr I likes* to sell fine ice-cream.

*Note: Tell the children not to be fooled when they see a word like **likes**. The magic is usually still there if they see this pattern: vowel–consonant–**e** before the **s**.

Long a: a–e, ai and ay

Materials
Picture Code Cards; Blends and Digraphs Songs; props (page 161)
✓ **Preparation**
Make onsets and rimes cards.

Listen first

● Play the Listen and Jump Game (page 162) as an *oral* activity. Children jump if they hear Mr A's name in a word: **ape**, **apron**, at, cat, **cape**, cap, **rain**, ran, **paint**, plan, **age**, apple, **page**, tractor, **make**, **take**, tap, **snake**.

Review a–e

Sammy Snake

Review the Silent Magic e concept (page 109):

● A silent **e** on the end of a word usually means the previous vowel will be a Vowel Man saying his name. We've seen its sparks make Mr A appear!

● Review **a–e** by picture-coding **Sammy Snake** on the board (page 109).

Live Spelling and dictation

● Dictate and /or Live Spell the following words, (see page 160):
plan → plane, at → ate, cap → cape, mad → made, tap → tape

Individual activity: onsets and rimes

● Give out prepared rimes cards containing: **–ake**, **–ame**, **–ate**, **–ape** and **–ade** and onsets cards containing consonants as well as blends and digraphs, like **sh**, **sn**, **pl** and **fl**. Children combine onsets and rimes and write down any resulting words.

Demonstration

rain

The second Vowel Man is always silent because he is too busy being the 'Look-out Man', looking out for robots who have a habit of running off with vowels. (The 'Look-out Man' reference prepares the way for explaining **r**-controlled vowels in later lessons, such as **–ar**, **–er**, **–air**, **–ear**, etc.)

Introducing the Vowels Out Walking

When two vowels go out walking,
the FIRST one does the talking.
The first one says his name,
but his friend won't do the same.

New concept

Phoneme count

● Write **rain** on the board, underline **ai** and do a phoneme count, demonstrating that *two letters* represent *one phoneme*.

● Which letter is silent? Why isn't Mr I saying anything in the word **rain**? .

Show the ai card and tell the ai story:

● When Mr A and I walk, Mr A talks
When Mr A and I go out walking,
Mr A does the talking.
He just says his name,
but his friend won't do the same.

● Picture-code **ai** words on the board: **rain**, **brain**, **train**, **paint**.

Demonstration

Review the Vowels Out Walking concept:
- When two vowels go out walking, the first one does the talking.
- But what is Yo-yo Man doing in these words? (**day**, **say**, **play**) This story explains how Yo-yo Man became a part-time Vowel Man.

Show the ay card and tell the ay story:
- When Mr A and Yo-yo Man go out walking, Mr A does the talking. Mr A's usual walking partner is Mr I. But when Mr A has to say his name at the END of a word it's no use taking Mr I with him – because Mr I always feels dizzy at the END of words! So Mr I and the Yo-yo Man have agreed that the Yo-yo Man will always take over as Mr A's silent Look-out Man at the END of words.
- Picture-code some **ay** words on the board: **say**, **day**, **today**, **play**. Now Yo-yo Man is your clue that Mr A will be saying his name.

Show me: ai and ay

Role-play and sing
- Two children play-act the **ai** story, walking in place, as the whole class sings the Vowels Out Walking Song. Mr A shoots up his arm when the whole class shouts out his name, 'A!' in line 3. The second Vowel Man is silent and mimes looking out for danger from vowel-stealing robots (causing exceptions like **air**). Repeat for **ay** using the same song and the **ay** *Picture Code Card*.

ay or ai?
- Using the picture-coded **ai** and **ay** words, help children to notice that **ai** NEVER occurs at the end of a word, but that **ay** ALWAYS* occurs at the end of words – and now we know why!

> *Note: If children spot **ay** inside some words, e.g. **payment** and **playing**, explain that Yo-yo Man is still helping Mr A to finish the main (or root) word.

Live Spelling

● Help the children to Live Spell these words:
rain → train → brain → paint → pay → say → stain → stay → stray → spray

Ask the **i**-child to mime feeling dizzy as soon as **n** and **t** leave the word **paint**, calling for the Yo-yo Man to take his place. Repeat for **stain/stay**.

Dictation

● Alternatively, dictate the Live Spelling words, or other **ai** and **ay** words:
nail, pay, paid, tray, trail, train, delay, relay, snail, tail, ray, rail, railway, stay, stain, afraid, today, brain.

Individual activity ideas: ai and ay

Picture-code

● Children copy and picture-code these words from the board, in two columns: **rain**, **brain**, **train**, **paint**, **say**, **day**, **today**, **play**.

Days of the week

● Give each child a piece of paper with the days of the week written in large text.

● Ask the children which day is Dippy Duck's favourite day. (Wednesday – because her letter appears in it twice!)

● Children picture-code the **d**'s in **Wednesday** as well as the **ay** digraph. They may like to write the first **d** and **e** in dots to show they are silent letters.

Extension

● Children picture-code the vowel pairs and Magic **e**'s in these instruction words and compound words:

make   trace   explain

railway   brainwave   gateway

Lesson 5 • PiPs Step 3.3, 6.1, 6.2, 6.3, 7.2

Long e: e–e, ee and ea

Materials
Picture Code Cards; Blends and Digraphs Songs; props (page 161)

Listen first

- Play the Listen and Jump Game (page 162) as an *oral* activity. If children hear Mr E saying his name in a word, they jump in the circle: **easy**, **cheese**, elephant, **eagle**, envelope, egg, leg, **queen**, **seed**, bed, **beads**, **green**, get, let, **leaf**, **read**, etc.

Review e–e

these

Review the Silent Magic e concept (page 109):

- A silent **e** on the end of a word usually means the previous vowel will be a Vowel Man saying his name. Sometimes a Magic **e** makes Mr E himself appear!
- Briefly review the **e–e** spelling pattern by picture-coding the words **these**, **complete** and **Pete** on the board.

Live Spelling and dictation

- Live Spell or dictate: **pet → Pete → compete → complete**

Individual activity: picture-code

- Praise any child who finds more of these very rare **e–e** words:

compete	eve	extreme	Pete	Chinese		delete
concrete	Eve	Irene	scene	Japanese	athlete	

Demonstration

feet

Review the Vowels Out Walking concept (page 111):

- Use **ee** in **feet** to review Vowels Out Walking. Count the phonemes.

Show the ee card and tell the ee story:

- When Mr E and his brother walk, Mr E talks.
  When two e's go out walking,   He just says his name, E!,
  the first Mr E does the talking.   but his brother won't do the same.
- Picture-code **fee**t on the board.

Show me

Role-play and sing

- Two children play-act **ee,** walking in place as the whole class sings the Vowels Out Walking Song. Mr E shoots up his arm as everyone shouts out his name, 'E!'. His brother silently mimes looking out for danger from vowel-stealing robots (causing exceptions like **deer**, **beer**).

Picture-code
● Ask some children to picture-code the following phrases on the board: green feet; sleepy green sheep; three green bees.

Individual activity ideas

Green book
● Make a group **ee** book using the colour green as a memory device.
● The children draw and label pictures of objects containing **ee** and colour them all green (see box on the left).
● These pictures can be collated into a class spelling book for the children to read and use as a spelling resource.

green feet, three green bees, a chimpanzee with green cheeks, sleepy green sheep, green cheese, green trees, greedy green geese, green teeth, green beetle, green sheets, etc.

Demonstration

Review the Vowels Out Walking concept (page 111):
● Write **leaf** on the board and underline **ea**. Who is talking in this word?
● Review the Vowels Out Walking rhyme (page 111).

Show the ea card and tell the ea story:
● **When Mr E and A walk, Mr E talks**
When Mr E and A go out walking,
Mr E usually does the talking.
He just says his name,
but his friend won't do the same.

Why? Let the children tell you. The second Vowel Man is looking out for robots.

Show me

Role-play and sing
● See the instructions for **ee** on the previous page.

Picture-code
● Ask some children to picture-code the following phrases on the board: foods for a f**ea**st, cr**ea**m cakes, p**ea**ches and cr**ea**m.

Phoneme count
● Do a phoneme count of each **ea** word.

Individual activity ideas

Letterland feast
● Give each child a different food (see box on the left) to draw, label and picture-code for a Letterland F**ea**st Mural: **ea** things to **ea**t.

cream cake; peaches and cream; lettuce leaves; bubble and squeak; dream dish; Mike's magnet meal; peanuts; peanut butter; meatballs; Easter eggs; steam pudding; heap of beans; heap of peas

Long i: i–e, ie, y and igh

Materials
Picture Code Cards; Blends and Digraphs Songs; props (page 161)
Preparation
Make plain letter cards for **b**, **f**, **h**, **l**, **m**, **n**, **r**, **s**, **t** and **igh** (one per child/pair).

Listen first

● Play the Listen and Jump Game (page 162) as an *oral* activity. If children hear Mr I saying his name in a word, they jump in the circle: **ice-cream**, **bike**, bit, **kite**, **life**, little, **prize**, **light**, dip, **Mike**, lip, **like**, lift, **shine**, **mine**, minute, trip, **try**, **night**.

Review i–e

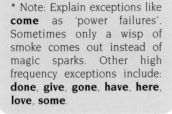

Review the Silent Magic e concept (page 109):

● A silent **e** on the end of a word usually means the previous vowel will be a Vowel Man saying his name. We've seen its sparks make Mr I appear.

● Review **i–e** by picture-coding these words on the board:

Invite Munching Mike to come* inside.

Live Spelling and dictation

● Live Spell or dictate these words:
pin → pine → pin → bit → bite → spin → spine → strip → stripe

● Additional dictation words: **alive**, **bike**, **fine**, **size**, **side**, **slide**, **smile**, **write**, **hide**, **inside**, **five**, **fire**, **lifetime**.

** Note: Explain exceptions like **come** as 'power failures'. Sometimes only a wisp of smoke comes out instead of magic sparks. Other high frequency exceptions include: **done**, **give**, **gone**, **have**, **here**, **love**, **some**.*

Individual activity: picture-code

● Children copy the following sentence and picture-code **i-e**:

Let's bite into a nice white ice-cream.

Demonstration

Review the Vowels Out Walking concept (page 111):

● When two vowels walk, the first one says his name.

● Write these words on the board: **lies**, **ties**, **cried**, **die**, **pie** and **fried**.

● Which Vowel Man could be saying his name in these words?

Show the ie card and tell the ie story:

● When Mr I and Mr E walk, Mr I usually talks
When Mr I and E go out walking,
Mr I usually* does the talking.
He just says his name, I!
But his friend won't do the same.

** Note: Mr E sometimes talks, e.g. in words like **believe**, **brief**, **chief**, **field**, **niece**, **piece**, **thief**, **Annie** (and other names).*

ties

● Picture-code **tie**s on the board.

Show me

Role-play and sing
- Two children play-act **ie**, walking in place as the whole class sings the Vowels Out Walking Song. Mr I shoots up his arm when the whole class shouts out his name, 'I!' in line 3. Mr E is silent and mimes looking out for robots.

Live Spelling, phoneme count and dictation
- pie → die → lies → ties → tries → cried → fried
- Do some phoneme counts showing that **ie** represents one phoneme.
- Follow up with a dictation of the Live Spelling words.

Individual activity ideas

Picture-code
- Children copy and picture-code this sentence:

Help! I can't untie my tie!

Demonstration

fly

Yo-yo Man, the part-time Vowel Man
- Yo-yo Man sometimes acts as a part-time Vowel Man.

Show the card and tell the story:
- **Why Yo–yo Man says 'I!' for Mr I**
  Yellow Yo–yo Man likes to appear in words, but there are not many words that begin with his 'yyy…' sound. Luckily, Mr I had an idea. "Yo-yo Man," said Mr I , "every time I stand at the end of a word I feel dizzy, as if I were about to fall off a cliff! Could you stand at the end of a few words and say my name for me?" Yo-yo Man was happy to help – he loves to appear at the end of words. So now Mr I gives him a free ice-cream as a reward, every time!
- Picture-code **y** (as in **fly**) on the board.

Show me

Role-play
- Children play-act this story with a yo-yo and paper ice-cream cone.

Individual activity ideas

Picture-code
- Children copy the following sentence and picture-code it:
  I'm going to fly in the sky all by myself, so goodbye!

| Firefighter Fred |
| Lucy Lamp Light |
| Munching Mike |

night

Listen first

- Read out the Letterland character names for **a** to **m**. If children hear Mr I saying his name in any of them, write the full name on the board. (**Firefighter Fred**, **Lucy Lamp Light**, **Munching Mike**.)
- Ask different children to picture-code Mr I in each character name.
- Ask which letters are silent in **fight** and **light**.

Demonstration

Show the igh card and tell the igh story:

- **An ice-cream for Golden Girl**
  When Mr I stands next to Golden Girl and the Hat Man in a word, he gives Golden Girl an ice-cream. Do you know why? It's because she is doing such a good job of being quiet beside the Hat Man. (We know how he hates noise.) So in words where you see these three letters **igh** you will only hear Mr I saying 'i' for 'ice-cream' as he hands Golden Girl a delicious ice-cream.
- Picture-code n**igh**t on the board.

Show me

Role-play

- Children play-act this brief **igh** story, with Mr I handing an ice-cream cone to Golden Girl, as he says his name, 'I'. She nods and smiles.

Live Spelling and phoneme count

- high → sigh → sight → night → bright → light
- Count the phonemes in each word.

Dictate and picture-code

- Dictate this sentence for children to picture-code:

It might not be right to have a fight late at night in the bright moonlight.

Individual activity ideas

Word building

- Give each child an **igh** card for them to picture code as well as a set of plain letter cards for **b**, **f**, **h**, **l**, **m**, **n**, **r**, **s** and **t**.
- The aim is to build 15 words. (They should include consonant blends **br**, **fl**, **fr**, **sl**, **th** and plurals.)
- Children record the words they make and use it as a spelling list.

Long o: o–e, oa and ow

Materials
Picture Code Cards; Blends and Digraphs Songs; props (page 161)

Listen first

● Play the Listen and Jump Game (page 162) as an *oral* activity: **old**, **bone**, top, **phone**, pot, **loaf**, hot, **goat**, **snow**, stop, **hole**, **mole**, **hope**, hop.

Review o–e

Review the Silent Magic e concept (page 109):
● A silent **e** on the end of a word usually means the previous vowel will be a Vowel Man saying his name.
● Review the **o–e** spelling pattern using **home**, **close**, **alone** and **joke**.

Live Spelling and dictation
● hop → hope → not → note → glob → globe → mop → mope
● Additonal dictation words:
  nose, **stone**, **rope**, **note**, **choke**, **broke**, **alone**, **hope**.

Individual activity: picture-code
● Children copy and picture-code this sentence:

Don't choke on the smoke from those burning pinecones!

Demonstration

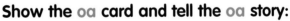

Review the Vowels Out Walking concept (page 111):
● Write the word **boat** on the board. Who could be talking in this word?

Show the oa card and tell the oa story:
● When Mr O and Mr A walk, Mr O talks
  When Mr O and A go out walking,
  Mr O does the talking.
  He just says his name, O!
  but his friend won't do the same.
● Picture code **boat** on the board.

Show me

Role-play and sing
● Two children play-act **oa**, walking in place as the whole class sings the Vowels Out Walking Song. Mr O shoots up his arm when the whole class shouts out his name, 'O!'. Mr A silently mimes looking out for robots.

Live Spelling
● boat → coat → coast → toast → throat

Dictation
● Follow up by dictating some of these **oa** words:

boat coast   goal   loaf   road   soap
coach   float   groan oatmeal   roasted   throat

● Children could make up sentences using at least three **oa** words.

Individual activity ideas

Picture-code
● Children copy and picture-code this sentence:

Oh no, goats on the road to the coast!

Demonstration

w-controlled vowels
Watch out when Walter Walrus is about! He usually causes trouble for any vowel beside him.

New concept

yellow

● Write **Yellow Yo-yo Man** on the board. Underline **ow**.
● Can children spot the trouble-maker? What could be happening?

Show the ow card and tell the ow story:
● Mr O stops Walter Walrus from teasing Oscar Orange by shouting 'O!' Mr O is an old man. He has been around for a long time and he knows a lot! Mr O knows that Walter Walrus likes to tease vowels by splashing them with salty water. So he rushes to protect Oscar Orange, crying out, "Oh no you don't!" before Walter can begin to tease him. In fact old Mr O cries "Oh!" so loudly that Walter Walrus is completely silenced. He's too surprised to make any sound at all.

● Picture-code **yellow** on the board.

Show me

Role-play
● Children play-act the **ow** story, making the actions and 'ow...' sound.

Live Spelling and dictation
● low → blow → slow → grow → show
● Other **ow** words: **row**, **below**, **snow**, **elbow**, **own**.

Individual activity ideas

Picture-code
● Children copy and picture-code this sentence:

I am the owner of two elbows.

Develop a Yellow Window display.

Long u: u–e, oo, ew and ue

Listen first

● Play the Listen and Jump Game (page 162) as an *oral* activity. If children hear Mr U saying his name, they jump into a circle: **use**, **uniform**, up, mud, **new**, nut, **grew**, **cube**, cub, tub, **boot**, foot, **moo**, us, **glue**, **moon**, hut, pup, **poodle**, **unicorn**, fuss, **perfume**, **confuse**.

Review u–e

Review the Silent Magic e concept (page 109):

● A silent **e** on the end of a word usually means the previous vowel will be a Vowel Man saying his name. Let's see how its sparks make Mr U appear.

● Review the **u–e** spelling pattern using the words **use** and **cube**.

Live Spelling and dictation

● cub → cube, tub → tube, cut → cute, us → use

Picture-code

● Children copy and picture-code this sentence:

Mr U played a fine tune on his flute.

Demonstration

● Now it's time to meet two Vowel Children, the Boot and Foot Twins. Let's find out what they say in words. First let's meet the Boot Twin.

● Write the word **boot** on the board, underline **oo** and read the word aloud. What sound are these two letters making in the word **boot**?

Show the o͞o card and tell the o͞o story:

● **The Boot and Foot Twins always fight over their boots**
Mr O has two grandsons. Everyone calls them the Boot and Foot Twins because they spend so much time arguing over their boots. When you hear the sound 'ooo …' in words like **bo͞ot** and **so͞on** and **zo͞o**, you know that the Boot twin is teasing his brother by saying '**OO**! I have your **bo͞ot**!'

Picture-code

● Demonstrate how to picture-code the Boot Twin on the board:

boot

That afternoon we all went to the zoo.

The Boot and Foot
Twins' Song

oo, oo, oo, oo,
oo, oo, oo, oo.
Boot and foot, boot and foot.
We are the boot and foot twins.
When we fight he always wins.
Boot and foot.
Boot and foot.

Show me

Shared reading and singing

- Use the Boot and Foot Twins Song lyrics as a shared reading text (for shared reading tips, see page 106). Then sing the song together, emphasising the long **oo** words. The focus on the Foot Twin's sound comes on page 135.

Read

- Picture-code some of these words on the board and help children to see that they can now decode: **balloon**, **boot**, **cool**, **hoop**, **kangaroo**, **moo**, **moon**, **soon**, **cocoon**, **droop**, **macaroon**, **noodles**, **racoon**, **rooster**, **swoop**, **shampoo**, **shoot**.

Live spelling, phoneme count and dictation

- Help the children Live Spell these words:
  boot → **too** → **tool** → **stool** → **spoon** → **moon**

Individual activity ideas

Boot Twin Words poster

- Write some **oo** words on the board.
- Give each child a piece of paper to make a **Boot Twin Words** poster.
- Ask them to ch**oo**se words that they can illustrate for the main section, and to write words they cannot illustrate on the bottom section.

Words cubes (o͞o)

- Write these words on a piece of paper and give one list to each pair of children:
  bloom, **boot**, **boost**, **booth**, **stool**, **cool**, **hoop**, **loot**, **moo**, **moon**, **root**, **shoot**, **soon**, **spoon**, **too**, **tool**, **tooth**, **zoo**.
- Prepare four cubes per pair of children.
  Cube 1: **r**, **b**, **c**, **h**, **m**, **s**
  Cube 2: **m**, **t**, **l**, **n**, **th**, **p**
  Cube 3: **l**, **n**, **s**, **t**, **z**
  Cube 4: **oo** × 6
- Children throw the four cubes to see how many words from the list they can make.
- They put a tick next to the word on the list when they have thrown the right combination.

Demonstration

Review the w-controlled vowel concept (page 120):

● You can hardly ever expect the vowel beside a **w** to be making its usual sound – no matter which side it is on! *

> *Note: For example, all words with **aw**, **ew**, **ow/ow** plus **–ward**, **word**, **wolf**, **work**, **worst**, **world**, **woman**, **women**, **two** and many more.

● Write the words **few** and **flew** on the board, underline **ew** and read them aloud.

Show the ew card and tell the ew story:

● This next story explains why **ew** can sound EITHER like 'oo' (as in flew) or 'you' (as in few).

● When Eddy surprises Walter Walrus, Walter cries, 'OO! You!'
We know Walter Walrus is a trouble-maker. He loves to tease, so when Eddy Elephant finds himself next to Walter Walrus in a word, he decides to act first. He uses his trunk to squirt water at Walter. That makes Walter cry out, 'Oo! You!' in surprise. That's why, when we see Eddy Elephant and Walter Walrus together in a word, we will always hear an 'oo' or a 'you' sound.

● Demonstrate how to picture-code **ew** on the board.

Show me

Role-play

● Children play-act this brief story as you talk them through the story explanation for both possible sounds: 'oo' and 'you'.

Shared reading and singing

● Use the **ew** Song lyrics as a shared reading text. Then sing the song together.

Live Spelling and dictation

● few → flew → blew → grew → chew

● Follow up with a dictation of these and other **ew** words.

Individual activity ideas

Picture-code

● Ask children to picture-code a large **ew** at the top of a piece of paper, followed by the sentence:

Eddy Elephant knew a few new tricks.

● They can write a list of **ew** words underneath their sentence, for example: **blew**, **brew**, **chew**, **flew**, **grew**, **jewel**, **threw**, **dew**, **few**, **knew**, **new**, **stew**.

Demonstration

Review the Vowels Out Walking concept (page 111):

● Write **blue** on the board, underline **ue** and read it aloud.

● Can anyone guess what might be happening in these words? Can you spot two Vowels Out Walking?

Show the ue card and tell the ue story:

● When Mr U and Mr E walk, Mr U talks
When Mr U and E go out walking,
Mr U does all the talking.
He just says his name, 'U!'
Or else he just says 'oo!'

● Demonstrate how to picture-code **ue** on the board.

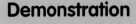

blue

Show me

Role-play

● Children play-act this brief story as you talk them through it again.

Live Spelling and dictation

● Children Live Spell these words:
true → blue → glue → clue → rescue

● Follow up with a dictation of the **ue** words above. (There aren't many others.)

Individual activity ideas

Picture-code

● Children copy and picture-code this sentence:

It's true that Mr U has blue glue.

Follow up

● You could consolidate the Vowels Out Walking concept by making a mural with a long road full of Vowel Men all out walking. Smaller pictures at the left, getting bigger towards the right, will create a real sense of perspective. You could also add speech bubbles with one example in each bubble.

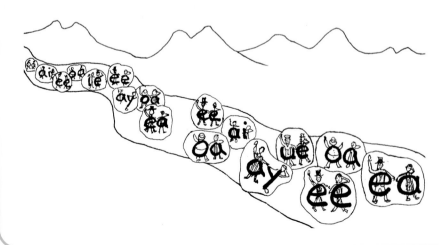

ar and or

Materials
Picture Code Cards; Blends and Digraphs Songs; props (page 161)
Preparation
Copymaster 7 for Listen and Sort Activities (page 126); Write up song lyrics for shared reading (page 106); prepare Getaway Car (page 126).

* Note: If you prefer to focus on one Vowel Stealer at a time, simply go through all the **ar** activities first, and the **or** ones later.

Listen first

- Tell children that they will meet two trouble-makers in Letterland today*. They are Arthur **Ar** and Orvil **Or**. Say each of their names a few times.
- Arthur Ar and Orvil Or are both members of Red Robot's Robber Band. They have a bad habit of running off with vowel sounds. So remember this:

Introducing r-controlled vowels

Watch out when there's a robot about! If there is a vowel behind a robot's back, don't expect that vowel to be making its usual sound.

New concept

Demonstration

Note: All the robots have torn sacks, which they can't be bothered to fix, so all the vowels eventually escape!

Show the ar card and tell the ar story:

- When Arthur Ar runs off with an apple, he shouts out "Ar!"
  When Arthur Ar runs off with an apple, the apple is too surprised to make any sound at all. So all you will be able to hear is Arthur Ar reporting back to Red Robot on a tiny mobile phone. He says just one word: his last name, "Ar!" as he runs to his getaway rad**ar** c**ar**.

- Demonstrate how to picture-code **ar**, using this sentence:

  Arthur Ar has a dark green scarf.

Demonstration

Show the or card and tell the or story:

- When Orvil Or runs off with an orange, he shouts out "Or!"
  Orvil Or is the robot robber who runs off with oranges. When he is around, don't expect an orange to make its usual 'ŏ …' sound. All you will hear is Orvil Or rep**or**ting back to Red Robot by saying his last name: "Or!" as he runs to his get-away boat that he keeps by the sh**or**e.

- Demonstrate how to picture-code **or** on the board, using this sentence:

  Did Orvil Or order forty pairs of shorts?

How to catch the Vowel Stealers:

The Vowel Stealers will try to stop you from reading the words they appear in. The best way to stop them is to become a detective! Whenever you see a **r**obot with an **a**pple or an **o**range behind his back, stop him before he can trick you into saying a short vowel sound. Instead call out that robber's last name: 'Ar!' or 'Or!'

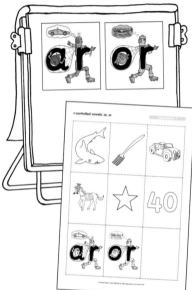

Show me: ar and or

Shared reading and singing

● Use the **ar** Song lyrics prepared as a shared reading text (see page 106 for shared reading tips). Then sing the song together.

● Do the same with the **or** Song.

Live Spelling

● Help the children Live Spell these words using *Picture Code Cards*:
  cat → car, had → hard → card → part → shark
  spot → sport → sort → horn → corn → short

Listen and sort activity

● When you have consolidated both **ar** and **or**, play Sort it Out! (page 165) as a whole-class activity. Use the pictures on *Copymaster 7*.

Individual activity ideas: ar and or

Listen and sort activity: ar and or

● You can also play Sort it Out! as an individual activity. Make a flapchart for each child and use the pictures on *Copymaster 7*.

Arthur Ar's getaway car: ar

● Draw a large outline of a car and give a photocopy to each child.

● Underneath the car, children picture-code the sentence:

Arthur Ar parks his car in a barn.

● They write in some other **ar** words on the picture.

Picture-code: or

● Children copy and picture-code this sentence from the board.

Did Orvil Or order forty pairs of shorts?

Note: Magic **e**'s magic sparks don't work in **ore** words because Orvil Or absorbs the sparks into his robot arm! See page 109 for more about Magic **e**.

oor (as in floor), **oar** (as in oar) and **our** (as in four)
Whether Orvil Or takes one vowel or two, it is all the same to him! He just goes on reporting back with his last name, "Or!" as he has always done before. (This includes **-oar** words and some but not all **-our** words, like **four**, **fourteen** (not forty!) and **your**.)

door

roar

four

ow and ou

✓ Materials
Picture Code Cards; Blends and Digraphs Songs; blank cards for displays (see individual activity ideas)

✓ Preparation
Write lyrics for shared reading (page 106); prepare displays.

Listen first

- Introduce the new sound of the day with this silly sentence: **Can a vowel howl like an owl?** Really exaggerate the **ow** sounds.

Demonstration

Review the w-controlled vowel concept (page 120):

- Watch out when there's a walrus about! Can the children spot a trouble-maker in the words **now** and **cow**?

Show the ow (as in cow) card and tell the ow story:

- When Oscar gets teased by Walter Walrus, they both shout "ow!" Whenever you see Walter Walrus next to Oscar Orange in a word, you can expect trouble. Sometimes old Mr O isn't on hand to protect Oscar. Then wily Walter Walrus starts splashing Oscar, even though he knows that oranges hate salty water.

  What Walter always forgets is that, when you tease someone, you can end up hurting yourself the most. Walter loses his balance. Now the trouble-maker is in trouble! Oscar has salty water in his eyes and Walter has bumped his chin, so they both howl, 'OW!' This happens in quite a few words. Will Walter ever learn to stop teasing?

- Demonstrate how to picture-code **ow** on the board.

Oscar Orange
and Walter Walrus

There are some things that aren't allowed
Like teasing different vowels,
But Walter Walrus breaks the rules.
He's breaking one right now!

The splashing Walrus showers me.
My eyes are stinging now.
But look, he's slipped and bumped his chin
So now we both howl, OW!

Show me

Role-play, Live Spelling and dictation

- Play act the **ow** story. The **w**-child uses a hand to mime Walter bumping his chin.
- Live Spell these words in front of the class, and/or dictate them:
  owl → howl → growl → brown → clown → power → shower

Shared reading and singing

- Use the **ow** Song lyrics as a shared reading text. Then sing the song together, emphasising **ow** words.

cloud

Demonstration

(This next story is a sequel, so tell the **ow** (as in cow) story first.)

● Write **Bouncy Ben** on the board. Can anyone underline the letters that make the **ou** sound? What has happened to Oscar Orange now?

Show the ou (as in ouch) card and tell the ou story:

● Oscar Orange gets teased again and both he and Walter shout "ou!" Walter has another wily way we need to be wary about. He sometimes does his teasing from another letter! One that can hold a lot of water. Yes, he takes Uppy Umbrella's letter, fills it up with salty water and flops into it with a big splash.

Now Oscar has salty water in his eyes and clumsy Walter has knocked himself on Uppy's letter again, so they both sh**out**, '**ou**!' (as in ouch!).

Picture-code

● Demonstrate how to picture-code **ou** on the board.

Show me

Role-play, Live Spelling and dictation

● Children play act the **ou** story, with actions and sound.

● Live Spell these words in front of the class, and/or use the same words for a dictation: **loud → cloud → ground → pound → pouch → ouch**

Shared reading and singing

● Use the **ou** Song lyrics as a shared reading text. Then sing the song.

Individual activity ideas: ow and ou

Picture-code words for ow and ou displays

● Give each child a suitable **ow** or **ou** word from the lists below to write in large letters, picture-code and illustrate.

● Use them to make a 'Brown owl' and an 'Our cloud words' display.

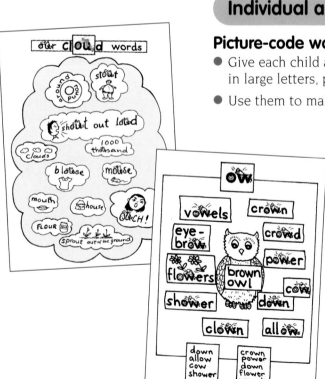

ow words: allow, brown, clown, cow, crowd, down, flower, frown, growl, how, owl, powder, shower, towel, town, vowel, power.

ou words: about, around, blouse, cloud, count, flour, found, ground, hour, house, loud, mouth, our, out, round, shout, sound, thousand.

Silly sentences

● Children create **ow** or **ou** sentences from the above word lists and underline the target sound in each one. For example: **A crowd of clowns rode into town on brown cows. I found a thousand blouses in our house.**

oy and oi

Materials
Picture Code Cards; Blends and Digraphs Songs; props (page 161)
Preparation
Write up song lyrics for shared reading (page 106).

Listen first

- Today we will meet a new character – a boy called Roy. Let's say his **oy** sound a few times together.

- Play the Listen and Jump Game (page 162). Children jump if they hear the 'oy' sound inside a word: **boy**, **enjoy**, **annoy**, about, **destroy**, hello, **joy**, jump, **toy**, top, **oil**, **Noisy** Nick, **boil**, **coin**, coat, **join**, **noise**, nose, note, **toilet**, toe, **voice**.

Demonstration

Show the oy card and tell the oy story:

- **The boy called Roy's 'oy game'**
There is a boy called Roy in Letterland. At the end of words, this boy called Roy enjoys leap-frogging over an **o** and into the Yo-yo Man's sack. He calls this leap-frog game his 'oy game' because he likes to shout "oy!" as he leaps. The Yo-yo Man pretends to be annoyed so he shouts out "oy!" every time Roy lands on him unexpectedly.

- Demonstrate how to picture-code **oy** on the board.

boy

Demonstration

Show the oi card and tell the oi story:

- **Roy and Mr I play the 'oi game' inside words**
From time to time Mr I likes to join Roy in playing the 'oy game' but only when they can play it INSIDE words. Why is that? Remember, Mr I always feels dizzy at the end of words. That's when he asks the Yo-yo Man to take over.

So now we know why we have two spellings for this one sound – Roy with Mr I INSIDE words and Roy with Yo-yo Man at the END*.

- Demonstrate how to picture-code **oi** on the board.

coin

*Note: Children might spot **oy** in the middle of a few words, but that will only be because a new ending like **–ing**, **–ed**, **–ment** or **–s** has been added on to the root word, just like the **ay/ai** rule (page xx).

Show me: oy and oi

Shared reading and singing

- Use the lyrics of Roy's Song as a shared reading text (see page 106). Sing the song together. Half the class can be Roy while the other half sings the ann**oy**ed responses of Yo-yo Man and Mr I.

- Ask two children to hold up the **oy** *Picture Code Card* as they sing 'Oy, oy, oy!' and another two to hold up the **oi** *Picture Card Card* as they sing 'Oi, oi, oi!' Sing the **oi** version in even more n**oi**sy and b**oi**sterous v**oi**ces.

Word sort listening activity

- Draw two columns on the board, one headed **oy** and one headed **oi**.
- Remind children that if they hear the **oy** sound at the END of a word, they will find Roy and the Yo-yo Man playing the 'oy game', but if they hear the **oi** sound INSIDE a word, they will find Roy and Mr I playing the 'oi game'.
- Slowly read out these words, emphasising each **oi/oy** sound. Children should tell you in which column you should write each word:
  Noisy Nick, Roy, boy, joy, coin, enjoy, join, boil, toy, destroy, spoil, point, pointed, toilet, oysters.

Live Spelling

- Help children to Live Spell these words using *Picture Code Cards*.
  boy → boil → coil → coin → coy → toy → toil

Read

- Read these longer words together: **employer, enjoyment, destroying, appointment, disjointed, rejoice, pointless, ointment**.

Individual activity ideas: oy and oi

Picture-code: oy and oi

- Write down these sentences, and picture-code or underline:

Roy enjoys oysters dipped in soy sauce.

The nurse put ointment on Roy's boil.

Review all vowel digraphs

Quick Dash

- Now is a good time to review all the vowel digraphs you have learnt so far:-
  Long a: a–e, ai, ay
  Long e: e–e, ee, ea
  Long i: i–e, ie, y, igh
  Long o: o–e, oa, ow
  Long u: u–e, oo, ew, ue
  ar, or; ow, ou; oi, oy
- Display one *Picture Code Card* at a time and ask for a volunteer to tell the story that explains why those letters make that sound when they are together.
- Then do a Quick Dash (page 155) through all the cards, and ask for the sound only.

er, ur and ir

Materials
Picture Code Cards; Blends and Digraphs Songs
Preparation
Write up song lyrics for shared reading for **er**, **ur**, **ir**.

The Er/Ur/Ir brothers

- It's time to meet three more members of Red Robot's band of Vowel Stealers. Their names are Ernest Er, Urgent Ur and Irving Ir. They call themselves the 'Robot Brothers'. All three brothers are trouble-makers. They all make the same 'er/ir/ur' sound. But they can't agree on how to spell it! So each one spells his last name differently. That could mean trouble for us whenever we want to read or spell a word with an er/ir/ur sound in it. The best way to stop the robots is to become detectives and catch these law-breakers in words!

Demonstration

Review the r-controlled vowel concept (page 125):
- Watch out when there's a robot about!
  If there is a vowel behind a robot's back,
  don't expect that vowel to be making its usual sound.

Show the er card and tell the er story:
- When Ernest Er runs off with an elephant he shouts out "Er!" Ernest Er is the robot robber who steals elephants. When you see Ernest Er in a word, don't expect to hear the elephant he has captured making its usual 'ĕ …' sound. All you will hear is Ernest Er calling out his last name, "Er!" as he reports back to Red Robot.

- Demonstrate how to picture-code **er** on the board.

Catching Ernest Er the Elephant Stealer:
Whenever you see an **e**lephant behind a robot's back, stop that robot by calling out "Er!" before he can trick you into making the wrong sound.

Show me

Shared reading and singing
- Use the prepared lyrics of the 'Ernest Er in Person' Song for a shared reading activity (page 106). Highlight all the **er**'s.

Live Spelling
- Help the children Live Spell these words using *Picture Code Cards*.
  hen → her → ever → clever → never → after → sister

Individual activity ideas

Picture-code: er
- Children copy this sentence from the board, and picture-code it:

  Ernest Er is faster than his other brothers.

Word detectives
- Each child skim-reads any book until they have found five **er** words. List them on the board as *Detective Work: Catch Ernest Er in words*. Children choose ten words, and picture-code them on a *Detective Sheet for Ernest Er*.

Demonstration

Review the r-controlled vowel concept (page 125):

● Watch out when there's a robot about!
  If there is a vowel behind a robot's back,
  don't expect that vowel to be making its usual sound.

● Let's take a closer look at the second Vowel Stealer, Urgent Ur.

Show the ur card and tell the ur story:

● Urgent Ur, the Umbrella Stealer, says, "Ur!"
  Urgent Ur steals umbrellas. When he does, he reports back to Red Robot
  with his last name, spelt: Ur! But you won't see him very often in words. He
  must have cold feet, because he always turns up wearing boots made of
  thick curly purple fur. They slow him down so he you hardly ever see him at
  the END of words.

● Demonstrate how to picture-code **ur** on the board.

Show me

Shared reading and singing

● Use the prepared lyrics of the 'Urgent Ur in Person' Song for shared
  reading (page 106). Highlight the **ur**'s. Then sing the song together,
  emphasising all **ur** words.

Live Spelling

● fun → fur → curl → hut → hurt → turn → bun → burn

Individual activity ideas

Purple Book

● Make a **Purple Book** of **ur** words to link them together in the children's
  minds. In it they put pictures of **ur** objects labelled and coloured
  purple. For example:
  curl, nurse, church, purse, curtain, turkey, fur, furniture, turtle.

Picture-code: ur

● Children copy and picture-code this sentence:

  Urgent Ur has boots of curly purple fur.

Word detectives

● Each child skim-reads any book until they have found five **ur** words.
  List them on the board as *Detective Work: Catching Urgent Ur in words*.
  Children choose five and write them down on a *Detective Sheet for
  Urgent Ur*.

Catch three robots in one word!

● Children picture-code the three Vowel Stealers in **furthermore**.

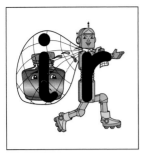

girl

Demonstration

Review the r-controlled vowel concept (page 125):

● Watch out when there's a robot about!
If there is a vowel behind a robot's back,
don't expect that vowel to be making its usual sound.

● It's time to meet the third robot brother, Irving Ir.

Show the ir card and tell the ir story:

● Irving Ir, the Ink Stealer says, 'Ir!'
Irving Ir is the thi**r**d 'Er/Ur/Ir brother'. He steals every colour ink he can find: black, blue, red, green or rainbow ink. Then he reports back to Red Robot with his last name, spelt: Ir! But he gets into far fewer words than either of his robot brothers, because most of the ink bottles in Letterland make themselves invisible when they see Irving Ir coming.

Just to teach him a lesson, they squi**r**t some of their invisible ink on his shirt. When it becomes visible again it makes his shi**r**t look very di**r**ty! Vi**r**tually every shi**r**t he owns has ink stains on it!

● Demonstrate how to picture-code **ir** on the board.

Irving Ir in Person

You'll recognise me,
Irving Ir, by my dirty shirt,
with lots of spots of ink on it,
and this is not
my first dirty shirt,
nor my second,
nor my third,
nor my thirteenth
nor my thirtieth
nor my thirty-first.

Show me

Shared reading and singing

● Use the prepared lyrics of the 'Irving Ir in Person' Song for a shared reading text (page 106). Highlight the **ir**'s before you sing the song together.

Live Spelling

● bid → bird → girl → fist → first → skirt → shirt

Individual activity ideas

Picture-code: ir

● Children copy and picture-code this sentence:

Irving Ir has more than thirty dirty shirts.

Word detectives

● Each child skim-reads any book until they have found five **ir** words. List them on the board as *Detective Work: Catching Irving Ir in words*. Children choose five, write them large and picture-code them on a *Detective Sheet for Irving Ir*.

Rhyming ir words

● Mix up this list of **ir** words on the board (see box on left). Children write them down in rhyming pairs. They could use the rhyming pairs to make up **ir** sentences.

Rhyming ir words

bird	shirt
girl	dirt
firm	thirst
third	skirt
swirl	squirt
squirm	first

Review of Er/Ur/Ir Brothers

Detective work: LOOK

- Look closely at *Picture Code Cards*: **er**, **ur**, **ir**. Notice they each run off with different letters. What else is different about each one?
- Observe their clothes. Ernest Er: train**er**s; Urgent Ur boots made of p**ur**ple c**ur**ly f**ur** and Irving Ir: an ink-splashed d**ir**ty sh**ir**t.

Detective work: LISTEN

- Read out the words in the box (see left).
- If children hear an Er/Ur/Ir Brother in a word, they shout out the brothers' last name – even if they don't know which Er/Ur/Ir brother it is yet! They could also shoot out one arm (like the robots).

Ernest Er's longer legs

- Ask the children to look closely again at the *Picture Code Cards*.
- Apart from their clothes and the fact that Irving Ir captures **i**nk, Urgent Ur captures **u**mbrellas and Ernest Er captures **e**lephants, there is one more important difference – Ernest Er's legs are long**er** than his oth**er** broth**er**s!
- That's why you find him at the END of so many words – because he can get there fast**er** than his slow**er** broth**er**s!

Picture-code and word sort

- Have ready some or all of the following words on large pieces of card: **burn, curl, curtain, disturb, fur, hurt, purple, turkey, turtle, bird, skirt, first, thirsty, squirt, girl, dirt, shirt, her, fern, brother, sister, faster, longer, slower, older, letter, circus.**
- Create three columns on a display, one for each spelling pattern.
- Give each child a word card.
- Children picture-code their word, then stick their card in the correct column.
- Finally, read each word together.

Vowel Stealer's Chart

- Each child makes their own Vowel Stealer's Chart showing Red Robot and his band of trouble-makers. Vowel Scene Posters are available from Letterland. www.letterland.com

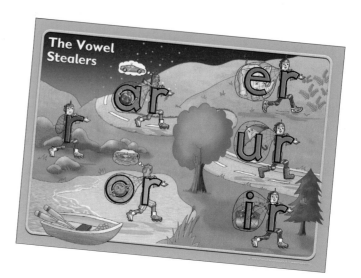

Word box (left margin)

purple, puppy, fun, **fur**, **curly**, cut, **shirt**, shed, **dirty**, **thirty**, **her**, head, **fern**, **turn**, toad, bed, **bird**, **skirt**, skate, late, **burn**, box, **clever**.

Er stories

Give the children a selection of **er** words from this list, and ask them to write an **er** story.
other, mother, brother, another, older, colder, bolder, whiter, lighter, brighter, cleaner, greener, meaner, better, letter, wetter, met her, dinner, thinner, winner, spinner, flippers, slippers.

o͝o and u

Materials
Picture Code Cards; Blends and Digraphs Songs

Preparation
Make plain letter cards for **b**, **f**, **p**, **ll**, **t**, **sh** and a picture-coded card for **u** (as in pull) (per child/pair). Write up song lyrics for shared reading (page 106).

Listen first

- Play the Listen and Jump Game, (page 162). If children hear **oo** (as in foot), they jump: **foot**, boot, **book**, **took**, too, cool, **good**, food, **hood**, **hook**, hoop, etc.

Demonstration

- Write **Boot and Foot Twins** on the board, and read the words aloud.
- Ask a child to underline the letters that make the Foot Twin's short o͝o sound.

Show the Foot Twin's card and tell the o͝o story:

- The Foot Twin steps in a puddle and says, "oo!"
Remember the Boot and Fo͝ot Twins are the grandsons of Mr O, the Old man. They spend a lot of time arguing over their boots. In most words you will hear the Boot Twin teasing his brother by saying, "O͞O! I have your bo͞ot!" Sometimes though, you will hear the second twin, the Fo͝ot Twin, complaining, "O͞O! Just lo͝ok at my fo͝ot!" as he steps in a puddle.
- Picture-code **foot** on the board.

Show me

Shared reading and singing

- Use the prepared lyrics for the Boot and Foot Twins Song for shared reading (page 106), this time emphasising the Foot Twin's sound. Then sing the song together.

Role-play, Live Spelling and dictation

- Children play-act this brief story. One child could remove both shoes.
- Live Spell and/or dictate: **foot** → **good** → **wood** → **wool** → **book**

Individual activity ideas

Foot Twin Poster (o͝o)

- Write some o͝o words on the board.
- Give each child paper to make a **Foot Twin Words** poster.

full

Demonstration

Another way to spell the Foot Twin's sound
- Write the high-frequency words **pull**, **push**, **put** and **full** on the board. Underline **u.**
- Read the words and encourage the children to notice that Uppy's letter is making the same sound as the Foot Twin's **'oo'** sound.

Show the card and tell the u (as in pull) story:
- If an umbrella is pushed into its letter upside down it will say "o͝o!"
  In Letterland there is giant called Giant Full. He helps Mr U by filling his letters full of umbrellas for him. The trouble is that he sometimes works so quickly that he pushes an umbrella in upside–down. Then you will hear that umbrella saying, "U!" Giant Full! You pushed me in! Please pull me out!".
- Picture-code this irregular **u** sound on the board.

Show me

Role-play, Live Spelling and dictation
- Children impersonate an annoyed umbrella saying, "**U!*** Giant Full! You pushed me in! Please pull me out!"
- Dictate and/or Live Spell these words: **full**, **bull**, **pull**, **push**, **bush**, **put**, **useful**, **pudding**.

Individual activity ideas

Little words with u*
- Give each child a set of homemade letter cards for **b**, **f** , **p**, **ll**, **t** and **sh** as well as a picture-coded **u** (as in **pull**) card.
- Children re-arrange the cards to see how many words they can build. Then they write them on a large piece of paper and picture code each **u** with an upside-down umbrella.

*(Pronounce as in pull.)

aw and au

Materials
Picture Code Cards; Blends and Digraphs Songs

Listen first

- Play the Listen and Jump Game (page 162): **awful**, **saw**, sat, **caught**, cat, **August**, clam, **claw**, **crawl**, jam, **jaw**, down, **draw**, pat, **paw**, **yawn**, etc.

Demonstration

Review the w-controlled vowels concept:

- Write **draw** and read it aloud. Why isn't Annie Apple making her usual sound. Who is next to her? Watch out when Walter is about! He is always changing the sounds that vowels make in words.

Show the aw card and tell the aw story:

- When Walter is awful to Annie she cries, "Aw!"
  Whenever you see that wily Walrus next to Annie Apple in a word, don't expect her to be saying 'ă…' anymore! That's because Walter Walrus teases her by splashing her with salty water! So instead we hear Annie crying out, " **AW!** Stop it Walter! Don't be so **aw**ful!"
- Picture-code **aw** on the board.

Demonstration

Show the au card and tell the au story:

- Walter hides in Uppy Umbrella's letter and makes Annie cry, "Aw!"
  Walter has another way of making trouble! He sometimes hides in Uppy Umbrella's letter, thinking we might not notice, and tries to tease Annie Apple from there! Often Golden Girl and the Hat Man are in the word as well, but they are too shocked to speak, seeing Walter Walrus being so n**au**ghty! So we just hear Annie Apple crying "AW!" again.
- Picture-code **au** on the board.

Show me: aw and au

Role-play, Live Spelling and dictation

- Children play-act these brief **aw** and **au** stories.
- Live Spell and/or dictate:
  **sat → saw → pat → paw → clap → claw → crawl → draw → awful
  because → sauce → saucer → laundry → haunted → fault
  caught → daughter → naughty → taught***

Individual activity ideas: aw and au

Picture-code: aw and au

- Children picture-code **aw** in the word **saw** and write more **aw** words around the border of the page.
- Do the same with **caught** and other **au** words.

*Note: Remind children of the **igh** story (page 118) when reading **augh** words.

air and ear (as in hair and hear)

> **Materials** ✓
> *Picture Code Cards*

Review concepts

● When two vowels go out walking the second one is silent. Do you remember why? He is too busy looking out for vowel-stealing robots. But sometimes the Vowels are not able to spot the robots in time and then the Vowel Stealers run off with them, changing the sounds they make in words.

Demonstration

Show the air (as in hair) card and tell the air story:

● When two vowels are captured, the robot does the talking. The silent look-out men are not always able to spot a robot in time. Sometimes the robot manages to sneak up on them and capture both Vowel Men at once. Carrying off two Vowel Men at once is heavy business. When a robot captures Mr A and Mr I, the robot always puffs out, "**Air**! I need **air**! I've caught a p**air**!"

● Picture-code the word **hair** on the board.

Demonstration

Show the ear (as in hear) card and tell the ear story:

● When two vowels are captured, the robot does the talking. Sometimes a silent look-out man is not able to spot a robot in time, so both Vowel Men are captured. But they don't go quietly! The robot looks away and pretends he can't hear them. He points to his ear and says sarcastically, "Oh D**EAR**! I F**EAR** my **EAR** can't H**EAR** you!"

● Picture-code the word **hear** on the board.

Show me

Role-play, Live Spelling and dictation

● Children play-act these brief stories.

● Live Spell and/or dictate:
  aim → **air**,   **fail** → **fair**,   **hail** → **hair**
  ear → **hear** → **hears** → **near** → **fear** → **appear** → **appeared**

Individual activity ideas

Picture-code: -air words

● Give each child a large piece of paper to make a label for their chair. For example, **Paul's chair**. They picture-code **air**. They could write other **air** words in the space around the label.

Picture-code: -ear words

● Children copy and picture-code some Live Spelling words. For example: **clearly**, **dear**, **disappear**, **dreary**, **weary**, **year**.

More Letterland stories

You have now covered all the spelling patterns required by PiPs! However, there are Letterland stories to explain many more spelling patterns. If you would like to continue using Letterland phonic fables to teach any of the following spelling patterns, please move on to the *Advanced* materials. See our website for further details. www.letterland.com

a (as in America)	**kn** (as in knee)
a (as in father)	**le** (as in table)
o (as in love)	**ly** (as in lovely)
all/al (as in all/allways)	**less/ness** (suffixes)
al/el (as in musical/angel)	**mb** (as in thumb)
ce/ci/cy (soft c stories)	**mn** (as in autumn)
ch (as in school)	**ough/ought**
dge (as in bridge)	**ous** (as in famous)
ed (the 3 sounds of)	**ph** (as in photograph)
ei (as in eight/height)	**que** (as in antique)
ei (as in receive)	**tion** (as in action)
ere (as in here/there/where)	**ture** (as in picture)
ey (as in they)	**wh** (as in when)
ey (as in donkey)	**wh** (as in who)
full/ful (as in useful)	**wr** (as in write)
ge/gi/gy (soft g stories)	**y** (as in bicycle)
gh (as in laugh)	**y to i** (as in cry/cries)

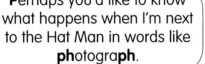

Perhaps you'd like to know what happens when I'm next to the Hat Man in words like **ph**otogra**ph**.

Want to know what happens when I meet up with Red Robot in words like **wr**ite?

Appendices

This section begins with Child and Teacher Strategies that combine with the pictogram mnemonics to make Letterland teaching fun, memorable and empowering. It also contains an Activity Bank, Reading and Spelling Lists, Song Lyrics, Copymasters and more.

Letterland strategies

This section models the key Letterland strategies in detail. It gives a clear overview of Letterland's storytelling teaching style, terminology and 'secret tricks'. You will be referred to specific strategies in the Lesson Plans, but you can also visit this section as a central resource whenever you need to.

Letterland's storytelling teaching style

A big part of the appeal of Letterland for many teachers is the way it engages children's imaginations. Children quickly grasp the alliterative principle when you model it for them by presenting Letterland in a storytelling style. For example, Do you think **M**unching **M**ike **m**ight like to **m**unch on this **m**assive piece of **m**etal? Or, Which Letterlander might like to have this **l**ovely **l**ittle **l**amb as a pet? and so on. Teachers find that children soon come up with some really imaginative ideas themselves! For example, one child told his teacher that the Hat Man would need a quiet pet (because he hates noise), so he could have a **h**ummingbird with **h**ardly any **h**um! Another child decided he would also be **h**appy with a **h**ibernating **h**edgehog.

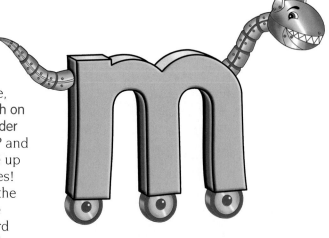

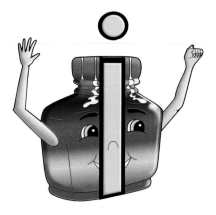

Throughout this section (and the rest of this *Teacher's Guide*) the blue text provides examples of how you might present key Letterland teaching points in a storytelling style. There's no need to present these scripts word for word – simply use whatever you find useful.

Language development

Teachers also find that the Letterland storytelling style enables them to introduce quite advanced language much earlier than they otherwise might. Even EFL children benefit from the language development opportunities afforded by Letterland. One EFL teacher wrote: 'I have also used the character names and associated vocabulary to get the children's tongues around English words... This has been beautiful as they have now acquired a really complex oral vocabulary. How many EFL kids know the meaning of the words 'clever', 'noisy' or 'quarrelsome'?'

Child strategies

Present Letterland's eight main child strategies as TRICKS that the Letterlanders have thought up to help children to become better readers and writers. (You will be referred to specific TRICKS in the Lesson Plans.) Encourage children to make the tricks their own and to use them during independent reading and writing, and during paired reading or peer-coaching sessions.

1 The SOUNDS TRICK

Objectives
- To discover **a–z** letter sounds.
- To match **a–z** letter sounds to the plain letter shapes.

The TRICK

The Letterlanders have a special trick to help us learn their letter sounds. The first sound of the Letterlander's name is the sound their letter makes in words!

To discover any letter sound, just START to say a Letterlander's name.

Munching Mike
(Show the picture.)

'mmm...'
(Show the plain letter.)

READ ME!

Whenever you talk about letter sounds, always **show the plain letter side** of your *Picture Code Card*.

Munching Mike is a good letter to use to introduce this strategy, because it is easy to separate his letter's 'mmm...' sound from the start of his name. To avoid adding an unwanted 'uh' sound, say his sound with a closed mouth: 'mmm...'.

After the children have grasped the principle of segmenting off the initial sound, you can use the same strategy to discover any **a–z** letter sound. Make use of both sides of the *Picture Code Card* for this TRICK, helping children to form an automatic association between the plain letter and the letter sound.

It is very important that the children get used to saying the letter sound in response to the plain letter, so after you have discovered the new Letterlander's sound, show the plain letter again, and ask children to respond *just with the sound*.

Note The children will soon come across words where the letters are not making their 'usual' sounds. For example, 'c...' in **c**ake <u>but</u> 'sss...' in **c**ircle and 'ch...' in **ch**ips. See Dealing with exceptions (page 161).

Letter sounds and letter names

Letter names are not much help to a child when it comes to blending words. The 21 consonant letter names (bee, see, dee, eff, jee, aitch, etc.) are *never* used in reading, and 15 letter names actually begin with *another letter's* sound (see, eff, aitch, ell, em, etc.).

Having the Letterland character names (Annie Apple, Bouncy Ben, Clever Cat, etc.) gives you a temporary alternative to the traditional alphabet names (aee, bee, see, etc.). Now you can talk about 'Clever Cat's letter shape' and 'Clever Cat's letter sound' if you want to avoid the confusions that may arise from teaching letter names and letter sounds at the same time.

If you prefer to introduce the letter names along with the letter sounds, you will find suggestions on page 155 for how to include letter names in your Letterland teaching from the start.

Teaching the concept of *letter sounds* vs *letter names*

If your children are completely new to the concepts of letter sounds and letter names, try using the following routine before you explain that the Letterlanders are going to help them learn all the *letter sounds*.

New concept

- Write the letters **a**, **t** and **m** randomly on the board. Also write the word **mat**.

- Ask, Which are the *letters* and which is the *word*? Can anyone name these letters? (em, ay, tee)

- Now attempt to read the word **mat** by blending the letter names: emaytee

- The letter names aren't helping me to read this word. What if I use each letter's sound: mmm…a…t, mmmat, mat!

- Talk about the difference between letter sounds and letter names.

- Talk about different strategies for reading words: using pictures, prediction, sight words and sounding out *using letter sounds*.

I am Mr A. I say my name in words! (ay)

I'm Annie Apple. I make my letter sound in words. (ă)

The five Vowel Men are the only Letterlanders who say their alphabet names in words.

All the other Letterlanders make their letter sounds in words.

The CAPITAL LETTER TRICK

Objectives
- To learn when capital letters are used.
- To learn capital letter shapes.

Teaching point
Each Letterlander has a special way of turning their letter into a capital. They are so proud at being given the important job of beginning someone's name or a sentence that they do their **CAPITAL LETTER TRICK**.

The TRICKS

A	In Letterland, the capital A shapes are called Applestands. The apples sit on the Applestand while they say 'ă...' at the start of important words, such as names like Anne, Andrew and Ashraf.
B	Bouncy Ben's head is still in the same position in his capital letter shape. The only difference now is that he is balancing his 'best blue ball' between his 'big brown ears'. Bouncy Ben shows off this trick whenever he starts an important word.
C	Whenever Clever Cat starts important words such as names, she takes a deep breath and gets bigger.
D	The funny shaped door with Dippy Duck's head poking out is Dippy Duck's very own duck door. This is her trick for making sure you know she is starting an important word.
E	Eddy Elephant is very proud of his 'elephant on end' trick. He sits down and points everything – his trunk and all his feet – in the Reading Direction whenever he starts an important word.
F	Firefighter Fred takes a deep breath and gets bigger to start an important word. His letter gets a bit sharper as well.
G	When Golden Girl is needed to start an important word, she gets out of her garden swing, gets into her go-cart and drives along in the Reading Direction. She always turns up in her go-cart twice to start the two words in her name, Golden Girl.
H	When the Hat Man has a chance to start a name, he is so happy that he does a handstand with his hat on!
I	When Impy Ink takes a deep breath, his letter gets so tall and thin that you can't see his ink spot any more. Instead, his letter looks long and thin like his ink pen.
J	Whenever Jumping Jim can start an important word, he is so pleased, that he does a big jump, and his head and his ball disappear in the clouds.
K	When Kicking King starts an important word, he takes a deep breath. His arm and kicking leg then get longer so he will look more important in that word.

L	Whenever Lucy Lamp Light starts important words, she takes a deep breath and gets bigger. Her legs also grow longer, so long in fact, that she has to kneel with her legs on the line.
M	Munching Mike may look big, but he's really only a little monster (too little to start important words), so his much bigger Mum does the job for him.
N	Nick starts important words with three big nails, which you can see in Noisy Nick's name.
O	When Oscar Orange is needed to start an important word, he takes a deep breath and gets bigger.
P	When Peter Puppy has a chance to start an important word he is so pleased that he pops up so that everyone can see him better. He hopes his ears will pop up too, but sadly they still droop.
Q	This very different capital letter shape is Quarrelsome Queen's Quiet Room. She likes to sit very quietly in it to start important words like her own name!
R	When he starts somebody's name, Red Robot takes a big breath and gets bigger. But the rascal changes his letter shape as well, just to make it more difficult to recognise him. So look very carefully and remember it is still Red Robot.
S	Whenever Sammy Snake has a chance to start an important word, like a name or a word on a sign, he takes a deep breath and gets bigger.
T	When Tess starts her name or a sentence, she takes a deep breath and grows so tall that her head disappears in the clouds. We still know it's Tess, though, because we can still see her arms.
U	Like everyone else in Letterland, Uppy Umbrella loves starting important words. All she has to do to get bigger is to take a deep breath.
V	Vicky Violet has discovered how to make her very own valuable Vase of Violets get bigger just by taking a deep breath herself! So that's what she does whenever an important word like a name or the first word in a sentence needs her sound.
W	When Walter Walrus takes a deep breath, his letter gets bigger. It even holds more water! He always makes his letter bigger when he has a chance to start an important word, like somebody's name.
X	Like many other Letterlanders, Fix-it Max just takes a deep breath to make his letter bigger. But you will hardly ever find his capital letter at the start of a word. The best place to look for it is in the important word EXIT.
Y	When the Yo-yo Man has a chance to be in an important word, he quickly empties out some of his yo-yos (which are heavy) so that he can step lightly up on to the line to show how important that word is.
Z	When Zig Zag Zebra has a chance to start an important word, she takes a deep breath and gets bigger. We don't see her looking big (or small) very often in words, however, because she is very shy.

3 The CHARACTER NAMES TRICK

Objectives
- To make use of noticeable recurring capital letters for the rapid identification of the 26 **a–z** Letterland character names as sight words.
- To use character names to read rhyming words by analogy.

Materials
- Enlarge and photocopy the *Character Name Flashcards* (*Copymaster 8*).

The TRICK
We always start a name with a capital letter, because names are important words. So in every Letterlander's name we will see their capital letter. But there is something special about their names:

Letterlanders appear TWICE in their capital letter shape in their own names!

Remember that and it will help you to read all the Letterlanders' names!

Teaching point
- Each Letterlander's name contains his or her capital letter shape TWICE. This visual fact makes it easier for children to link a name they already know to the words that represent it.

- Why should children read the character names? The 26 character names contain 35 common words, such as apple, cat, duck, elephant, girl, etc. They are therefore extremely useful words to teach as sight words.

- You can use these same very familiar words to unlock many more words through the strategy of reading by analogy. (See page 152.)

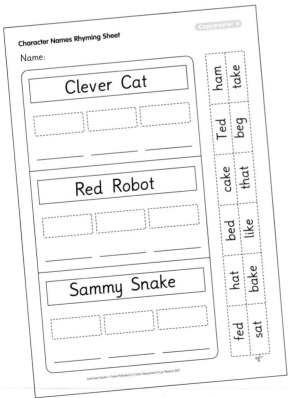

Character Names Rhyming Sheet
(*Copymaster 4*)

Character Name Flashcards
(*Copymaster 8*)

4 The ACTIONS TRICK

Objective
- To develop multi-sensory (kinaesthetic–auditory–oral–visual) memory cues for letter sounds.

Teaching point
There are so many supportive cues built into Letterland teaching that the actions for each letter can be considered as an optional extra.

Explain to the children that each Letterlander has given us an action to help us remember their letter sound. To begin with, encourage children to *make the sound each time they make the action*, so that the action and sound become firmly associated. Later on you could try using the actions in various activities. For example:

- A child makes an action and the rest of the class say the corresponding sound.
- Children play an Actions Game (page 162) where they make each action in alphabetical order.
- Some children spell a word using actions only. The others convert the actions into sounds to build the word.

The TRICKS
The actions are designed to be performed either sitting or standing. Where relevant, children should be facing in the Reading Direction.

The Action Tricks are available on a poster too!

a Bite an imaginary apple.	**b** Shoot arms up for ears and wiggle them.	**c** Stroke whiskers across cheeks.	**d** Flap elbows like a waddling duck.

e Spread out hands behind ears and flap like elephant ears.	**f** Hold and direct imaginary hose towards fire.	**g** Mime holding tipped glass of grape juice in 'glug, glug' position.	**h** Breathe on to hand in front of mouth. OR: Put on imaginary hat.

Letterland Teacher's Guide Published by Collins Educational © Lyn Wendon 2003

 **i** Touch fingers to thumb on the same hand as if sticky with ink and make an 'icky' face.

 **j** Juggle imaginary balls.

 **k** Lift one arm and one foot in a **k**-shape. If sitting, use arms only.

 **l** Touch finger tips above head to suggest Lucy's lamp-shade hat.

 **m** Rub tummy.

 **n** Bang one fist on the other, as if hammering a nail.

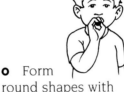 **o** Form round shapes with both mouth and hand and adopt a surprised look.

 **p** Stroke down long imaginary ears.

 **q** Point index finger up as if ordering 'Quiet!', while saying 'qu...'.

 **r** Make a running movement with arms.

 **s** Make snake movements with hand and arm.

 **t** Lift arms horizontally at shoulder height in **t**-shape.

 **u** Hold up imaginary umbrella with one hand low and the other above the head.

 **v** Hold hands together in **v**-shape.

 **w** Flick both hands up and away as if splashing water, ending with arms in a **w**-shape.

 **x** Cross arms on chest in **x**-shape.

 **y** Move hand up and down as if controlling a yo-yo.

 **z** Tilt head and rest against hands to mime falling asleep.

Long vowel action
Each Vowel Man punches the air with his right hand as he calls out his name enthusiastically.

5 The ALLITERATION TRICK and The ALLITERATION GAME

Objective
● To develop phonemic awareness of initial sounds.

Teaching point
The alliterative 'logic' of Letterland adds an engaging discovery factor to phonemic awareness activities. In Letterland, the characters love things that start with their sounds.

The activity of searching for alliterative words enables children to have creative input as they build up a bigger picture of each character. Children feel like they are discovering new things about their Letterland friends. This element of discovery has proved a real strength of the Letterland programme, making the children highly motivated to learn more about their Letterland friends.

The TRICK
Do you know how you can tell what each Letterland character likes? Let me give you a clue. Listen carefully… Firefighter Fred's fffavourite fffood is fffresh fffish. Munching Mike likes mmmushrooms and mmmelons. Lucy Lamp Light loves lllettuce lllleaves and lllemon lllollipops. Can you guess what the Letterland ALLITERATION TRICK is? How can we tell what each character likes?

Each Letterlander likes things that start with his or her sound.

The ALLITERATION GAME
● Children supply their own alliterative information about a Letterlander. You can help them with hints, for example: I'm thinking of a long, thin, crunchy, orange vegetable (carrot) that Clever Cat likes to eat.

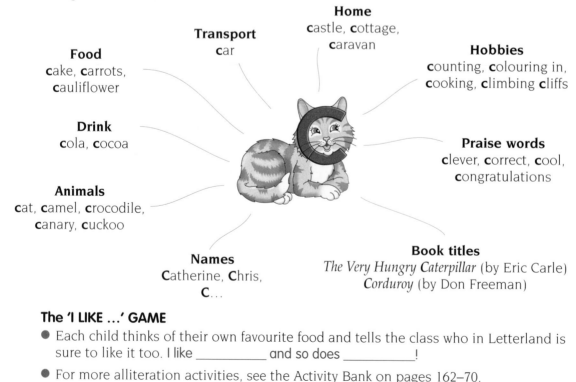

Home
castle, cottage, caravan

Transport
car

Food
cake, carrots, cauliflower

Hobbies
counting, colouring in, cooking, climbing cliffs

Drink
cola, cocoa

Praise words
clever, correct, cool, congratulations

Animals
cat, camel, crocodile, canary, cuckoo

Names
Catherine, Chris, C…

Book titles
The Very Hungry Caterpillar (by Eric Carle)
Corduroy (by Don Freeman)

The 'I LIKE …' GAME
● Each child thinks of their own favourite food and tells the class who in Letterland is sure to like it too. I like _____ and so does _____!

● For more alliteration activities, see the Activity Bank on pages 162–70.

6 The ROLLERCOASTER TRICK

Objective
- To blend individual sounds into words.

Teaching point
The **ROLLERCOASTER TRICK** is a multi-sensory strategy to help children move on from just saying individual sounds to running sounds together to **read** words.

The TRICK
- Write down a regular word on the board, but don't read it aloud, e.g. **dog**.
- Draw this 'rollercoaster' shape on the board.

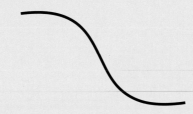

- Next, write the letters **d, o** and **g** on the rollercoaster as shown.

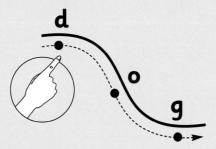

- Finger-trace the shape of the rollercoaster as you all say each sound. (The children can use a hand action miming a rollercoaster gaining speed as it rushes down the tracks.)

  ✓ On the first ride, say each individual sound; d... o... g....
  ✓ On the second ride, pick up speed as you blend the sounds together to make a word; do... g.
  ✓ Finally, take a fast ride down the rollercoaster and blend the whole word; dog.

- The children can use this blending trick any time they are having trouble reading a phonically regular word. They might like to use one arm (from shoulder to hand) as the rollercoaster, using the other hand to 'ride' the rollercoaster as they blend the sounds.

- Later on, they can use the same strategy to blend more advanced words, e.g. c...oa...ch, coach.

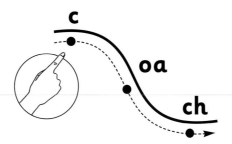

The SLOW-SPEAK TRICK

Objective
- To segment words into individual sounds.

Teaching point
The **SLOW-SPEAK TRICK** helps children to break up spoken words into their individual phonemes, in order to aid spelling.

> **The TRICK**
> - Teach children to stretch out any word by saying it so slowly that they can hear each sound. Slow down your voice to emphasise each sound in a word, e.g. **hhha...t, hhha...mmm, mmma...t, sssa...d, sssa...t**
> - Children might like to accompany this stretching-out technique with a hand movement. Start with hands together and move the right hand further and further away with each new sound, as if stretching out a giant rubber band.

The RHYMING WORDS TRICK

Objective
- To spell and read by analogy.

> **The TRICK**
> If I can read ___ I can also read ___, ___, ___, and ___.
> If I can spell ___ I can also spell ___, ___, ___ and ___.

Teaching point
One of the strategies children should consciously use when attempting to read or write a new word is to identify a spelling pattern in a word they already know. (You will need to control the use of this strategy, so that children are not making incorrect analogies.)

Section 2 focuses on developing reading and spelling by analogy, using three main resources:

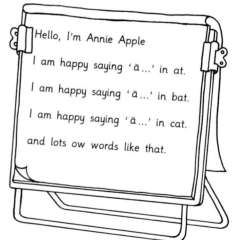

1 Rhyming chants
For example:

I am happy saying 'ă...' in at.
I am happy saying 'ă...' in bat.
I am happy saying 'ă...' in cat,
and lots of words like that.

2 Vocabulary Cards

You will find rhyming words on the backs of most of these 78 picture cards.
Help children to read these rhyming words by analogy, first using the *Vocabulary Cards* and then the 6 photocopiable *Rhyming Words Lists* on the insert accompanying the *Vocabulary Cards* pack which contains all 450+ rhyming words.

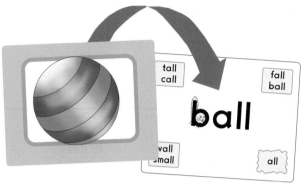

bed	ball	blue
red	tall	blue
bed	call	glue
fed	ball	true
ted	wall	clue
led	fall	flue
sled	small	rescue
	all	

cake	car	cat
bake	bar	at
cake	car	bat
fake	far	mat
lake	hard	hat
snake	dark	sat
awake	park	that

Rhyming Words Lists

3 Character names

Once children recognise the Letterlanders' names by sight, they will be able to read many more words by analogy. You can help children to deduce certain spelling patterns from these words. For example:

See page 147 for more ideas on how to use character names to develop the strategy of reading and spelling by analogy.

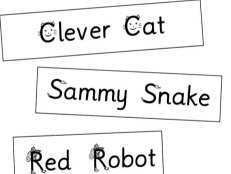

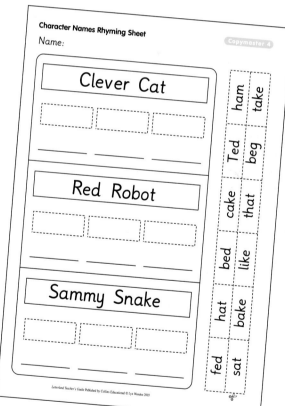

Character Names Rhyming Sheet

Name:

Copymaster 4

Clever Cat

Red Robot

Sammy Snake

ham take
Ted beg
cake that
bed like
hat bake
fed sat

Letterland Teacher's Guide Published by Collins Educational © Lyn Wendon 2003

Teacher strategies

Here are Letterland's ten main teaching strategies, as well as a letter sounds pronunciation guide for teachers who are new to phonics. You will be referred to specific strategies in the Lesson Plans, but you can visit these strategies as a central resource whenever you need to. A quick read through all the strategies before you begin your Letterland teaching will give you a good overview of the Letterland methodology.

Letter sounds pronunciation guide

Pronunciation models
- *Letterland Alphabet Songs* (**a–z** sounds and long vowels)
- *Letterland Blends and Digraphs Songs* (consonant blends, consonant digraphs, vowel digraphs)

Pronunciation

Accurate pronunciation of each letter sound is a vital factor in teaching children how to access print. Inaccurate pronunciation can lead to a delay in reading and predictable spelling inaccuracies, such as **bt** for **butter**.

The three simple categories set out below are guidelines for pronouncing sounds accurately in Live Reading, Live Spelling and dictation activities.

1 Whispered sounds are never spoken with voice, ('c...' not 'cuh').

2 Prolonged sounds can be extended, (fff...). They are helpful for independent spelling and **SLOW-SPEAK** dictation (page 152).

3 Almost closed mouth sounds are the hardest to say. Although they contain a small amount of voice, try to avoid adding an unwanted 'uh' sound by keeping your mouth almost closed.

1 Quick Dash

Objectives
- To revise previously learned Letterland character names and letter sounds.
- To give letter sound in response to the plain letter shape.
- To give letter name in response to plain letter (optional).

Materials
Letterland Picture Code Cards

Procedure
- Review all the letters you have taught so far.
- Hold up each *Picture Code Card* in turn. Show the picture-coded side and ask for the character name.
- Next, quickly turn the card over, showing the plain letter side. Ask for the sound only.
- Next, do a dash through the plain letter side of each card and ask the children to give you just the sounds.
- Turn to the picture-coded side only to confirm the children's answers.
- Increase the pace as children become more familiar with the routine, aiming for a 'Quick Dash' through all the letter sounds.

Teacher	Pupils
Who is this?	Clever Cat
What sound does she make in words?	'c...'
And who is this?	Annie Apple
What sound does she make?	'ă...'

Letter names
If you are teaching the traditional letter names at the same time, you could add a third question to this routine: **What is his/her letter name?** For a more detailed discussion of when to introduce letter names, please see page 144.

Phonemic awareness follow-up
After you have completed the Quick Dash as explained, build in a phonemic awareness strand as follows:

- Hand out *Vocabulary Cards* for letters you have revised in the Quick Dash.
- Show the plain side of each *Picture Code Card* and ask for the letter sound.
- Ask, Who has a word that starts with Annie Apple's sound? Children holding **a**nt, **a**pple and **a**crobat should stand up . Each one says their word, emphasising the beginning sound.

Character names follow-up
- You could also do a Quick Dash through the *Character Names Flashcards*.

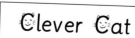

Digraphs
- Follow the same routine using the digraphs *Picture Code Cards*, as a review strategy in Section 5.

② Order Please!

Objectives
- To recreate a sequence of three sounds (words or non-words).
- To identify the position of each sound in an oral sequence.

Materials
Any or all *Picture Code Cards* you have introduced so far.

Procedure
- Hand out the *Picture Code Cards*. Explain that this is a **listening** game.
- Call out a sequence of three alphabet letter sounds (e.g. 'a …', 'c…', 'd…').
- Children holding matching cards line up in the same sequence in the Reading Direction.
- The class checks that the three children have lined up in the correct order.
- Ask: Which is the beginning sound? Which is the final sound? Which is the middle sound?
- Call out the same three sounds in a different order.
- Children quickly rearrange themselves.
- Call out three new sounds.
- Repeat the procedure a few more times.

Note: Use a maximum of three sounds when you play Order Please! so the children listen out for sounds in beginning, final and middle positions – a skill they will need when they start building CVC words in Section 2.

Variations
Use character names, whole words, numbers or *Letterland Vocabulary Cards* (picture sides or word sides).

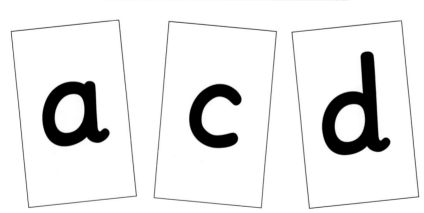

③ Picture-coding

Objectives

● To draw attention to the shape and orientation of individual letters.

● To draw attention to target sounds in selected words.

● To draw attention to all the sounds in selected words.

Teaching point

Picture-coding is the process of adding Letterland pictogram details to a letter shape. It can be done by teachers and children. It can be used for arts and craft, for board work and for object labels.

Procedure

● Children add pictogram details to plain letters. They can draw individual pictogram characters or picture-code whole words.

● To begin with, you may like to provide the plain letter shapes for children to picture-code.

● The children can also make spelling pictures by selecting regular words that can also be illustrated, e.g. cat, red, sun.

● You can also use picture-coding to draw attention to target sounds in words. You don't have to be an artist – simply 'hand-code' the letters by adding stick figures of simple details to the target letters.

Reading Direction

Objectives
- To help children to read and build words from left to right.
- To help children form letters correctly, avoiding common reversal problems like **b/d** and **p/q**.

Materials

Prepare a Reading Direction sign with arrows and stick it up on a wall behind the area where the children will be building Live Spelling words. A chalked arrow line on the floor in front of their feet can also be helpful at first.

Procedure
- Point to the Reading Direction sign on the front wall of the classroom. When you are introducing letter shapes, explain that most of the Letterlanders like to look, bounce, walk, hop, jump, etc. in the Reading Direction*, because they always want to see who is going to be next in any word.

  *Except for g, q and z – and there are good Letterland reasons for these exceptions!

- Use the Reading Direction sign when you are building words during Live Reading (page 159) and Live Spelling (page 160) by encouraging the children to enter words from the Reading Direction and by blending sounds in the Reading Direction.

- Also use the Reading Direction sign when you are air tracing, but make sure that you are facing the same direction as the children, in the Reading Direction. If you face the class, they will see you making a letter in reverse.

 NLS High-frequency Words List 1a

My Letterland Reading Booklet

Objectives
- To read and illustrate sentences containing:
  - ✓ NLS high-frequency words from List 1a
  - ✓ A selection of the decodable ('blending') words introduced in Section 1
  - ✓ 26 **a–z** Letterland character names.

Materials

My Letterland Reading Booklet For a free download of this photocopiable booklet, visit www.letterland.com.

Teaching point
- *My Letterland Reading Booklet* corresponds with the teaching order and 'blending' vocabulary in Section 1 of this *Teacher's Guide*.
- It features one or two sentences per page, and covers most of the 45 high-frequency words on NLS High-frequency Words List 1a.

Procedure
- Read the sentence together.
- Ask the children to draw a picture to match the sentence. (OR: On the pages where the focus is on segmenting, children spell words to match a picture.)
- The children complete a page after most lessons. They re-read all previous pages whenever they add a new page.

- Each time children complete a new page they can read over the previous pages as a paired reading exercise, using their own illustrations to help them read each sentence.

- When the book is complete, they can take the booklet home and read it to their parents.

⑥ NLS High-frequency Words List 1b

The look-say-cover-write-check strategy

Objective
- To learn and practice the correct spelling of words.

Materials
pen/pencils; paper

Procedure
- Dictate a word for the children to write down.

- Write the correct spelling on the board right after the children have written each word and ask them to check their spelling.

- Using the look-say-cover-write-check process, the children: 1) copy the words in a list/on the board; 2) study and read each word carefully as many times as they need to; 3) say it slowly out loud; 4) cover it and write the word again.

- They can then check for themselves whether they have written the word correctly.

Look/say	Cover/write	Check✓	Write again

⑦ Live Reading

Objectives
- To model the blending process.
- To blend words as a whole-class activity.

Materials
Picture Code Cards

Procedure
- Hand out *Picture Code Cards* and arrange children in a word at the front of the classroom (e.g. **cat**). Children can imagine that they are the letters on a big blank page behind them.

- Stand behind the children.

- To help the watching children blend the words you have created, point to each letter child in turn (e.g. 'c...a...t'). If you would like the children to blend two sounds together, point to two children at once (e.g. 'ca...t').

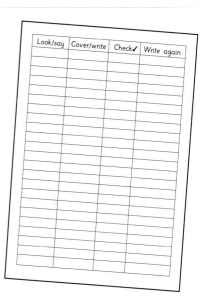

8 Live Spelling

Objectives
- To model the segmenting process.
- To spell words as a whole class activity.
- To check the resulting word by blending it as a whole class activity.

Materials
Picture Code Cards; costumes (optional)

Procedure
- Hand out *Picture Code Cards* for all the words that you would like the children to build.
- **SLOW-SPEAK** a word (e.g. 'mmmannn').
- Children repeat the word in **SLOW-SPEAK** and decide which letter sounds they can hear.
- Children decide whether the letter they are holding is needed in the word. If so, they come up and stand in position at the front.
- The rest of the class checks the word by blending the resulting word.
- Most Lesson Plans contain a Live Spelling 'word chain' (e.g. **tip → ship → shop → chop**), where changing only one or two letters results in a new word. For example, after building **ship**, ask Who needs to come up to build the word shop?

9 Dealing with exceptions

> **For additional stories, see page 139.**

Objective
- To avoid confusion caused by letters that represent more than one sound.

Procedure
- Explain early on that letters sometimes change the sound they make in words.
- Tell the children that first of all, they will be using the **SOUNDS TRICK** to discover each letter's *usual* sound. Later on they will hear stories that explain why letters sometimes change their sounds in different words.
- Congratulate any child who notices any exceptions. If you think the child is ready, you may choose to tell the appropriate Letterland story for that exception.
- In the meantime, a nice way of making the exception 'safe' is to put a wavy line under it or surround it with a box. Encourage children to understand that when they spot a Letterlander not making his or her usual sound in a word, there will usually be a story (or a new character) to make sense of the new sound.

turn   news   chips

circle   enjoy

Cross-curricular opportunities

Objectives
- To make conceptual links between target sounds and other subjects.
- To broaden the learning experience.

Procedure
- Relate the Letterlanders to arts and craft, e.g. make masks or puppets of the Letterlanders out of card or papier mâché. Alternatively, use modelling dough with thick letters in one colour and the characters' features in other colours.
- Make large murals of the imaginary place called Letterland. Encourage the children to plan where each character might live and add appropriate alliterative landmarks or objects around them.
- Organise a Letterland Day or Event. For example an assembly, a Letterland Dressing-up Day, a Letterland Olympics or a Letterland Fête, bringing in artwork, crafts, puppetry and storytelling.
- Incorporate Letterland into any Science and Technology lesson, e.g. study light or electricity with Lucy Lamp Light or magnetism with Munching Mike.
- Relate individual Letterlanders to other activities that begin with their sound, e.g. count with Clever Cat or do sums with Sammy Snake.

Costumes and props

a–z
Annie Apple Apple leaf hat; red t-shirt
Bouncy Ben Big, brown ears
Clever Cat Yellow ears
Dippy Duck Headband with picture of Dippy Duck's head
Eddy Elephant Elephant ears
Firefighter Fred Firefighter helmet; hose; raincoat
Golden Girl Long blond ponytail made of wool; green glasses
Harry Hat Man Hairy green hat or hat picture on a headband
Impy Ink Headband with yellow dot; yellow letter on blue t-shirt
Jumping Jim Jeans jacket or a red and yellow jacket
Kicking King Crown and cape
Lucy Lamp Light Lampshade hat
Munching Mike Cardboard monster mask covered in foil, or headband
Noisy Nick Toy hammer and tinfoil nails
Oscar Orange Orange on a headband
Peter Puppy Long droopy ears
Quarrelsome Queen Crown and cape; plain 'royal' umbrella
Red Robot Square, red cardboard headgear; red sack
Sammy Snake Snake headband

Talking Tess Headphones and phone
Uppy Umbrella Small umbrella hat or real umbrella
Vicky Violet Violet t-shirt; flower necklace
Walter Walrus Grey flippers
Fix-it Max Toy tools and cap
Yellow Yo-yo Man Yellow cap; yellow t-shirt; yellow yo-yo
Zig Zag Zebra Ears on headband; black and white-striped clothing

Vowel Men
Mr A Red and white striped apron
Mr E Top hat featuring the letter **e**
Mr I Ice-cream cone made of rolled up paper
Mr O White beard
Mr U Official hat

Other
Silent magic e Red crepe paper wand
Arthur Ar Green cardboard headgear
Orvil Or Orange cardboard headgear
Ernest Er Purple cardboard headgear
Urgent Ur Purple cardboard headgear and boots of purple fur
Irving Ir Purple cardboard headgear and an ink-splashed shirt

Activity Bank

'Listen first!' activity

Listen and Jump Game

Objective
- To listen for a target sound in initial, final or medial position.

Materials
List of words (some contain the target sound, some do not); rope or mat.

Procedure
- Children stand on the outside of a rope circle or mat.
- Choose a target sound and say it together.
- Call out one word at a time from your word list. If the word contains the target sound, children jump into the circle or on the mat.
- If the next word you read starts with the target sound, they stay where they are. If not, they jump back out.

Phonemic awareness and review activities

Actions Game

Objectives
- To reinforce **a–z** letter sounds; to reinforce alphabetical order.

Materials
Picture Code Cards; **ACTIONS TRICK** (pages 148–149) for **a–z** actions

Procedure
- Hold up a *Picture Code Card*. Children make the letter sound and the action.
- After you have been through all the letters you have introduced so far, try the sequence again, but this time go through your cards as quickly as possible.
- Once the children know **a–z** (or **a–m**), use a third round to challenge the children to perform the sounds and actions in alphabetical order, without the help of the cards.

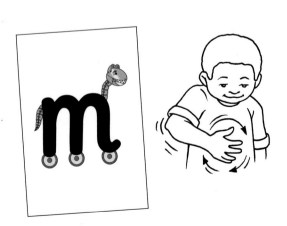

Alliterative Story Sentences

Objective
- To reinforce initial phonemes.

Procedure
- Children compose their own alliterative stories, along the lines of the Letterland Jingles (page 164).
- For example, 'I like **s**inging and **s**o does **S**ammy **S**nake' or '**S**ammy **S**nake went to **s**it in the **s**un by the **s**ea last **S**aturday'.

Human Sound Machine

Objective
- To reinforce initial sounds in words.

Materials
Sound bag or *Vocabulary Cards*

Procedure
- Choose three children to stand facing the class.
- Show each of them a different letter and ask them to whisper the phoneme in your ear, so that the rest of the class cannot hear.
- Give another child an object or *Vocabulary Card* that starts with one of these three phonemes.

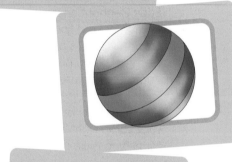

- The child with the object (or card) taps each child at the front, who then says their sound out loud.
- They hand over the object to the child who says the matching initial sound.
- The game continues with a new object and a new set of phonemes.

Knock Knock

Objective
- To reinforce initial sounds.

Procedure
- Play as a class or in pairs.
    A: Knock, knock.
    B: Who's there?
    A: I like fishing and flowers. Who am I?
    B: Firefighter Fred!

Letterland Jingles

Objective
- To complete an alliterative pattern.

Materials
Vocabulary Cards and/or **a–z** objects from a 'sound bag' (a bag containing objects starting or ending with target sounds)

Procedure
- Hand out *Vocabulary Cards* or sound bag objects to each child.
- Read out the alliterative jingles below.
- The child holding a card or object that completes the pattern stands up and says the word.

Annie Apple asks for an...	Noisy Nick needs a...
Bouncy Ben buys a...	Oscar Orange likes to ride on his pet...
Clever Cat carries a...	Peter Puppy plays with a...
Dippy Duck draws a...	Quarrelsome Queen asks questions about a...
Eddy Elephant enjoys an...	Red Robot runs away with a...
Firefighter Fred finds a...	Sammy Snake sees a...
Golden Girl gets a...	Talking Tess touches a...
Harry Hat Man has a...	Uppy Umbrella likes going...
Impy Ink imagines an interesting...	Vicky Violet visits a...
Jumping Jim juggles with...	Walter Walrus wins a...
Kicking King is keen on...	Fix-it Max is... years old.
Lucy Lamp Light likes...	Yo-yo Man sees a yellow...
Munching Mike moves a...	Zig Zag Zebra zooms to the...

Letter Sounds Train Game

Objective
- To reinforce the sound/symbol link.

Materials
Homemade 'tickets'/plain letter cards; *Picture Code Cards*

Procedure
- Hand out 'tickets' for each child. Each ticket shows the plain letter(s) for a sound that has been taught. Several children should have the same letter on their ticket.
- One child holds a picture-coded ticket for the target sound and 'is' the train.
- Announce the target sound, e.g. 'mmm.....': The train arriving at Platform One is the 'mmm...' train.
- Children with the matching ticket get on the train and hold up their tickets for the rest of the class to check.
- After checking, the train circles the classroom making the target sound.
- Repeat for each sound being reviewed.

Sounds Box

Objective
- To reinforce letter sounds.

Materials
Picture Code Cards

Procedure
- Place a *Picture Code Card* for each phoneme you have taught so far in a box labelled the Sounds Box.
- Throughout the day, ask different children to take out a card and hold it up.
- Invite the rest of the class to fill the classroom with the letter's sound.

Sound Pops

Objective
- To reinforce the sound/symbol link.

Materials
Picture Code Cards

Procedure
- Give each child a *Picture Code Card*.
- Call out a letter sound. (See page 154 for pronunciation tips.)
- The child holding the corresponding *Picture Code Card* pops up and says, 'Firefighter Fred says fff…'.

Sort it Out! (Suitable for informal assessment.)

Objective
- To sort pictures according to target sounds.

Materials
A variety of pictures containing the target sounds (*Vocabulary Cards* or images on the Copymasters in this *Teacher's Guide*).

Procedure
a) Whole-class activity
- Choose up to three target sounds and place pictures representing all three sounds in a box.
- Stick three 'pockets' on a flipchart or blackboard. Label the pockets with the Letterland pictograms representing those sounds.
- Select a child to pick a card from the box.
- The child names the picture aloud, identifies the target sound and puts the card in the appropriate pocket.
- The class decides if the card is in the correct pocket.

b) Individual activity
- Provide children with their own page of the photocopiable pictures.
- Help them to make flaps on a piece of construction paper, as shown.
- Children cut out the pictures one at a time, then stick each picture under the appropriate flap.

Tray/Hoop Game

Objective
- To reinforce the sound/symbol link for beginning or final sounds.

Materials

Vocabulary Cards or a sound bag of objects (one object/card per child); tray/hoop; *Picture Code Cards*

Procedure
- Choose a target sound and place its *Picture Code Card* in the tray/hoop.
- Give each child a *Vocabulary Card* or an object from the sound bag.
- Each child says the name of their object/card, emphasising the initial sound.
- If the initial sound matches the *Picture Code Card*, they put their object/card in the tray/hoop.
- Children may like to tell a short story about the Letterlander and their object, e.g. 'Sammy Snake has seven pairs of smelly **socks**.'
- You could also use this activity to focus on final sounds.

Who Likes...?

Objective
- To reinforce initial sounds and Letterland character names.

Materials

Picture Code Cards; *Vocabulary Cards* or a range of objects.

Procedure
- Give each child a *Picture Code Card*.
- Show one *Vocabulary Card* or object at a time. Ask, for example, Who likes cake?
- The child holding the appropriate *Picture Code Card* stands up and says, 'Clever Cat likes cake. 'c...' cake.'

Who's Missing?

Objective
- To reinforce alphabetical order and Letterland character names.

Materials

Picture Code Cards

Procedure
- Display some *Picture Code Cards* in alphabetical order.
- Ask the children to close their eyes.
- Then take a card away and ask, Who's missing?

Activities for reinforcing letter shapes

Letter Hunt

Objective
- To recognise letter shapes in words.

Materials
Photocopied sheets of text

Procedure
- Give each child an enlarged piece of text from a newspaper, magazine or book.
- Call out a letter and ask the children to find and circle each one on their paper. Children could use a different colour for every letter you call out.

Ring the Words

Objective
To recognise letter shapes in words.

Procedure
- Write a list of words on the board, e.g. **frog**, **sun**, **cat**, **apple**, **six**. Ask a child to come up and ring the words that start with the target letter (for example, Sammy Snake's letter in the initial position).

Activities for blending CVC words

Vowels-Go-Round

Objectives
- To reinforce short vowel in medial position.
- To blend CVC words.

Materials
Picture Code Cards: **d**, **g**, **h**, **p**, **t**, **a**, **e**, **i**, **o**, **u** (short vowels)

Procedure
- Two children hold *Picture Code Cards* **p** and **t**.
- Five children line up with *Picture Code Cards* for each of the short vowels.
- The vowel children take turns to appear in the middle position, e.g. p**a**t, p**e**t, p**i**t, p**o**t, p**u**t*.
- The rest of the class blend the sounds to read the word out loud, and decides, 'word or non-word'.
- Repeat with **d__g** and **h__t**.

* To explain the irregular **u** sound (as in put and pull), see page 135.

Short Vowels Bingo

Objective
● To blend phonemes to read CVC words in non-rhyming sets.

Materials
Create up to six plain letter Bingo Boards using the word lists below; counters

Sheet 1: **pin pen pan; dog dig dug**
Sheet 2: **pit pat pet; mit mat met**
Sheet 3: **hot hat hit; ten tan tin**
Sheet 4: **bed bad bud; bat but bit**
Sheet 5: **rug rag rig; bug bag big**
Sheet 6: **met mat mit; ham hum him**

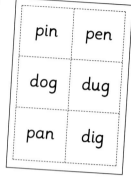

Sheet 1

Procedure

a) Whole-class activity
● Each child gets a Bingo Board and some counters.
● Put a copy of each word in a hat, and call out one word at a time. You could put each word in a sentence, e.g. 'I am happy saying 'a…' in hat'.
● The first child to fill their board with counters calls out 'Bingo!'

b) Small group activity
● Record all the words in random order on a short cassette until full. Repeat the list in a different order each time, so you can start playing the cassette at any point, and the same board doesn't win every time.
● Children play in small groups of up to six. Each child has a different board and markers.
● Children start the tape and cover each word as it is read out.

Full Circle Game

Objective
● To manipulate phonemes.

Materials
List of words (page 169); *Picture Code Cards* (or play without cards, choosing children to write on the board).

Procedure
● Hand out *Picture Code Cards*, one per child (as listed on following page).
● Read the first word on the list. Ask the children with letters in that word to come to the front and make the word.
● Everybody says the word, emphasising each phoneme, then the whole word.
● Write the word on the board and tell the children that they will make different words but when they come back to the word on the board they must shout 'Full circle!'
● Say the next word. Ask the children which letter has to go and which new letter is needed to make the new word.
● Ask the children to swap places. As before, everyone says the new word and it is written on the board.
● Repeat until the game goes 'full circle'.

Note: To maximise the number of children involved in a game, divide the class into two groups and hand out two of each card. The two groups make their words in different places at the same time. Any children without a card can participate by looking for any letters which are out of place or missing from a word.

Robot Red's Game
b–d–r–a–e–i

red
bed
bad
bid
rid
red

Bouncy Ben's Game
B–g–n–p–t–e–i

Ben
ten
tin
pin
pig
peg
pen
Ben

Jumping Jim's Game
ch–b–d–g–h–J–m–t–a–i

Jim
him
ham
hat
chat
bat
bag
big
dig
dim
Jim

Kicking King's Game
ch–k–ng–p–r–s–sh–th–i–o

king
thing
ring
rich
rip
ship
shop
chop
chip
sip
sing
king

Dippy Duck's Game
ch–ck–d–m–s–t–u

duck
dust
must
much
muck
duck

Talking Tess's Game
b–ck–l–m–ng–s–ss–T–e–o

Tess
mess
bless
less
loss
lock
long
song
sock
block
mock
moss
mess
Tess

Firefighter Fred's Game
b–d–F–ll–m–ng–r–s–sh–t–e–u

Fred
shed
shell
bell
bull
bush
bung
bust
must
mud
bud
bed
Fred

Golden Girl's Game
b–f–g–l–m–r–t–i–oa
–oo–ir

girl
goal
goat
boat
boot
root
room
roam
foam
foal
goal
girl

Quarrelsome Queen's Game
f–j–k–l–m–n–qu–r–s–t–a
i–ee–oo

queen
seen
soon
moon
main
train
trail
jail
sail
fail
feel
keel
keen
queen

Munching Mike's Game
k–l–M–n–p–s–t–a–e–i

Mike
spike
like
line
lane
late
plane
plate
lake
like
Mike

Sammy Snake's Game
d–f–g–k–l–m–n–s–sh–t–
v–w–a–e–i

snake
shake
shave
gave
game
same
tame
time
lime
life
wife
wide
wade
wake
snake

Silly Questions

Objective
- To read words in context.

Materials
Set out the questions below on large cards; make **yes** and **no** cards for each child

Procedure
- Give every child a **yes** and **no** card.
- Hold up a silly question.
- Ask the children to read the question and answer it by holding up their **yes** or **no** card. Repeat.

Note: These questions may not always have an obvious 'yes' or 'no' answer. Some of them may be a matter of opinion, and could provide opportunities for discussion, reasoning and even starting points for creative writing. Children also love to write their own silly questions.

Bouncy Ben's Questions

Is Ben a dog?
Is Ben a cat?
Is Ben a hen?
Is Ben red?
Can Ben run with a fox?

Clever Cat's Questions

Has the cat got red legs?
Is the cat as a big as a man?
Can the cat get up a hill?
Can the cat hop on a bus?
Can the cat fit in a big box?

Harry Hat Man's Questions

Can the Hat Man sing?
Has the Hat Man got a hat?
Can the Hat Man fix a van?
Can the Hat Man say sh?
Is the Hat Man a boy?

Dippy Duck's Questions

Can the duck run with a fox?
Can the duck peck?
Has the duck got six wings?
Can the duck hop in a shop?
Is the duck in the mud?

Jumping Jim's Questions

Will Jim jump in a pond?
Is Jim fit and well?
Has Jim put his socks on his hands?
Has Jim got ten legs?
Can Jim stand on a clock?

Noisy Nick's Questions

Can Nick lift up the king?
Is Nick rich?
Is Nick a boy?
Has Nick got a thick neck?
Can Nick hit things?

Firefighter Fred's Questions

Has Fred got a flat hat?
Has Fred got a pet crab?
Has Fred got a long neck?
Is Fred a thin man?
Can Fred pick up big things?

Kicking King's Questions

Can the king kick?
Is the king a sad man?
Has the king got long legs?
Has the king got rings on his hands?
Can the king stand on a plant?

Quarrelsome Queen's Questions

Is the queen having toast?
Can the queen make a loud sound?
Has the queen seen a shark on her roof?
Will the queen shout at the king?
Can the queen sleep on a hard bed?

Golden Girl's Questions

Can the girl start her go-cart?
Has the girl got short hair?
Has the girl got big green feet?
Are you a girl?
Have you tried the girl's go-cart?

Sammy Snake's Questions

Has Sammy Snake got hairy legs?
Can Sammy Snake stick things with glue?
Does Sammy Snake like to be noisy?
Will Sammy Snake fight with Harry Hat Man?
Is Sammy Snake nine on his next birthday?

Munching Mike's Questions

Can Mike play with Clever Cat?
Does Mike eat sharp things each day?
Has Mike got fur?
Is Mike a monster?
Can Mike fly a kite high in the sky?

Reading and Spelling Lists

Alliterative Words Grid

These words match the images on the *Letterland Vocabulary Cards*. Use them for a sight words vocabulary with strong ideational links. Most of the examples in the second column are also easy to sound out.

Annie Apple	ant	apple	acrobat
Bouncy Ben	bed	ball	blue
Clever Cat	cat	car	cake
Dippy Duck	duck	dog	dinosaur
Eddy Elephant	egg	elbow	elephant
Firefighter Fred	fish	fire	flowers
Golden Girl	green	goat	grapes
Harry Hat Man	hat	horse	house
Impy Ink	in	insect	ink
Jumping Jim	jacket	juice	jigsaw
Kicking King	kite	key	kangaroo
Lucy Lamp Light	lamp	leg	lighthouse
Munching Mike	magnet	milk	monkey
Noisy Nick	nest	nuts	nine
Oscar Orange	octopus	orange	ostrich
Peter Puppy	pink	parrot	pig
Quarrelsome Queen	quilt	question	quill
Red Robot	red	ring	rocket
Sammy Snake	sun	seven	snake
Talking Tess	ten	telephone	tiger
Uppy Umbrella	up	umbrella	under
Vicky Violet	van	vase	vegetables
Walter Walrus	web	water	window
Fix-it Max	box	fox	six
Yellow Yo-yo Man	yo-yo	yellow	yoghurt
Zig Zag Zebra	zebra	zero	zoo

SECTION 1 List 1 (Lesson 3)

High-frequency words

this   my   dad
is   mum

Sentences

This is Clever Cat.
This is Annie Apple.
This is Dippy Duck.
This is my mum.
This is my dad.

SECTION 1 List 2 (Lesson 6)

High-frequency words

I   like
am

Sentences

I am Clever Cat.
I am Annie Apple.
I am Dippy Duck.
I like Harry Hat Man.
I like Munching Mike.
I like Talking Tess.

SECTION 1 List 3 (Lesson 7)

Blending words

cat   hat
mat   ham

High-frequency words

this   is   a

Sentences

This is a cat.
This is a hat.
This is a mat.
This is ham.

SECTION 1 List 4 (Lesson 10)

Blending Words

cats   hats   mats

High-frequency words

I   can
see   the

Sentences

I can see the cats.
I can see the hats.
I can see the mats.

SECTION 1 List 5 (Lesson 13)

Blending words

him	his	miss
dig	hiss	did
is	mess	can
handstand		

High-frequency words

going

to

see

Sentences

Sammy Snake is going to see Impy Ink.

Impy Ink is going to see Noisy Nick.

Noisy Nick is going to see Golden Girl.

Letterland Teacher's Guide Published by Letterland International © Letterland International 2005

SECTION 1 List 6 (Lesson 18)

Blending words

pat	pot	pet
pit	hot	hit
hat	man	men

High-frequency words

can	I
play	said

Sentences

"Can I play?" said Oscar Orange.

"Can I play?" said Mr O.

"Can I play?" said Peter Puppy.

"Can I play?" said Eddy Elephant.

"Can I play?" said Mr E.

Letterland Teacher's Guide Published by Letterland International © Letterland International 2005

SECTION 1 List 7 (Lesson 22)

Blending words

kick   lick   sick

stick   duck   sock

pack   king   sing

song

High-frequency words

how   are

you

Sentences

How are you, Uppy Umbrella?

How are you, Mr U?

How are you, Kicking King?

Letterland Teacher's Guide Published by Letterland International © Letterland International 2005

SECTION 1 List 8 (Lesson 25)

Blending words

ship   shop   chip

chop   shin   chin

thin   shell   lunch

munch

High-frequency words

can   you

see   the

Sentences

Look! Can you see the ship?

Look! Can you see the shop?

Look! Can you see the chip?

Look! Can you see the shell?

Letterland Teacher's Guide Published by Letterland International © Letterland International 2005

Blending words

fit	lift	cliff
puff	sniff	bell
doll	spell	jump
jet		

High-frequency words

look	up
it's	a

Sentences

Look up! It's Lucy Lamp Light.

Look up! It's Firefighter Fred.

Look up! It's Bouncy Ben.

Look up! It's Jumping Jim.

Letterland Teacher's Guide Published by Letterland International © Letterland International 2005

Blending words

red	run	running
ran	quick	quilt
have	give	live

High-frequency words

went	to
see	he
	love

Sentences

Quarrelsome Queen went to see Vicky Violet.

Vicky Violet went to see Red Robot.

Look at Red Robot! He is running away.

Letterland Teacher's Guide Published by Letterland International © Letterland International 2005

Blending words

wind	six	fix
fox	box	next
yes	yet	wet
zip		

High-frequency words

is	it
you	go
away	getting

Sentences

Is it you, Fix-it Max?

Is it you, Yellow Yo-yo Man?

Is it you, Zig Zag Zebra?

Go away, Walter Walrus!

I am getting wet!

Letterland Teacher's Guide Published by Letterland International © Letterland International 2005

SECTION 2 List 1

cat
hat
man
can
hand
band
am
ham
bad
sad

Letterland Teacher's Guide Published by Letterland International
© Letterland International 2005

SECTION 2 List 2

bed
red
beg
leg
Ben
men
get
jet
bell
well

Letterland Teacher's Guide Published by Letterland International
© Letterland International 2005

SECTION 2 List 3

fin
pin
hip
lip
dig
pig
fit
sit
fill
hill

Letterland Teacher's Guide Published by Letterland International
© Letterland International 2005

SECTION 2 List 4

hop
mop
dot
got
dog
log
bug
hug
fun
sun

Letterland Teacher's Guide Published by Letterland International
© Letterland International 2005

SECTION 3 List 1 (Lesson 6)

back
pack
sock
deck
neck
lick
pick
sick
lock
clock

Letterland Teacher's Guide Published by Letterland International
© Letterland International 2005

SECTION 3 List 2 (Lesson 7)

off
bell
well
will
doll
shell
tell
hiss
kiss
mess

Letterland Teacher's Guide Published by Letterland International
© Letterland International 2005

SECTION 3 List 3 (Lesson 8)

ring
sing
wing
bring
sting
bang
fang
hang
long
song

Letterland Teacher's Guide Published by Letterland International
© Letterland International 2005

SECTION 3 List 4 (Lesson 9)

click
puff
sang
dress
ill
king
sniff
less
black
well

Letterland Teacher's Guide Published by Letterland International
© Letterland International 2005

Take-home Lists

S4 List 1 (Lesson 1)

flip
flag
black
block
clock
clap
glad
slip
slim
plan

Letterland Teacher's Guide Published by Letterland International © Letterland International 2005

Take-home Lists

S4 List 2 (Lesson 2)

bring
brush
cross
crash
grab
grunt
truck
from
drink
present

Letterland Teacher's Guide Published by Letterland International © Letterland International 2005

Take-home Lists

S4 List 3 (Lesson 3)

scab
scan
skip
skin
desk
disk
spin
spell
stand
stick

Letterland Teacher's Guide Published by Letterland International © Letterland International 2005

Take-home Lists

S4 List 4 (Lesson 4)

smell
smash
snap
sniff
snack
swim
swing
twin
twist
dwell

Letterland Teacher's Guide Published by Letterland International © Letterland International 2005

Take-home Lists

S4 List 5 (Lesson 5)

scratch
scrap
splash
split
spring
sprint
string
shrug
shrimp
thrill

Letterland Teacher's Guide Published by Letterland International © Letterland International 2005

Take-home Lists

Review

blot
click
smash
grip
split
strap
fresh
shrink
splendid
scrub

Letterland Teacher's Guide Published by Letterland International © Letterland International 2005

SECTION 5 List 1 (Lesson 2)
Silent Magic e

cake
take
these
likes
line
mine
joke
those
use
refuse

Letterland Teacher's Guide Published by Letterland International
© Letterland International 2005

SECTION 5 List 2 (Lesson 3)
a-e ay ai

late
date
came
play
way
away
train
afraid
again
straight

Letterland Teacher's Guide Published by Letterland International
© Letterland International 2005

SECTION 5 List 3 (Lesson 4)
e-e ee ea

these
complete
Chinese
green
meet
between
feast
clean
meat
teach

Letterland Teacher's Guide Published by Letterland International
© Letterland International 2005

SECTION 5 List 4 (Lesson 6)
i-e ie y igh

five
hide
tried
cried
my
cry
try
light
fight
high

Letterland Teacher's Guide Published by Letterland International
© Letterland International 2005

SECTION 5 List 5 (Lesson 7)

o-e oa ow

bone
hope
those
boat
float
goat
coach
low
show
pillow

Letterland Teacher's Guide Published by Letterland International
© Letterland International 2005

SECTION 5 List 6 (Lesson 8)

u-e o̅o̅ ew ue

use
cube
tube
moon
soon
flew
knew
blue
glue
true

Letterland Teacher's Guide Published by Letterland International
© Letterland International 2005

SECTION 5 List 7 (Lesson 9)

ar or oor

arm
car
dark
star
start
fork
short
north
floor
door

Letterland Teacher's Guide Published by Letterland International
© Letterland International 2005

SECTION 5 List 8 (Lesson 10)

ow ou

cow
now
down
frown
flower
shout
out
loud
cloud
sound

Letterland Teacher's Guide Published by Letterland International
© Letterland International 2005

S5 List 9 (Lesson 11)

oi oy

boil
soil
Noisy Nick
noise
point
boy
toy
joy
enjoy
enjoying

S5 List 10 (Lesson 12)

er ir ur

longer
faster
other
brother
third
dirt
shirt
turn
curl
fur

S5 List 11 (Lesson 13)

o͝o u

foot
book
look
hook
took
stood
full
bull
push
put

S5 List 12 (Lesson 14)

aw au

jaw
paw
saw
straw
awful
seesaw
draw
caught
taught
naughty

S5 List 13 (Lesson 15)

air ear

fair
hair
pair
stair
chair
ear
clear
dear
fear
hear

Review

join
further
skirt
woods
awful
pair
fulfil
hear
market
round

I	come	up	day
look	the	we	dog
like	big	and	my
on	mum	at	no
for	dad	he	all
is	get	to	was
go	went	you	me
are	of	this	see
going	she	they	yes
away	it	play	
a	can	am	
cat	said	in	

NLS LIST 1b

about	could	him	much	put	too
after	did	his	must	ran	took
again	do	home	name	saw	tree
an	don't	house	new	school	two
another	dig	how	next	seen	us
as	door	if	night	should	very
back	down	jump	not	sister	want
ball	first	just	now	so	water
be	from	last	off	some	way
because	girl	laugh	old	take	were
bed	good	little	once	than	what
been	got	live(d)	one	that	when
boy	had	love	or	their	where
brother	half	made	our	them	who
but	has	make	out	then	will
by	have	man	over	there	with
call(ed)	help	many	people	these	would
came	her	may	push	three	your
can't	here	more	pull	time	

Letterland Teacher's Guide Published by Letterland International © Letterland International 2005

Character changes

Some changes have been made in response to feedback from teachers and parents and the introduction of new teaching strategies based on character names. You might like to explain these changes to children as follows.

- **Red Robot** You will still see Robber Red in books that were written before he was finally caught and sent to prison. Everyone was pleased – until they discovered that Robber Red had secretly been making a brand new **r**obot to do his **r**unning and stealing for him. Now this Red Robot is behaving just as badly in Letterland as Robber Red did!

- **Walter Walrus** You will still see Letterland's Water Witch in some books before she made a big mistake. One day while testing one of her special **w**alrus spells on a **w**iggly **w**orm, she accidentally **w**obbled and turned *herself* into a **w**alrus! Now she can't turn herself back! So instead of the Water Witch you will see a **w**et old **w**alrus called Walter in her **w**ater **w**ells.

- **Harry Hat Man** One summer day the Hat Man decided his beard was too **h**ot so he shaved it off – but he still always wears **h**is **h**airy **h**at! That is why his nickname is Hairy Hat Man. His real name is Harry Hat Man, but he'll be **h**appy, no matter which name you choose to call him.

- **Impy Ink** Impy has changed colour because he has **i**nvented a way to make some **i**ncredible new multi-coloured **i**nk! You will sometimes still see him with blue **i**nk **i**nside.

- **Lucy Lamp Light** One day Lucy decided she wanted the word <u>light</u> in her name, so now instead of Lucy Lamp Lady she **l**ikes people to call her Lucy Lamp Light. She also has a new hairstyle which makes her **l**ook quite different, and even more **l**ovely.

- **Noisy Nick** It can't be too difficult to guess how Naughty Nick got his **n**ew **n**ickname, considering how much he loves banging around with his hammer and **n**ails.

- **Peter Puppy** This little **p**up is often sad because his ears won't **p**rick up like a **p**olice dog's ears. Then **p**eople call him Poor Peter. But he is often happy, too. Then **p**eople call him by his real name, Peter Puppy.

- **Talking Tess** Ticking Tess has a new nickname, **t**oo. It is Talking Tess, because she is always **t**alking on the **t**elephone. She also has a new hairstyle, a new **t**op and a new pair of **t**an **t**rousers.

- **Vicky Violet** Vicky is new to Letterland and already all the children think that she is a **v**ery lo**v**ely new friend. Vicky lo**v**es **v**iolets and has promised to look after all the little **v**ases of **v**iolets we find in words!

- **Firefighter Fred** One day Fireman Fred realised that the word 'fireman' doesn't tell us what **f**iremen do. That's why now Fred likes to be called Firefighter Fred.

- **Fix-it Max** Maxine is still Max's best friend but she is not always on hand to make the 'kss' sound in the letter **x**. So she leaves it to Max who is quite happy to make the sound by himself as he fi**x**es things.

Handwriting songs

Annie Apple

At the leaf begin.
Go round the apple this way.
Then add a line down,
so Annie won't roll away.

Bouncy Ben

Brush down Ben's
big, long ears.
Go up and round his head
so his face appears!

Clever Cat

Curve round Clever Cat's
face to begin.
Then gently tickle her
under her chin.

Dippy Duck

Draw Dippy Duck's back.
Go round her tum.
Go up to her head.
Then down you come!

Eddy Elephant

Ed has a headband.
Draw it and then
stroke round his head
and his trunk to the end.

Firefighter Fred

First draw Fred's helmet.
Then go down a way.
Give him some arms
and he'll put out the blaze.

Golden Girl

Go round Golden Girl's head.
Go down her golden hair.
Then curve to make her swing,
so she can sit there.

Harry Hat Man

Hurry from the Hat Man's head
down to his heel on the ground.
Go up and bend his knee over,
so he'll hop while he makes
his sound.

Impy Ink

Inside the ink bottle
draw a line.
Add an inky dot. That's fine!

Jumping Jim

Just draw down Jim,
bending his knees.
Then add the one ball
which everyone sees.

Kicking King

Kicking King's body
is a straight stick.
Add his arm, then his leg,
so he can kick!

Lucy Lamp Light

Lucy looks like
one long line.
Go straight from head to foot
and she's ready to shine!

Munching Mike

Make Munching Mike's
back leg first,
then his second leg,
and third,
so he can go munch-munching
in a word.

Noisy Nick

'Now bang my nail,'
Noisy Nick said.
'Go up and over
around my head.'

Oscar Orange

On Oscar Orange
start at the top.
Go all the way round him,
and... then stop.

Peter Puppy

Pat Peter Puppy properly.
First stroke down his ear,
then up and round his face
so he won't shed a tear.

Quarrelsome Queen

Quickly go round the
Queen's cross face.
Then comb her beautiful
hair into place.

Red Robot

Run down Red Robot's body.
Go up to his arm
and his hand.
Then watch out for this robot
roaming round Letterland.

Sammy Snake

Start at Sam's head
where he can see.
Stroke down to his tail,
oh so care-ful-ly!

Talking Tess

Tall as a tower make
Talking Tess stand.
Go from head to toe,
and then from hand to hand.

Uppy Umbrella

Under the umbrella
draw a shape like a cup.
Then draw a straight line
so it won't tip up.

Vicky Violet

Very neatly, start at the top.
Draw down your vase,
then up and stop.

Walter Walrus

When you draw the
Walrus wells,
with wild and wavy water,
whizz down and up
and then...,
whizz down and up again.

Fix-it Max

Fix two sticks, to look
like this.
That's how to draw a
little kiss.

Yo-yo Man

You first make the yo-yo sack
on the Yo-yo Man's back,
and then go down to his toes
so he can sell his yo-yos.

Zig Zag Zebra

Zip along Zig Zag's nose.
Stroke her neck...,
stroke her back...
Zzzoom! Away she goes.

Alphabet songs

Annie Apple

(To the tune of *London bridge is falling down*)

Annie Apple, she says 'ă...',
she says 'ă...', she says 'ă...'.
Annie Apple, she says 'ă...'.
She belongs to Mr A.

Bouncy Ben

(To the tune of *Polly put the kettle on*)

Bouncy Ben says 'b...' in words.
Bouncy Ben says 'b...' in words.
Bouncy Ben says 'b...' in words,
before he bounces home.

Clever Cat

(To the tune of *Merrily we roll along*)

Clever Cat says 'c...' in words,
'c...' in words, 'c...' in words.
Clever Cat says 'c...' in words,
and cuddles close to me.

She also makes another sound,
another sound, another sound.
She also makes another sound.
Just you wait and see.*

Dippy Duck

(To the tune of *London Bridge is falling down*)

'D..., d..., d...' goes Dippy Duck,
Dippy Duck, Dippy Duck.
'D..., d..., d...' goes Dippy Duck.
All Duck down!

Eddy Elephant

(To the tune of *Oh the grand old Duke of York*)

Here comes Eddy El-e-phant
to talk to you and me.
He just says 'ĕ...', he just says 'ĕ...'.
He belongs to Mr E.

Firefighter Fred

(To the tune of *Here we go round the mulberry bush*)

Firefighter Fred goes 'fff..., fff..., fff...',
Firefighter Fred, Firefighter Fred.
Firefighter Fred goes 'fff..., fff..., fff...',
fighting fires with foam.

Golden Girl

(To the tune of *Merrily we roll along*)

Golden Girl says 'g...' in words,
'g...' in words, 'g...' in words.
Golden Girl says 'g...' in words,
giggling merrily.

Her girlfriend makes another sound,
another sound, another sound.
Her girlfriend makes another sound.
Just you wait and see.**

Harry Hat Man

(To the tune of *The wheels on the bus*)

Harry Hat Man whispers 'hhh...',
whispers 'hhh...', whispers 'hhh...'.
Harry Hat Man whispers 'hhh...'.
He never talks out loud.

Impy Ink

(To the tune of *London Bridge is falling down*)

Impy Ink says 'ĭ...' in words,
'ĭ...' in words, 'ĭ...' in words.
Impy Ink says 'ĭ...' in words.
He belongs to Mr I.

Jumping Jim

(To the tune of *Old MacDonald had a farm*)

Jumping Jim says 'j...' in words,
as he jumps along.
Jumping Jim says 'j...' in words,
as he jumps along.
With a 'j..., j...' here, and a 'j..., j...' there;
here a 'j...', there a 'j...',
everywhere a 'j..., j...'.
Jumping Jim says 'j...' in words
as he jumps along.

Kicking King

(To the tune of *Merrily we roll along*)

Kicking King says 'k...' in words,
'k...' in words, 'k...' in words.
Kicking King says 'k...' in words,
as he kicks along.

Lucy Lamp Light

(To the tune of *Twinkle, twinkle, little star*)

Look, look, look, that lovely light.
It is Lucy's light so bright.
Listen, 'lll...' is what she'll say,
'lll...' for lamp, both night and day.
Look, look, look, that lovely light.
It is Lucy's light so bright.

* The soft **c** sound (ni**ce**, **ci**rcle, i**cy**). See page xx.
** The soft **g** sound (**ge**ntle, **gi**nger, **gy**m) whenever
the next letter is **e**, **i** or **y**. (See page 139.)

Munching Mike

(To the tune of *Humpty Dumpty*)

'Mmm...', that monster Munching Mike.
My, he has an appetite.
'Mmm...', he hums contentedly,
munching mouthfuls merrily.

Noisy Nick

(To the tune of *Muffin man*)

Noisy Nick says 'nnn…' in words,
'nnn…' in words, 'nnn…' in words.
Noisy Nick says 'nnn…' in words,
you can hear it nnnow!

Oscar Orange

(To the tune of *Polly put the kettle on*)

Oscar Orange, he says 'ŏ...'.
Oscar Orange, he says 'ŏ...'.
Oscar Orange, he says 'ŏ...'.
He belongs to Mr O.

Peter Puppy

(To the tune of *The wheels on the bus*)

Peter Puppy just says 'p...',
just says 'p...', just says 'p...'.
Peter Puppy just says 'p...',
his poor ears droop.

Quarrelsome Queen

(To the tune of *Here we go round the mulberry bush*)

Quarrelsome Queen says 'qu...' in words,
'qu...' in words, 'qu...' in words.
Quarrelsome Queen says 'qu...' in words.
She must have her umbrella.

Red Robot

(To the tune of *Three blind mice*)

Red Robot, Red Robot.
See how he runs. See how he runs.
He rrreally makes a growling sound.
He's always heard, but he's never found.
Have you ever seen such a rascal around!
'Rrr..., rrr..., rrr...'.

Sammy Snake

(To the tune of *Sing a song of sixpence*)

Sammy Snake says 'sss...' in words,
hissing all the time.
Sammy Snake says 'sss...' in words,
hissing all the time.
Hissing with a 'sss..., sss...',
hissing with a 'sss...'.
Sammy Snake says 'sss...' in words,
he's hissing all the time.

Talking Tess

(To the tune of *Old MacDonald had a farm*)

Talking Tess says 't...' in words,
talking all the time.
Talking Tess says 't...' in words,
talking all the time.
With a 't..., t...' here and a 't..., t...' there;
here a 't...', there a 't...',
everywhere a 't..., t...'.
Talking Tess says 't...' in words,
talking all the time.

Uppy Umbrella

(To the tune of *Here we go round the mulberry bush*)

Uppy Umbrella says 'ŭ...' in words,
'ŭ...' in words, 'ŭ...' in words.
Uppy Umbrella says 'ŭ...' in words.
She belongs to Mr U.

Vicky Violet

(To the tune of *Here we go round the mulberry bush*)

Vicky's violets say 'vvv…' in words,
'vvv…' in words, 'vvv…' in words.
Vicky's violets say 'vvv…' in words.
'vvv…, vvv…, vvv…'!

Walter Walrus

(To the tune of *Row, row, row your boat*)

'Www..., www', what's that we hear?
Is Walter Walrus near?
'Www..., www…!' Yes, that's him!
You may get wet, I fear!

Fix-it Max

(To the tune of *Old MacDonald had a farm*)

Now let's whisper, whisper 'k-ss',
whisper, whisper 'k-ss'.
Now let's whisper, whisper 'k-ss',
whisper, whisper 'k-ss'.
With a 'k-ss', 'k-ss' here
and a 'k-ss', 'k-ss' there;
here a 'k-ss', there a 'k-ss',
everywhere a 'k-ss', 'k-ss'.
Now let's whisper, whisper 'k-ss',
whisper, whisper 'k-ss'.

Yo-yo Man

(To the tune of *Baa, baa, black sheep*)

Yo-yo Man says 'yyy...' in words.
Yyyes sir, yes sir, 'yyy...' in words.
Yellow yo-yos he will sell,
and work for other men as well.

Zig Zag Zebra

(To the tune of *Humpty Dumpty*)

Zig Zag Zebra is very shy,
saying 'zzz...' while zzzipping by.
Zebras often seem to be shy,
but we'll never really know why.

Vowel Sounds Song

I am Annie Apple.
I am a talking apple.
I say 'ă..., ă..., ă...'
I say 'ă..., ă..., ă...'.

(*Chorus*)
We are the vowel sounds.
There are lots of us around.
In fact, have you heard;
we're in almost every word!

I am Eddy Elephant.
I am a talking elephant.
I say 'ĕ..., ĕ..., ĕ...'
I say 'ĕ..., ĕ..., ĕ...'.

(*Repeat chorus*)

I am Impy Ink.
I am a talking ink bottle.
I say 'ĭ..., ĭ..., ĭ...'
I say 'ĭ..., ĭ..., ĭ...'.

(*Repeat chorus*)

I am Oscar Orange.
I am a talking orange.
I say 'ŏ..., ŏ..., ŏ...'
I say 'ŏ..., ŏ..., ŏ...'.

(*Repeat chorus*)

I am Uppy Umbrella.
I am a talking umbrella.
I say 'ŭ..., ŭ..., ŭ...'
I say 'ŭ..., ŭ..., ŭ...'.

We are the vowel sounds.
There are lots of us around.
In fact, have you heard;
we're in almost every word.

Oh, all five of us are vowel sounds
and there's lots of us around.

Vowel Men Song

I am a Vowel Man.
My name is Mr A.
I wear an apron,
an apron everyday.
All five of us are Vowel Men,
and I am Mr A!
All five of us are Vowel Men,
and I am Mr A!

I am a Vowel Man.
My name is Mr E.
My magic tricks
are marvellous to see.
All five of us are Vowel Men,
and I am Mr E!
All five of us are Vowel Men,
and I am Mr E!

I am a Vowel Man.
My name is Mr I.
I sell ice cream
for you to come to buy.
All five of us are Vowel Men,
and I am Mr I!
All five of us are Vowel Men,
and I am Mr I!

I am a Vowel Man.
My name is Mr O.
I am an old man
but I'm still full of go.
All five of us are Vowel Men,
and I am Mr O!
All five of us are Vowel Men,
and I am Mr O!

I am a Vowel Man.
My name is Mr U.
I have a uniform
a uniform that's blue.
All five of us are Vowel Men,
and I am Mr U!
All five of us are Vowel Men,
and I am Mr U!

We're glad to meet you.
We hope you understand:
you all are welcome
here in Letterland!
Oh, all of you all are welcome
here in Letterland!

Cut out and use with *Fast Track* Activity Sheet 1: a–f

Cut out and use with *Fast Track* Activity Sheet 2: g–l

Cut out and use with *Fast Track* Activity Sheet 3: m–r

Cut out and use with *Fast Track* Activity Sheet 4: s–w

Letterland Teacher's Guide Published by Letterland International
© Letterland International 2005

Letterland Teacher's Guide Published by Letterland International
© Letterland International 2005

Name: _____

a

b

c

d

e

f

Assessment outcome Sort words according to initial sounds: **a–f**

Letterland Teacher's Guide Published by Letterland International
© Letterland International 2005

Name: _____

Assessment outcome Sort words according to initial sounds: **g–l**

Letterland Teacher's Guide Published by Letterland International © Letterland International 2005

Name: _____

m

n

o

p

qu

r

Assessment outcome Sort words according to initial sounds: **m–r**

Letterland Teacher's Guide Published by Letterland International © Letterland International 2005

Name: _____

s

t

u

v

w

Assessment outcome Sort words according to initial sounds: **s–w**

Letterland Teacher's Guide Published by Letterland International © Letterland International 2005

Name: _____

Circle the objects that END with Max's 'k-ss' sound.

  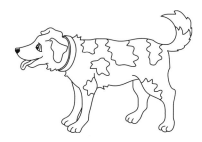

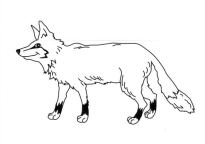  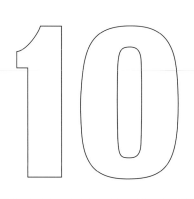

Circle the objects that start with the Letterlander's sound.

 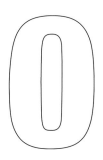  

Assessment outcome Sort words according to initial sounds: **x–z**

Letterland Teacher's Guide Published by Letterland International © Letterland International 2005

Name: _____

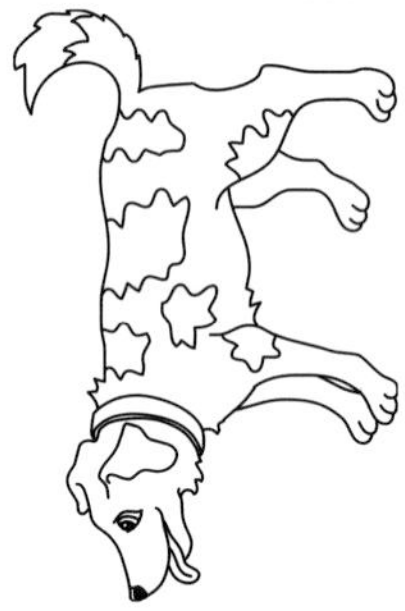

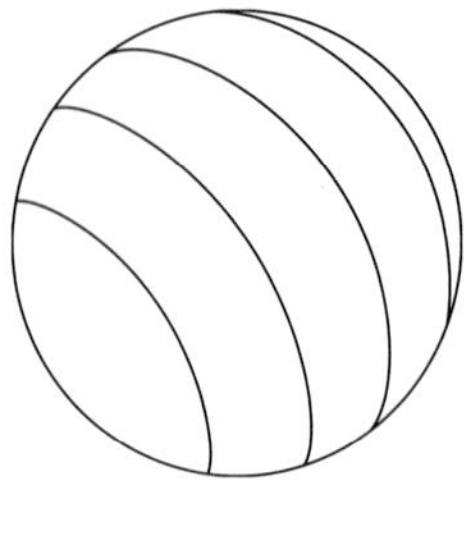

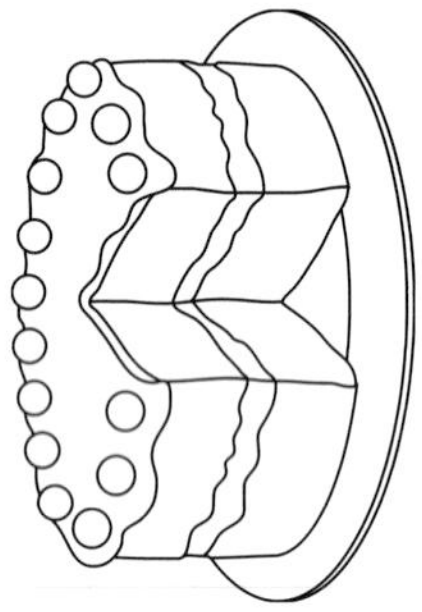

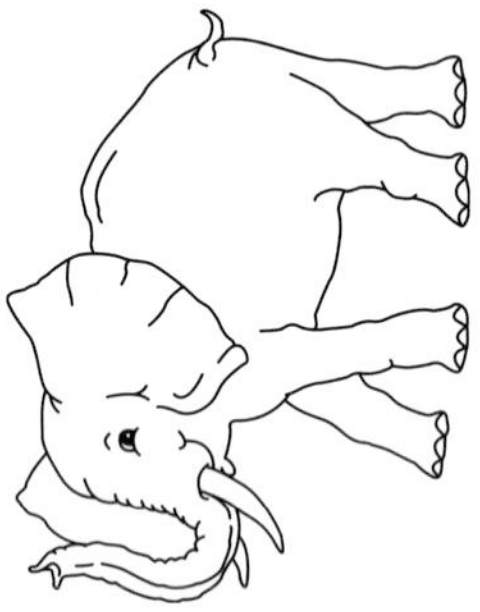

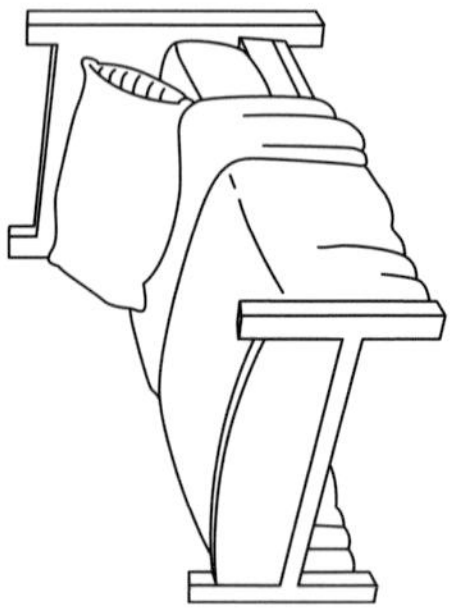

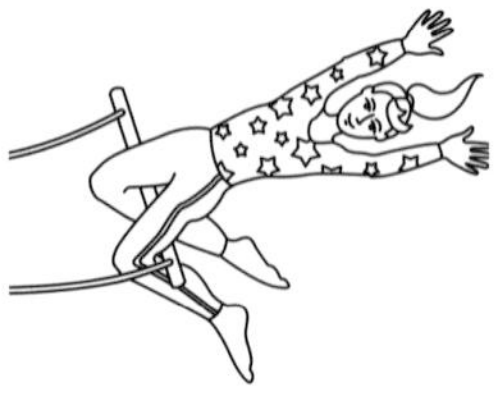

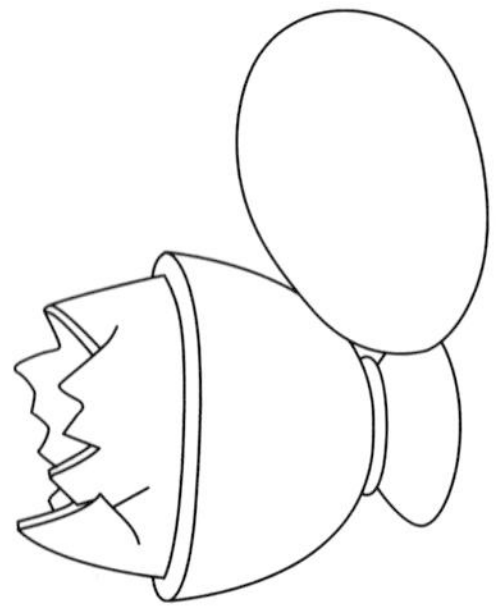

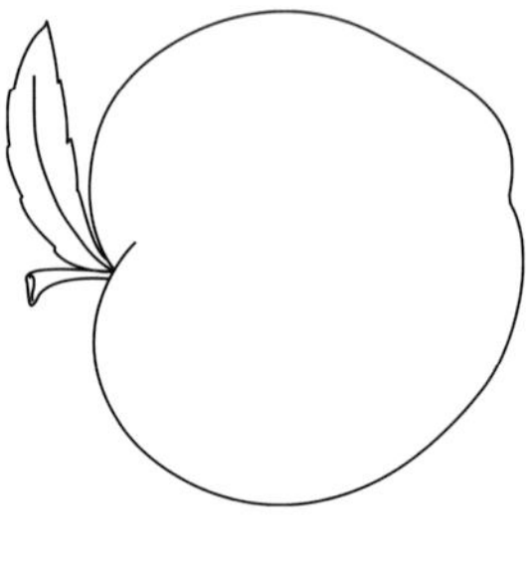

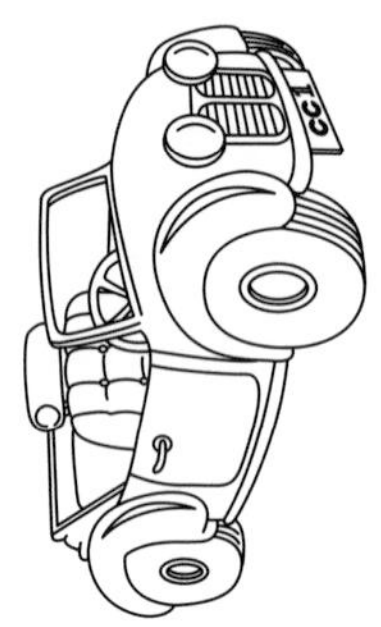

Assessment outcome Write initial letter in response to picture: **a–f**

Letterland Teacher's Guide Published by Letterland International © Letterland International 2005

Name: _____

Assessment outcome Write initial letter in response to picture: **g–l**

Letterland Teacher's Guide Published by Letterland International © Letterland International 2005

Name: _____

Assessment outcome Write initial letter in response to picture: **m–r**

Letterland Teacher's Guide Published by Letterland International © Letterland International 2005

Name: _____

Assessment outcome Write initial letter in response to picture: **s-z**

Letterland Teacher's Guide Published by Letterland International © Letterland International 2005

Name: _____

Dippy Duck

Firefighter Fred

Bouncy Ben

Golden Girl

Annie Apple

Eddy Elephant

Clever Cat

Assessment outcome Read Letterland character names

Letterland Teacher's Guide Published by Letterland International © Letterland International 2005

Name: _____

Impy Ink		
Kicking King		
Noisy Nick		
Harry Hat Man		
Munching Mike		
Lucy Lamp Light		
Jumping Jim		

Assessment outcome Read Letterland character names

Letterland Teacher's Guide Published by Letterland International © Letterland International 2005

Name: _____

Red Robot		
Talking Tess		
Oscar Orange		
Quarrelsome Queen		
Peter Puppy		
Sammy Snake		

Assessment outcome Read Letterland character names

Letterland Teacher's Guide Published by Letterland International © Letterland International 2005

Name: _____

Yellow Yo-yo Man

Zig Zag Zebra

Vicky Violet

Uppy Umbrella

Fix-it Max

Walter Walrus

Assessment outcome Read Letterland character names

Letterland Teacher's Guide Published by Letterland International © Letterland International 2005

Vowel Flip-overs

Rhyming Bingo (cut boards apart)

Board 2

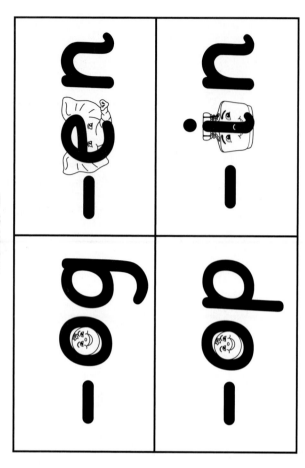

-en	-og
-un	-op

Board 4

-ip	-un
-ell	-op

Board 1

-ell	-at
-ip	-un

Board 3

-at	-en
-un	-og

Letterland Teacher's Guide Published by Letterland International © Letterland International 2005

Character Names Rhyming Sheet

Copymaster 4

Name: _____

Letterland Teacher's Guide Published by Letterland International © Letterland International 2005

Name: _____

  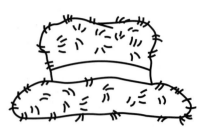

_at   _at   _at

_ en   _ en   _en

_op   _op   _op

ch, sh, th words

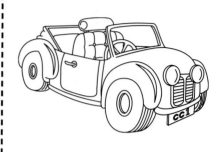

Annie Apple	Noisy Nick
Bouncy Ben	Oscar Orange
Clever Cat	Peter Puppy
Dippy Duck	Quarrelsome Queen
Eddy Elephant	Red Robot
Firefighter Fred	Sammy Snake
Golden Girl	Talking Tess
Harry Hat Man	Uppy Umbrella
Impy Ink	Vicky Violet
Jumping Jim	Walter Walrus
Kicking King	Fix-it Max
Lucy Lamp Light	Yo-Yo Man
Munching Mike	Zig Zag Zebra

PiPs coverage

NLS Progression in Phonics (PiPs), Framework for Teaching

Step	Skill		Letters
1	Hearing and discriminating general sounds, speech sounds and patterns		
2	1. To be able to continue a rhyming string 2. To hear and say phonemes in initial position: /s/, /m/, /k/, /t/, /g/, /h/ 3. To know phoneme-grapheme correspondences: **s**, **m**, **c**, **t**, **g**, **h**	Knowledge of simple letter-sound correspondences and some consonant digraphs, e.g. **ch**, **ll**, **ck**, **ng**	**s**, **m**, **c**, **t**, **g**, **h**
3	1. To hear and say phonemes in final position: /s/, /m/, /k/, /t/, /g/ 2. To consolidate previously learned phoneme-grapheme correspondences recognizing that some alter in final position, e.g. **ss**, **ck** 3. To know more phoneme-grapheme correspondences: **l**, **n**, **d**, **k**, **sh**, **ch**		**ss**, **ck**, **l**, **n**, **d**, **k**, **sh**, **ch**
4	1. To hear and say phonemes in medial position: /a/, /e/, /i/, /o/, /u/ 2. To know more phoneme-grapheme correspondences: **a**, **e**, **i**, **o**, **u**, **f**, **qu**, **b**, **r**, **j**, **p**, **th**, **ng** 3. To segment to spell CVC words 4. To blend to read CVC words		**a**, **e**, **i**, **o**, **u**, **f**, **qu**, **b**, **r**, **j**, **p**, **th**, **ng**
5	1. To hear phonemes within consonant clusters 2. To know more phoneme-grapheme correspondences: **v**, **w**, **x**, **y**, **z** 3. To segment to spell words containing consonant clusters in initial position (CCVC) and final position (CVCC) 4. To blend to read words containing consonant clusters in initial position (CCVC) and final position (CVCC)		**v**, **w**, **x**, **y**, **z**
6	1. To know one representation of each of ten vowel phonemes: digraphs **ai**, **ee**, **ie**, **oa**, **oo**, **or**, **ar**, **ir**, **oi**, **ou** 2. To segment to spell words containing vowel phonemes represented by more than one letter 3. To blend to read words containing vowel phonemes represented by more than one letter	Knowledge of vowel digraphs and trigraphs	**ai**, **ee**, **ie**, **oa**, **oo**, **or**, **ar**, **ir**, **oi**, **ou**
7	1. To segment to spell words containing vowel digraphs and trigraphs: **ay**, **a-e**, **ea**, **igh**, **y**, **i-e**, **o-e**, **oe**, **ew**, **ue**, **u-e**, **oy**, **ow**, **er**, **ur**, **aw**, **air**, **ear**, **oo** 2. To blend to read words containing the same vowel digraphs and trigraphs		**ay**, **a-e**, **ea**, **igh**, **y**, **i-e**, **o-e**, **oe**, **ew**, **ue**, **u-e**, **oy**, **ow**, **er**, **ur**, **aw**, **air**, **ear**, **oo**

PiPs © Crown Copyright 1999 and 2000

PiPs coverage in Lesson Plans

		PiPs Step/Skill			PiPs Step/Skill
Section 1: a–z Word Building			Lesson 12	**Nn**	1, 2.2, 3.3
Lesson 1	**Cc**	1, 2.1, 2.2, 2.3	Lesson 13	**Gg**	1, 2.2
Lesson 2a	**Aa** (short vowel)	1, 2.2	Lesson 14	Segmenting	2.1, 2.2, 3.1, 4.1, 4.3, 4.4
Lesson 2b	**Aa** (long vowel)	1, 2.2, 4.1			
Lesson 3	**Dd**	1, 2.2, 3.3	Lesson 15a	**Oo** (short vowel)	1, 2.2, 4.2
Lesson 4	**Hh**	1, 2.2	Lesson 15b	**Oo** (long vowel)	1, 2.2, 4.1, 4.2, 4.4
Lesson 5	**Mm**	1, 2.2	Lesson 16	**Pp**	1, 2.2, 4.2
Lesson 6	**Tt**	1, 2.2	Lesson 17	Segmenting	1, 2.2, 3.3, 4.3, 4.4
Lesson 7	First blends	4.1, 4.3, 4.4	Lesson 18a	**Ee** (short vowel)	1, 2.2, 4.1, 4.2
Lesson 8	**Ss**	1, 2.2	Lesson 18b	**Ee** (long vowel)	1, 2.2, 4.1, 4.2, 6.1
Lesson 9	Blending with endings: **s**, **s** & **ss**	3.1, 3.2, 4.3, 4.4	Lesson 19	Blending and segmenting	1, 3.1, 3.3, 4.1, 4.2, 4.3, 4.4
Lesson 10	First segmenting words	2.1, 2.2, 3.1, 4.3			
Lesson 11a	**Ii** (short vowel)	1, 2.2, 4.2	Lesson 20a	**Uu** (short vowel)	1, 2.2, 4.2
Lesson 11b	**Ii** (long vowel)	1, 2.2	Lesson 20b	**Uu** (long vowel)	1, 2.2, 4.1, 4.2

	PiPs Step/Skill			PiPs Step/Skill
Section 1: a–z Word Building (continued)		Lesson 29	**Bb**	1, 2.2, 4.2
Lesson 21	**Kk**	1, 2.2, 3.3	Lesson 30	**Jj**	1, 2.2, 4.2
Lesson 22	Blending and segmenting: **-ck** & **-ng**	1, 3.2, 4.1, 4.2, 5.3, 5.4	Lesson 31	Blending and segmenting	4.3, 4.4
Lesson 23	Sounds only: **sh**, **ch** & **th**	1, 3.3, 4.2	Lesson 32	**Rr**	1, 2.2, 4.2
Lesson 24	Sounds and spellings: **sh** & **th**	1, 3.3, 4.2, 5.3	Lesson 33	**Qq**	1, 2.2, 4.2
Lesson 25	Sounds and spellings: **th** & **th**	1, 4.2, 5.4	Lesson 34	**Vv**	1, 2.2, 5.2
Lesson 26	**Ll**	1, 2.2, 3.3	Lesson 35	Blending and segmenting: **-ve**	2.2, 3.1, 4.3, 5.3, 7.1, 7.2
Lesson 27	**Ff**	1, 2.2, 4.2	Lesson 36	**Ww**	1, 2.2, 5.2
Lesson 28	Blending and segmenting: **ff** & **ll**	1, 2.1, 3.1, 3.2, 4.1, 5.3, 5.4	Lesson 37	**Xx**	1, 3.1, 5.2
			Lesson 38	**Yy**	1, 2.2, 5.2
			Lesson 39	**Zz**	1, 2.2, 5.2

	PiPs Step/Skill		PiPs Step/Skill
Section 2: Onsets and Rimes			
Rhyming Chants and Live Spelling	2.1, 4.1, 4.3, 4.4	Using the Letterland Vocabulary Cards	2.1, 4.4
Word sort	2.1, 4.1, 4.4		
Rhyming bingo	2.1, 4.1, 4.4	Using the Letterland character names	2.1, 4.4, 5.4
Word challenge	2.1, 4.3, 4.4		

		PiPs Step/Skill			PiPs Step/Skill
Section 3: Beginnings, Middles and Endings					
Lesson 1	Introduction to initial sounds	2.2, 2.3, 3.3, 4.2, 5.2,	Lesson 6	**-ck**	3.2, 5.3, 5.4
Lesson 2	Segmenting initial sounds	2.2, 2.3, 3.3, 4.2, 4.3, 4.4, 5.2	Lesson 7	**-ff**, **-ll**, **-ss**	3.2, 5.3
			Lesson 8	**-ng**	4.2
Lesson 3	Initial sounds: **sh** & **ch**	3.3, 4.1, 5.3	Lesson 9	Blending medial sounds	2.2, 3.3, 4.1, 4.2
Lesson 4	Initial sounds: **th**, **th**, **sh** & **ch**	3.3, 4.2	Lesson 10	Blending CVC words	4.4
Lesson 5	Endings: **-t** and **-g**	3.1	Lesson 11	Segmenting CVC words	4.1, 4.3, 4.4

		PiPs Step/Skill			PiPs Step/Skill
Section 4: Consonant Blends					
Lesson 1	**bl**, **cl**, **fl**, **gl**, **pl** & **sl**	2.2, 2.3, 3.3, 4.2, 5.1, 5.3	Lesson 4	**sm**, **sn** & **sw**	2.3, 3.3, 5.1, 5.2
Lesson 2	**br**, **cr**, **dr**, **fr**, **gr**, **pr**, & **tr**	2.2, 2.3, 3.3, 5.1, 5.3, 5.4	Lesson 5	**scr**, **spl**, **spr**, **squ** & **str**	2.3, 3.3, 4.2, 5.3, 5.4
Lesson 3	**sc**, **sk**, **sp** & **st**	2.3, 5.1, 5.3	Lesson 6	**shr** & **thr**	3.3, 4.2, 5.3, 5.4

		PiPs Step/Skill			PiPs Step/Skill
Section 5: Digraphs and Trigraphs					
Lesson 1	Review long vowels	4.2	Lesson 8	Long u: **u-e**, **oo**, **ew** and **ue**	2.2, 3.1, 6.1, 6.2, 6.3, 7.1, 7.2
Lesson 2	Long vowels in common words	4.2, 5.3	Lesson 9	**ar** and **or**	6.1, 6.2, 6.3
Lesson 3	The **Silent Magic e** concept	4.2, 6.2, 6.3, 7.1, 7.2	Lesson 10	**ow** and **ou**	6.1, 6.2, 6.3, 7.1, 7.2
			Lesson 11	**oy** and **oi**	6.1, 6.2, 6.3, 7.1, 7.2
Lesson 4	Long a: **a–e**, **ai** and **ay**	3.3, 4.1, 5.1, 6.1, 6.2, 6.3, 7.1, 7.2	Lesson 12	**er**, **ur** and **ir**	4.1, 6.1, 6.3, 7.1, 7.2
Lesson 5	Long e: **e-e**, **ee** and **ea**	3.3, 6.1, 6.2, 6.3, 7.2	Lesson 13	**o͞o** and **u**	4.2, 6.1, 6.2, 6.3
			Lesson 14	**aw** and **au**	4.1, 6.2, 7.1, 7.2
Lesson 6	Long i: **i-e**, **ie**, **y** and **igh**	2.2, 3.1, 4.1, 5.1, 6.2, 6.3, 7.1	Lesson 15	**air** and **ear** (hair, hear)	6.2, 7.1, 7.2
Lesson 7	Long o: **o-e**, **oa** and **ow**	6.2, 6.3, 7.1, 7.2			

Index